Department of Economic & Social Affairs

United Nations
Model Double Taxation
Convention between
Developed and
Developing Countries

United Nations
New York, 2001

NOTE

Symbols of United Nations documents are composed of capital letters combined with figures. Mention of such a symbol indicates a reference to a United Nations document.

The designations employed and the presentation of the material in this publication do not imply the expression of any opinion whatsoever on the part of the Secretariat of the United Nations concerning the legal status of any country or territory or of its authorities, or concerning the delimitation of its frontiers or boundaries.

ST/ESA/PAD/SER.E/21

UNITED NATIONS PUBLICATION

Sales No. E.01.XVI.2

ISBN 92-1-159097-3

CONTENTS

Part One
Articles of the United Nations Model Double Taxation Convention between Developed and Developing Countries

Part Two
Commentaries on the articles of the United Nations Model Double Taxation Convention between Developed and Developing Countries

INTRODUCTION

A. ORIGIN OF THE UNITED NATIONS MODEL CONVENTION

1.   The desirability of promoting greater inflows of foreign investment to developing countries on conditions which are politically acceptable as well as economically and socially beneficial has been frequently affirmed in resolutions of the General Assembly and the Economic and Social Council of the United Nations and the United Nations Conference on Trade and Development. The countries participating in the Paris Conference on International Economic Co-operation held in 1963-1964 recognized that foreign private capital flows and investment play an important complementary role in the economic development process, particularly through the transfer of resources, managerial and administrative expertise and technology to the developing countries, the expansion of productive capacity and employment in those countries and the establishment of export markets.

2.   The growth of investment flows from developed to developing countries depends to a large extent on what has been referred to as the international investment climate. The prevention or elimination of international double taxation—i.e., the imposition of similar taxes in two or more States on the same taxpayer in respect of the same base—whose effects are harmful to the exchange of goods and services and to the movement of capital and persons, constitutes a significant component of such a climate. Broadly, the general objectives of bilateral tax conventions may today be seen to include the full protection of taxpayers against double taxation (whether direct or indirect) and the prevention of the discouragement which taxation may provide for the free flow of international trade and investment and the transfer of technology. They also aim to prevent discrimination between taxpayers in the international field, and to provide a reasonable element of legal and fiscal certainty as a framework within which

international operations can be carried on. With this background, tax treaties should contribute to the furtherance of the development aims of the developing countries. In addition, the treaties have as an objective the improvement of cooperation between taxing authorities in carrying out their duties.

3.   Substantial progress towards the elimination of double taxation has been made through unilateral relief measures and more particularly through bilateral tax conventions, which have emerged since the 1960s as a salient feature of inter-State economic relations. However, until 1965, only a relatively small number of treaties had been concluded between developed and developing countries, the reason being probably the fact, acknowledged in 1965 by the Fiscal Committee of the Organisation for Economic Co-operation and Development, that "the traditional tax conventions have not commended themselves to developing countries".[1] According to that Committee, "the essential fact remains that tax conventions which capital-exporting countries have found to be of value to improve trade and investment among themselves and which might contribute in like ways to closer economic relations between developing and capital-exporting countries are not making sufficient contributions to that end . . . Existing treaties between industrialized countries sometimes require the country of residence to give up revenue. More often, however, it is the country of source which gives up revenue. Such a pattern may not be equally appropriate in treaties between developing and industrialized countries because income flows are largely from developing to industrialized countries and the revenue sacrifice would be one-sided. But there are many provisions in existing tax conventions that have a valid place in conventions between capital-exporting and developing countries too."[2]

4.   The desirability of encouraging the conclusion of bilateral tax treaties between developed and developing countries was recognized

---

[1] Organisation for Economic Co-operation and Development, *Fiscal Incentives for Private Investment in Developing Countries: Report of the OECD Fiscal Committee* (Paris, 1965), para. 164.
[2] Ibid., paras. 163 and 165.

by the Economic and Social Council of the United Nations, which in its resolution 1273 (XLIII) adopted on 4 August 1967 requested the Secretary-General "to set up an ad hoc working group consisting of experts and tax administrators nominated by Governments, but acting in their personal capacity, both from developed and developing countries and adequately representing different regions and tax systems, with the task of exploring, in consultation with interested international agencies, ways and means for facilitating the conclusion of tax treaties between developed and developing countries, including the formulation, as appropriate, of possible guidelines and techniques for use in such tax treaties which would be acceptable to both groups of countries and would fully safeguard their respective revenue interests". Pursuant to that resolution, the Secretary-General set up in 1968 the Ad Hoc Group of Experts on Tax Treaties between Developed and Developing Countries, composed of tax officials and experts from developed and developing countries, appointed in their personal capacity.

5.   The Group of Experts completed the formulation of guidelines for the negotiation of bilateral treaties between developed and developing countries in the course of seven meetings, from 1968 to 1977, which were attended by members from Argentina, Brazil, Chile, France, Federal Republic of Germany, Ghana, India, Israel, Japan, the Netherlands, Norway, Pakistan, the Philippines, Sri Lanka, the Sudan, Switzerland, Tunisia, Turkey, the United Kingdom of Great Britain and Northern Ireland and the United States of America. These meetings were also attended by the observers from Austria, Belgium, Finland, the Republic of Korea, Mexico, Nigeria, Spain, Swaziland and Venezuela and from the following international organizations: the International Monetary Fund, the International Fiscal Association, the Organisation for Economic Co-operation and Development, the Organization of American States and the International Chamber of Commerce. The guidelines are contained in the *Manual for the Negotiation of Bilateral Tax Treaties between Developed and Developing Countries.*[3] According to Economic and Social Council

---

[3]United Nations publication, Sales No. E.79.XVI.3.

resolution 1541 (XLIX), the guidelines should represent "an important form of technical assistance for the conclusion of future treaties".

6.   At its Seventh Meeting, the attention of the Group of Experts was drawn to the fact that the Group of Eminent Persons appointed in 1974 by the Secretary-General pursuant to Economic and Social Council resolution 1721 (LIII) had stated in its report to the Secretary-General that "If, through the work of the Group of Experts on Tax Treaties, the provisions of these treaties could be standardized, with only a small number of clauses to be negotiated in particular cases, they would in fact amount to an international agreement on taxation, which . . . [the Group of Eminent Persons considers] to be the final objective".[4]

7.   The Group of Experts took the view that the worldwide multilateral tax agreement recommended by the Group of Eminent Persons would not seem feasible during the forthcoming decade but, recognizing the seriousness and urgency of many of the issues singled out by the latter, agreed that it was imperative that those issues be dealt with through an adequate network of bilateral tax treaties. According to the Group of Experts, it would therefore seem appropriate for the competent United Nations bodies to urge Member States to embark as soon as possible on a policy of entering into such treaties. In that connection, the Group of Experts expressed readiness to consider a draft model bilateral convention between a developed and a developing country based on the guidelines already developed by the Group, which the United Nations Secretariat might wish to prepare as a follow-up to the work of the Group at its first seven meetings.

8.   In his report to the first regular session of 1978 of the Economic and Social Council on the work of the Group of Experts at its Seventh Meeting, the Secretary-General expressed the view that "the completion of a model bilateral convention for possible use by developed

---

[4]*The Impact of Multinational Corporations on Development and on International Relations* (United Nations publication, Sales No. E.74.II.A.5), p. 92.

and developing countries constitutes a logical follow-up to the work done by the Group of Experts relating to the formulation of guidelines and would moreover be consonant with the recommendation of the Group of Eminent Persons that "bilateral tax treaties should be as uniform as possible so as to prepare the way for an international tax agreement" (see E/1978/36, para. 15). At that session, the Economic and Social Council adopted decision 1978/14, in which it welcomed the position of the Secretary-General as set forth above and requested the Group of Experts "to complete its consideration of a draft model bilateral convention at its Eighth Meeting in 1979".

9.   The United Nations Secretariat therefore prepared a draft model convention (ST/SG/AC.8/L.29) consisting of articles reproducing the guidelines formulated by the Group of Experts, together with Commentaries thereon incorporating the views of the members of the Group as expressed at its various meetings and also reproducing, where appropriate, the Commentaries on the Articles of the 1977 Model Double Taxation Convention on Income and on Capital of the Organisation for Economic Co-operation and Development, hereafter referred to as the OECD Model Convention. It may be recalled that in preparing the aforementioned guidelines the Group of Experts had decided to use the OECD Model Convention as its main reference text in order to take advantage of the accumulated technical expertise embodied in that Convention and the Commentary thereon, and also for reasons of practical convenience stemming from the fact that the Convention was being used by OECD member countries in the negotiation of tax treaties not only with each other but also with developing countries. However, it was fully understood that there was no presumption of correctness to be accorded to the OECD Model Convention, and that the decisions of the Group were in no way required to be governed by the OECD text.

10.   The Group of Experts reviewed the draft United Nations Model Convention at its Eighth Meeting, held at Geneva from 10 to 21 December 1979, and adopted the final text of the Convention and of the Commentary thereon. In 1980, the United Nations published the *United Nations Model Double Taxation Convention between De-*

veloped and Developing Countries, which was preceded in 1979 by the *Manual for the Negotiation of Bilateral Tax Treaties between Developed and Developing Countries*. By its resolution 1980/13 of 28 April 1980, the Economic and Social Council renamed the Group of Experts as "Ad Hoc Group of Experts on International Cooperation in Tax Matters". At present, the Group of Experts is composed of 25 members—10 from developed countries and 15 from developing countries and economies in transition.

11.   In the 1990s, the Ad Hoc Group of Experts on International Cooperation in Tax Matters recognized that significant changes had taken place in the international economic, financial and fiscal environment. In addition, there has been the advent of new financial instruments, transfer pricing mechanisms, the growth of tax havens and the globalization affecting international economic relations as well as the subsequent OECD Model Convention revision and updates in 1992, 1994, 1995 and 1997. Consequently, the Eighth Meeting of the Group of Experts held in Geneva in December 1997 established a Focus Group consisting of five members and four alternates, to proceed with the revision and update of both the *United Nations Model Double Taxation Convention between Developed and Developing Countries* and the *Manual for the Negotiation of Bilateral Tax Treaties between Developed and Developing Countries.*

12.   Accordingly, following its Seventh Meeting (Geneva, 11-15 December 1995), Eighth Meeting (Geneva, 15-19 December 1997), and the Focus Group meetings (New York, 9 and 10 December 1998, and Amsterdam, 22-25 March 1999), the Group of Experts reviewed the amendments suggested by its members to the Articles and Commentary of the *United Nations Model Double Taxation Convention between Developed and Developing Countries*. These amendments were consolidated in the draft revised United Nations Model Convention presented before the Ninth Meeting of the Group of Experts held in New York from 3 to 7 May 1999. The Group of Experts adopted the revised *United Nations Model Double Taxation Convention between Developed and Developing Countries*, subject to editorial changes. The comments and suggestions received from the

members of the Group of Experts on these changes were examined by a Steering Committee during its meeting held in New York from 12 to 14 April 2000. The meeting was attended by Mr. Antonio Hugo Figueroa (Argentina), who was appointed Chairman, Mr. Mayer Gabay (Israel), Mr. Noureddine Bensouda (Morocco), Mr. Mike Waters (United Kingdom) and Mr. Mordecai S. Feinberg (United States). The Secretariat was represented by Mr. Abdel Hamid Bouab and Mr. Suresh Shende, Secretary and Assistant Secretary of the Group of Experts, respectively. The final text of the United Nations Model Convention as so modified was adopted on a consensual basis by the Steering Committee. It was decided that after the editorial changes had been effected, a revised version of the United Nations Model Convention would be published. Thus, the revision and update of the *United Nations Model Double Taxation Convention between Developed and Developing Countries* was undertaken by the Group of Experts, Focus Group and Steering Committee under the overall guidance and supervision of Mr. Abdel Hamid Bouab, Officer-in-Charge, Public Finance and Private Sector Development Branch, Department of Economic and Social Affairs, United Nations, and Secretary, Ad Hoc Group of Experts, assisted by Mr. Suresh Shende, Interregional Adviser in Resource Mobilization and Assistant Secretary of the Group of Experts. The Steering Committee expressed its gratitude to Mr. Abdel Hamid Bouab for his knowledge, leadership and negotiating skills which contributed to the successful revision of the United Nations Model Double Taxation Convention between Developed and Developing Countries.

13.   The main objectives of the revision of the United Nations Model Convention were to take account of developments since 1980 in the globalization of trade and investment and in the international tax policies of developed and developing countries.

14.   The process of revision and update of the *United Nations Model Double Taxation Convention between Developed and Developing Countries* was initiated in 1995 and culminated in 1999 at the Ninth Meeting of the Group of Experts. The Ninth Meeting was attended by the following members: Antonio Hugo Figueroa (Argen-

tina), Iraci Kahan (Brazil), Adélaïde Nare (Burkina Faso), Yukang Wang (People's Republic of China), Abdoulaye Camara (Côte d'Ivoire), Mona M. A. Kassem (Egypt), Hillel Skurnik (Finland), Helmut Krabbe (Germany), Seth E. Terkper (Ghana), Ravi Kant (India), Arie Soelendro (Indonesia), Mayer Gabay (Israel), William W. Adler (Jamaica), Karina Pérez Delgadillo (Mexico), Abdelali Benbrik (Morocco), Ernst Bunders (the Netherlands), Atef Alawneh (Palestine Authority), María Pastor (Spain), Daniel Luthi (Switzerland), John Brian Shepherd (United Kingdom) and Mordecai S. Feinberg (United States).

Members from France, Japan, Nigeria and Pakistan did not attend the meeting.

15.   The Meeting was attended by the following observers:

(a)   Ken Allen (Australia), Claudine Devillet (Belgium), Carlos dos Santos Almeida (Brazil), Sandra Benedetto (Chile), Shubin Mu (People's Republic of China), Marcellin-Edgard Mebalet (Gabon), Dieudonné Bouddhou (Gabon), Vijay Mathur (India), Brahim Kettani (Morocco), Igor Yuri Noskov (Russian Federation), Babou Ngom (Senegal), Mike Waters (United Kingdom);

(b)   Jacques Sasseville (OECD), Jeffrey P. Owens (OECD), Willem F. J. Wijnen (International Bureau of Fiscal Documentation), Francisco Alfredo Garcia Prats (University of Valencia, Spain), Marcus V. Föllmi (International Chamber of Commerce), Stephen R. Crow (International Association of University Presidents, United States).

16.   The Group unanimously elected Antonio Hugo Figueroa and Hillel Skurnik as Chairman and Rapporteur, respectively. Abdel Hamid Bouab, Officer-in-Charge of Public Finance and Private Sector Development Branch, served as Secretary; Suresh Shende, Interregional Adviser in Resource Mobilization, as Assistant Secretary; and Paul McDaniel as resource person.

17.   The United Nations Model Convention represents a compromise between the source principle and the residence principle, al-

though it gives more weight to the source principle than does the OECD Model Convention. As a correlative to the principle of taxation at source the articles of the Model Convention are predicated on the premise of the recognition by the source country that (*a*) taxation of income from foreign capital would take into account expenses allocable to the earnings of the income so that such income would be taxed on a net basis, that (*b*) taxation would not be so high as to discourage investment and that (*c*) it would take into account the appropriateness of the sharing of revenue with the country providing the capital. In addition, the United Nations Model Convention embodies the idea that it would be appropriate for the residence country to extend a measure of relief from double taxation through either foreign tax credit or exemption as in the OECD Model Convention.

18.   In using the United Nations Model Convention, a country should bear in mind the fact that the relationship between treaties and domestic law may vary from country to country and that it is important to take into account the relationship between tax treaties and domestic law. Tax treaties affect the tax rules prevailing under the domestic tax laws of the Contracting States by establishing which Contracting State shall have jurisdiction to subject a given income item to its national tax laws and under what conditions and with what limitations it may do so. Consequently, countries wishing to enter into bilateral tax treaty negotiations should analyse carefully the applicable provisions of their domestic tax laws in order to assess the modifications that might be required if the treaty were applied.

19.   It may also be noted that domestic tax laws in their turn exert an influence on the content of bilateral tax treaties. Thus, although there was general agreement in OECD about the principles embodied in the OECD Model Convention and although most existing bilateral tax treaties conform by and large to the latter, there are often substantial variations from one treaty to another, due to differences in the domestic laws of the various Contracting States.

B. HISTORICAL SETTING OF THE UNITED NATIONS MODEL CONVENTION

20. The United Nations Model Double Taxation Convention between Developed and Developing Countries forms part of the continuing international efforts aimed at eliminating double taxation. These efforts begun by the League of Nations and pursued in the Organisation for European Economic Co-operation (OEEC) (now known as the Organisation for Economic Co-operation and Development (OECD)) and in regional forums, as well as in the United Nations, have in general found concrete expression in a series of model or draft model bilateral tax conventions.

21. In 1921, the League of Nations, acting through its Financial Committee in response to an appeal by the 1920 Brussels International Financial Conference for action aimed at eliminating double taxation, entrusted a team of four economists (from Italy, the Netherlands, the United Kingdom and the United States of America) with the task of preparing a study on the economic aspects of international double taxation.

22. In 1922, the Financial Committee of the League invited a group of seven high-level tax officials (from Belgium, Czechoslovakia, France, Italy, the Netherlands, Switzerland and the United Kingdom) to study the administrative and practical aspects of international double taxation and international tax evasion. In 1925, the group was enlarged to include officials from Argentina, Germany, Japan, Poland and Venezuela. In 1927, an official from the United States of America joined the group. In the course of sessions held from 1923 to 1927, the group drafted Bilateral Conventions for the Prevention of Double Taxation in the Special Matter of Direct Taxes dealing with income and property taxes, a Bilateral Convention for the Prevention of Double Taxation in the Special Matter of Succession Duties, a Bilateral Convention on Administrative Assistance in Matters of Taxation and a Bilateral Convention on [Judicial] Assistance in the Collection of Taxes. The conventions, with their commentaries, were sent to the various Governments, Members and non-members of the

League, which were invited to send representatives to discuss them at a General Meeting of Government Experts. The latter meeting, held at Geneva in October 1928, included representatives of 27 countries.

23. In 1929, pursuant to a recommendation of the General Meeting of Government Experts, the Council of the League of Nations appointed a permanent Fiscal Committee. The latter devoted considerable attention to the question of formulating, for tax purposes, rules for allocation of the business income of undertakings operating in several countries. Within the framework of those activities, a Draft Convention for the Allocation of Business Income between States for the Purposes of Taxation was formulated, first at meetings of a subcommittee held in New York and Washington under the auspices of the American Section of the International Chamber of Commerce, and then at the full meeting of the Fiscal Committee in June 1933. The Draft Convention was revised by the Fiscal Committee in June 1935.[5]

24. In 1940, the Fiscal Committee held a subcommittee meeting in the Netherlands to review the progress made with regard to tax treaties since the 1928 General Meeting of Government Experts. Soon afterwards, it began consolidating the 1928 Model Conventions and the 1935 Draft Convention. The results of its work were reviewed at a Regional Tax Conference convened in June 1940 at Mexico City, reconvened in July 1943, likewise at Mexico City, and attended by representatives from Argentina, Bolivia, Canada, Chile, Colombia, Ecuador, Mexico, Peru, the United States of America, Uruguay and Venezuela. The Second Regional Conference adopted a Model Bilateral Convention for the Prevention of the Double Taxation of Income and a Protocol thereto, and a Model Bilateral Convention for the Establishment of Reciprocal Administrative Assistance for the Assessment and Collection of Direct Taxes and a Protocol thereto.

---

[5]For further details, see Mitchell B. Carroll, *Global Perspectives of an International Tax Lawyer* (Hicksville, New York, Exposition Press, 1978). Mr. Carroll was a former President of the Fiscal Committee of the League of Nations and the International Fiscal Association.

25.   In March 1946, the Fiscal Committee of the League of Nations convened in London for its tenth session, at which it reviewed and re-drafted the Mexico model bilateral tax conventions. The Committee stated that the general structure of the model conventions drafted at the tenth session was similar to that of the Mexico models; a number of changes had been made in the wording, and some articles had been suppressed because they contained provisions already in other clauses. The Committee observed that virtually the only clauses where there was an effective divergence between the views of the 1943 Mexico meeting and those of the London meeting were those "relating to the taxation of interest, dividends, royalties, annuities and pensions". The Committee added that it was aware of the fact that the provisions contained in the 1943 model conventions might appear more attractive to some States—in Latin America for in-stance—than those which it had agreed during its current sessions and that it thought "that the work done both in Mexico and in London could be usefully reviewed and developed by a balanced group of tax administrators and experts from both capital-importing and capital-exporting countries and from economically-advanced and less-advanced countries, when the League work on international prob-lems is taken over by the United Nations".[6]

26.   It was against that background that the Economic and Social Council of the United Nations, in its resolution 2 (III) of 1 October 1946, set up a Fiscal Commission which was requested to "study and advise the Council in the field of public finance, particularly in its le-gal, administrative and technical aspects". After the Fiscal Commis-sion and its Committee on International Tax Relations stopped functioning in 1954, the focus of action in the field of international taxation shifted to OEEC.

27.   The Council of OEEC adopted its first recommendation con-cerning double taxation on 25 February 1955; that recommendation subsequently resulted in the establishment of the OEEC Fiscal Com-

---

[6]League of Nations, *Fiscal Committee: Report on the Work of the Tenth Session of the Committee, held in London from March 20th to 26th, 1946* (C.37.M.37.1946.II.A), p. 8.

mittee in March 1956. In July 1958, the Fiscal Committee was instructed to prepare a draft convention for the avoidance of double taxation with respect to taxes on income and capital as well as concrete proposals for the implementation of such a convention. In the words of the Fiscal Committee: "Since the work of the League of Nations, the value of a Model Convention has been universally recognized not only by the national authorities but also by the taxpayers themselves."[7]

28. From 1958 to 1961, the Fiscal Committee prepared four reports, published under the title "The elimination of double taxation", in which the Committee proposed a total of 25 Articles. After OEEC became the Organisation for Economic Co-operation and Development (OECD) in September 1961, the mandate of the Fiscal Committee was confirmed; the Committee subsequently agreed on a number of new Articles and all the Articles were embodied in a report entitled "Draft Double Taxation Convention on Income and on Capital", published in 1963.

29. In July 1963, OECD, recognizing that the effort to eliminate double taxation between member countries needed to go beyond the field of periodic taxes on income and capital, instructed the Fiscal Committee to work out a draft convention which would provide a means of settling on a uniform basis the most common problems of double taxation of estates and inheritances. The "Draft Convention for the Avoidance of Double Taxation with Respect to Taxes on Estates and Inheritances" was published in 1966.

30. In 1967 the Fiscal Committee—renamed in 1971 "Committee on Fiscal Affairs"—began revising the 1963 "Draft Double Taxation Convention". That revision was considered necessary in order to take account of "experience gained by Member countries in negotiating new conventions or in their practical working" and also of "the changes in systems of taxation and the increase in international fiscal

---

[7]Organisation for Economic Co-operation and Development, *Draft Double Taxation Convention on Income and Capital: Report of the OECD Fiscal Committee* (Paris, 1963), p. 25, para. 49.

relations on the one hand and, on the other, the development of new sectors of business activity and the increasingly complex forms of organization adopted by enterprises for their international activities". The revision of the 1963 "Draft Convention" ultimately led to the publication of the 1977 "Model Double Taxation Convention on Income and on Capital". It has recently undergone revisions in 1992, 1994, 1995 and 1997.

31.   As it had done for the 1963 "Draft Convention", the Council of OECD, in a recommendation based on a suggestion by the Committee on Fiscal Affairs and adopted on 23 October 1997, recommended to the Governments of member countries ". . . to pursue their efforts to conclude bilateral tax conventions on income and on capital with those Member countries, and where appropriate with non-member countries, with which they have not yet entered into such conventions, and to revise those of the existing conventions that may no longer reflect present-day needs, and when concluding new bilateral conventions or revising existing bilateral conventions to conform to the Model Tax Convention, as interpreted by the Commentaries thereon". The Council instructed the Committee on Fiscal Affairs "to proceed to periodic reviews of situations where double taxation may occur, in the light of experience gained by member countries and to make appropriate proposals for its removal".

32.   In the mid-1960s, the United Nations began to take a renewed interest in the problem of double taxation, as a result of the continued increase in the number of developing Member States and as part of its action aimed at promoting the flow of foreign investment to developing countries. That renewed interest led to the activities described in section 1 above, which have culminated in the preparation of the United Nations Model Convention.

33.   Action relating to double taxation has also been taken at the regional and subregional levels. At the regional level, a Group of Experts of the Latin American Free Trade Association (LAFTA) adopted in 1976 criteria for the avoidance of double taxation between LAFTA and member countries and countries outside the region. At the subregional level, the Commission of the Cartagena Agreement

adopted in November 1971 the "Model Convention for the Avoidance of Double Taxation between Member Countries and Other Countries outside the Andean Subregion" and also the "Convention for the Avoidance of Double Taxation within the Andean Group". Furthermore, in November 1972, a Convention on Administrative Assistance in Tax Matters was concluded by Denmark, Finland, Iceland, Norway and Sweden; the Convention was amended in 1973 and again in 1976. The Nordic Convention on Income and Capital entered into by Denmark, Finland, Iceland, Norway and Sweden, which was concluded in 1983, was replaced in 1987, 1989 and 1996. The Convention on Mutual Administrative Assistance in Tax Matters was drawn up within the Council of Europe on the basis of a first draft prepared by the Committee on Fiscal Affairs. This Convention entered into force on 1 April 1995.

C. RATIONALE AND SIGNIFICANCE OF THE UNITED NATIONS MODEL CONVENTION

34.   The rationale of the preparation of bilateral tax conventions was cogently expressed by the Fiscal Committee of the League of Nations in the following terms:

> "The existence of model draft treaties . . . has proved of real use . . . in helping to solve many of the technical difficulties which arise in [the negotiation of tax treaties]. This procedure has the dual merit that, on the one hand, in so far as the model constitutes the basis of bilateral agreements, it creates automatically a uniformity of practice and legislation, while, on the other hand, inasmuch as it may be modified in any bilateral agreement reached, it is sufficiently elastic to be adapted to the different conditions obtaining in different countries or pairs of countries."[8]

35.   Like all model conventions, the United Nations Model Convention is not enforceable. Its provisions are not binding and furthermore should not be construed as formal recommendations of the United Nations. The United Nations Model Convention is intended

primarily to point the way towards feasible approaches to the resolution of the issues involved that both potential contracting parties are likely to find acceptable. Its aim is to facilitate the negotiation of tax treaties by eliminating the need for elaborate analysis and protracted discussion of every issue *ab origine* in the case of each treaty. Indeed, in preparing for negotiations a participating country may wish to review the provisions of bilateral double taxation treaties entered into by the other country in order to survey the latter's treaty practice and in particular the concessions it has granted in the past. In bilateral negotiations, room of course should be left to insert in the treaty provisions adapted to special situations.

36.   If the negotiating parties decide to use in a treaty wording suggested in the United Nations Model Convention, it is to be presumed that they would also expect to derive assistance in the interpretation of that wording from the relevant Commentary. The Commentaries, which may prove to be very useful in the implementation of a treaty concluded by the negotiating parties and in the settlement of any dispute relating thereto, are not intended to be annexed to such a treaty, the text of which in itself would constitute the legally binding agreement.

37.   Since the United Nations Model Convention reproduces many Articles of the OECD Model Convention together with the Commentaries thereon, the Group of Experts have taken a decision in 1999 that the observations and reservations would be noted, wherever necessary, at appropriate places.

38.   With regard to the observations on the Commentaries, the OECD Committee on Fiscal Affairs has noted that they "have sometimes been inserted at the request of some member countries who were unable to concur in the interpretation given in the Commentary on the Article concerned. These observations thus do not express any disagreement with the text of the Convention, but furnish a useful in-

---

[8]League of Nations, *Fiscal Committee: Report to the Council on the Fifth Session of the Committee, held in Geneva from June 12th to 17th, 1935* (C.252.M.124.1935.II.A), chapter II, section B, para. 4.

dication of the way in which those countries will apply the provisions of the Article in question."[9]

39.   The OECD Model Convention now includes, in Volume II, observations and reservations spelling out the positions with respect to the Model Convention of a number of non-member countries. The following countries' positions are included:

Argentina	Israel	Romania	Ukraine
Belarus	Latvia	Russia	Viet Nam
Brazil	Lithuania	Slovakia	
China	Malaysia	South Africa	
Estonia	Philippines	Thailand	

D.   RATIONALE AND METHODOLOGY FOR THE 1999 REVISION OF THE UNITED NATIONS MODEL CONVENTION

40.   In the 19 years since the publication of the United Nations Model Convention in 1980, several major developments have suggested a need to revise the document.

41.   The importance of the discussion set out in the Commentaries, of the issues identified in the preceding paragraphs can scarcely be overemphasized. Not only do the Commentaries explain the reasons that underlie particular formulations adopted in the text of the Model Articles, but that they also set out suggested alternative wordings to cover non-standard approaches to certain international taxation issues which may fall to the consideration of treaty negotiators in order to deal with the special circumstances that can arise in the economic relations between pairs of countries. The tendency towards globalization, together with the increasing pace of economic and, especially technological change, means that, in order to maintain its

---

[9]Organisation for Economic Co-operation and Development, *Model Double Taxation Convention on Income and on Capital: Report of the Fiscal Committee* (Paris, 1977), para. 27.

relevance, the discussion of these issues in the Commentaries needs to be continuously reviewed and updated. To meet this challenge the Group of Experts unanimously recommended that the *United Nations Model Double Taxation Convention between Developed and Developing Countries* should be updated periodically.

42.   The increasing focus on international trade, reflected by the establishment of the World Trade Organization (WTO), creates additional incentives to reduce other barriers, to exchanges of goods and services and the international movement of capital and persons.

43.   The emergence of the transitional economies, with their contribution to the world economy, and the need for these countries to mobilize domestic financial resources for development suggest major efforts in the areas of tax policy, tax administration and international taxation.

44.   There is a need for international and regional organizations to provide guidelines to facilitate conclusion of tax treaties with a view to promoting trade liberalization and expansion as well as socio-economic growth. By its resolution 1980/13 of 28 April 1980 the Economic and Social Council recognized the importance of international cooperation to combat international tax evasion and avoidance in consultation with other international agencies.

45.   The primary goals behind the 1999 revision of the United Nations Model Convention are establishing fiscal guidelines for trade liberalization and expansion with a view to releasing additional resources for sustainable growth and promoting bilateral tax coordination. In the light of these goals, the work of the Group reflects: (i) the 1992, 1994, 1995 and 1997 revisions to the OECD Model Convention, which continues to be the basis for many provisions of the United Nations Model Convention, (ii) recent developed/developing country treaty practice, which has shown increasing sophistication, (iii) scholarship in the tax treaty field, and (iv) the comments of those who have negotiated and administered tax treaties under the United Nations Model Convention and those who engage in international trade and commerce with developing countries.

46.   It is hoped that the United Nations Model Convention will contribute to the conclusion of an increasing number of bilateral tax
treaties, not only between developed and developing countries but
also between developing countries. It is also hoped that the Model
Convention will contribute to the standardization of the provisions of
such treaties. The creation of a network of bilateral tax treaties based
on a common model will be an important step on the way leading to
the eventual conclusion of regional or subregional conventions for
the avoidance of double taxation.

Part One

ARTICLES OF THE UNITED NATIONS MODEL DOUBLE TAXATION CONVENTION BETWEEN DEVELOPED AND DEVELOPING COUNTRIES

SUMMARY OF THE CONVENTION

Title and Preamble

CHAPTER I
Scope of the Convention

CHAPTER II
Definitions

CHAPTER III
Taxation of income

CHAPTER IV
Taxation of capital

CHAPTER V
Methods for elimination of double taxation

CHAPTER VI
Special provisions

CHAPTER VII
Final provisions

TITLE OF THE CONVENTION

Convention between (State A) and (State B) with respect to taxes on income and on capital[10]

PREAMBLE OF THE CONVENTION[11]

---

[10]States wishing to do so may follow the widespread practice of including in the title a reference to either the avoidance of double taxation or to both the avoidance of double taxation and the prevention of fiscal evasion.

[11]The Preamble of the Convention shall be drafted in accordance with the constitutional procedures of the Contracting States.

Chapter I

SCOPE OF THE CONVENTION

Article 1

PERSONS COVERED

This Convention shall apply to persons who are residents of one or both of the Contracting States.

Article 2

TAXES COVERED

1.   This Convention shall apply to taxes on income and on capital imposed on behalf of a Contracting State or of its political subdivisions or local authorities, irrespective of the manner in which they are levied.

2.   There shall be regarded as taxes on income and on capital all taxes imposed on total income, on total capital, or on elements of income or of capital, including taxes on gains from the alienation of movable or immovable property, taxes on the total amounts of wages or salaries paid by enterprises, as well as taxes on capital appreciation.

3.   The existing taxes to which the Convention shall apply are in particular:

   (*a*)   (in State A): ....

   (*b*)   (in State B): ....

4.   The Convention shall apply also to any identical or substantially similar taxes which are imposed after the date of signature of the Convention in addition to, or in place of, the existing taxes. The competent authorities of the Contracting States shall notify each other of significant changes made to their tax law.

Chapter II

DEFINITIONS

Article 3

GENERAL DEFINITIONS

1. For the purposes of this Convention, unless the context otherwise requires:

   (*a*) The term "person" includes an individual, a company and any other body of persons;

   (*b*) The term "company" means any body corporate or any entity that is treated as a body corporate for tax purposes;

   (*c*) The terms "enterprise of a Contracting State" and "enterprise of the other Contracting State" mean respectively an enterprise carried on by a resident of a Contracting State and an enterprise carried on by a resident of the other Contracting State;

   (*d*) The term "international traffic" means any transport by a ship or aircraft operated by an enterprise that has its place of effective management in a Contracting State, except when the ship or aircraft is operated solely between places in the other Contracting State;

   (*e*) The term "competent authority" means:

   (i) (In State A): ....

   (ii) (In State B): ....

   (*f*) The term "national" means:

   (i) Any individual possessing the nationality of a Contracting State

   (ii) Any legal person, partnership or association deriving its status as such from the laws in force in a Contracting State.

2.   As regards the application of the Convention at any time by a Contracting State, any term not defined therein shall, unless the context otherwise requires, have the meaning that it has at that time under the law of that State for the purposes of the taxes to which the Convention applies, any meaning under the applicable tax laws of that State prevailing over a meaning given to the term under other laws of that State.

Article 4

RESIDENT

1.   For the purposes of this Convention, the term "resident of a Contracting State" means any person who, under the laws of that State, is liable to tax therein by reason of his domicile, residence, place of incorporation, place of management or any other criterion of a similar nature, and also includes that State and any political subdivision or local authority thereof. This term, however, does not include any person who is liable to tax in that State in respect only of income from sources in that State or capital situated therein.

2.   Where by reason of the provisions of paragraph 1 an individual is a resident of both Contracting States, then his status shall be determined as follows:

(*a*)   He shall be deemed to be a resident only of the State in which he has a permanent home available to him; if he has a permanent home available to him in both States, he shall be deemed to be a resident only of the State with which his personal and economic relations are closer (centre of vital interests);

(*b*)   If the State in which he has his centre of vital interests cannot be determined, or if he has not a permanent home available to him in either State, he shall be deemed to be a resident only of the State in which he has an habitual abode;

(*c*)   If he has an habitual abode in both States or in neither of them, he shall be deemed to be a resident only of the State of which he is a national;

(*d*) If he is a national of both States or of neither of them, the competent authorities of the Contracting States shall settle the question by mutual agreement.

3.   Where by reason of the provisions of paragraph 1 a person other than an individual is a resident of both Contracting States, then it shall be deemed to be a resident only of the State in which its place of effective management is situated.

Article 5

PERMANENT ESTABLISHMENT

1.   For the purposes of this Convention, the term "permanent establishment" means a fixed place of business through which the business of an enterprise is wholly or partly carried on.

2.   The term "permanent establishment" includes especially:
 (*a*) A place of management;
 (*b*) A branch;
 (*c*) An office;
 (*d*) A factory;
 (*e*) A workshop;
 (*f*) A mine, an oil or gas well, a quarry or any other place of extraction of natural resources.

3.   The term "permanent establishment" also encompasses:
 (*a*) A building site, a construction, assembly or installation project or supervisory activities in connection therewith, but only if such site, project or activities last more than six months;
 (*b*) The furnishing of services, including consultancy services, by an enterprise through employees or other personnel engaged by the enterprise for such purpose, but only if activities of that nature continue (for the same or a connected project) within a

Contracting State for a period or periods aggregating more than six months within any twelve-month period.

4.   Notwithstanding the preceding provisions of this article, the term "permanent establishment" shall be deemed not to include:

    (*a*) The use of facilities solely for the purpose of storage or display of goods or merchandise belonging to the enterprise;

    (*b*) The maintenance of a stock of goods or merchandise belonging to the enterprise solely for the purpose of storage or display;

    (*c*) The maintenance of a stock of goods or merchandise belonging to the enterprise solely for the purpose of processing by another enterprise;

    (*d*) The maintenance of a fixed place of business solely for the purpose of purchasing goods or merchandise or of collecting information, for the enterprise;

    (*e*) The maintenance of a fixed place of business solely for the purpose of carrying on, for the enterprise, any other activity of a preparatory or auxiliary character.

    (*f*) The maintenance of a fixed place of business solely for any combination of activities mentioned in subparagraphs (*a*) to (*e*), provided that the overall activity of the fixed place of business resulting from this combination is of a preparatory or auxiliary character.

5.   Notwithstanding the provisions of paragraphs 1 and 2, where a person—other than an agent of an independent status to whom paragraph 7 applies—is acting in a Contracting State on behalf of an enterprise of the other Contracting State, that enterprise shall be deemed to have a permanent establishment in the first-mentioned Contracting State in respect of any activities which that person undertakes for the enterprise, if such a person:

    (*a*) Has and habitually exercises in that State an authority to conclude contracts in the name of the enterprise, unless the activities of such person are limited to those mentioned in paragraph 4 which, if exercised through a fixed place of business, would not make this fixed place of business a permanent establishment under the provisions of that paragraph; or

(*b*) Has no such authority, but habitually maintains in the first-mentioned State a stock of goods or merchandise from which he regularly delivers goods or merchandise on behalf of the enterprise.

6.   Notwithstanding the preceding provisions of this article, an insurance enterprise of a Contracting State shall, except in regard to re-insurance, be deemed to have a permanent establishment in the other Contracting State if it collects premiums in the territory of that other State or insures risks situated therein through a person other than an agent of an independent status to whom paragraph 7 applies.

7.   An enterprise of a Contracting State shall not be deemed to have a permanent establishment in the other Contracting State merely because it carries on business in that other State through a broker, general commission agent or any other agent of an independent status, provided that such persons are acting in the ordinary course of their business. However, when the activities of such an agent are devoted wholly or almost wholly on behalf of that enterprise, and conditions are made or imposed between that enterprise and the agent in their commercial and financial relations which differ from those which would have been made between independent enterprises, he will not be considered an agent of an independent status within the meaning of this paragraph.

8.   The fact that a company which is a resident of a Contracting State controls or is controlled by a company which is a resident of the other Contracting State, or which carries on business in that other State (whether through a permanent establishment or otherwise), shall not of itself constitute either company a permanent establishment of the other.

Chapter III

TAXATION OF INCOME

Article 6

INCOME FROM IMMOVABLE PROPERTY

1.   Income derived by a resident of a Contracting State from immovable property (including income from agriculture or forestry) situated in the other Contracting State may be taxed in that other State.

2.   The term "immovable property" shall have the meaning which it has under the law of the Contracting State in which the property in question is situated. The term shall in any case include property accessory to immovable property, livestock and equipment used in agriculture and forestry, rights to which the provisions of general law respecting landed property apply, usufruct of immovable property and rights to variable or fixed payments as consideration for the working of, or the right to work, mineral deposits, sources and other natural resources; ships, boats and aircraft shall not be regarded as immovable property.

3.   The provisions of paragraph 1 shall also apply to income derived from the direct use, letting or use in any other form of immovable property.

4.   The provisions of paragraphs 1 and 3 shall also apply to the income from immovable property of an enterprise and to income from immovable property used for the performance of independent personal services.

Article 7

BUSINESS PROFITS

1.   The profits of an enterprise of a Contracting State shall be taxable only in that State unless the enterprise carries on business in the other Contracting State through a permanent establishment situated therein. If the enterprise carries on business as aforesaid, the profits of the enterprise may be taxed in the other State but only so much of them as is attributable to (*a*) that permanent establishment; (*b*) sales in that other State of goods or merchandise of the same or similar kind as those sold through that permanent establishment; or (*c*) other business activities carried on in that other State of the same or similar kind as those effected through that permanent establishment.

2.   Subject to the provisions of paragraph 3, where an enterprise of a Contracting State carries on business in the other Contracting State through a permanent establishment situated therein, there shall in each Contracting State be attributed to that permanent establishment the profits which it might be expected to make if it were a distinct and separate enterprise engaged in the same or similar activities under the same or similar conditions and dealing wholly independently with the enterprise of which it is a permanent establishment.

3.   In the determination of the profits of a permanent establishment, there shall be allowed as deductions expenses which are incurred for the purposes of the business of the permanent establishment including executive and general administrative expenses so incurred, whether in the State in which the permanent establishment is situated or elsewhere. However, no such deduction shall be allowed in respect of amounts, if any, paid (otherwise than towards reimbursement of actual expenses) by the permanent establishment to the head office of the enterprise or any of its other offices, by way of royalties, fees or other similar payments in return for the use of patents or other rights, or by way of commission, for specific services performed or for management, or, except in the case of a banking enterprise, by way of interest on moneys lent to the permanent establishment. Likewise, no account shall be taken, in the determination of the profits of

a permanent establishment, for amounts charged (otherwise than towards reimbursement of actual expenses), by the permanent establishment to the head office of the enterprise or any of its other offices, by way of royalties, fees or other similar payments in return for the use of patents or other rights, or by way of commission for specific services performed or for management, or, except in the case of a banking enterprise, by way of interest on moneys lent to the head office of the enterprise or any of its other offices.

4.   In so far as it has been customary in a Contracting State to determine the profits to be attributed to a permanent establishment on the basis of an apportionment of the total profits of the enterprise to its various parts, nothing in paragraph 2 shall preclude that Contracting State from determining the profits to be taxed by such an apportionment as may be customary; the method of apportionment adopted shall, however, be such that the result shall be in accordance with the principles contained in this article.

5.   For the purposes of the preceding paragraphs, the profits to be attributed to the permanent establishment shall be determined by the same method year by year unless there is good and sufficient reason to the contrary.

6.   Where profits include items of income which are dealt with separately in other articles of this Convention, then the provisions of those articles shall not be affected by the provisions of this article.

(NOTE: The question of whether profits should be attributed to a permanent establishment by reason of the mere purchase by that permanent establishment of goods and merchandise for the enterprise was not resolved. It should therefore be settled in bilateral negotiations.)

Article 8

SHIPPING, INLAND WATERWAYS TRANSPORT AND AIR TRANSPORT

Article 8 *(alternative A)*

1.   Profits from the operation of ships or aircraft in international traffic shall be taxable only in the Contracting State in which the place of effective management of the enterprise is situated.

2.   Profits from the operation of boats engaged in inland waterways transport shall be taxable only in the Contracting State in which the place of effective management of the enterprise is situated.

3.   If the place of effective management of a shipping enterprise or of an inland waterways transport enterprise is aboard a ship or a boat, then it shall be deemed to be situated in the Contracting State in which the home harbour of the ship or boat is situated, or, if there is no such home harbour, in the Contracting State of which the operator of the ship or boat is a resident.

4.   The provisions of paragraph 1 shall also apply to profits from the participation in a pool, a joint business or an international operating agency.

Article 8 *(alternative B)*

1.   Profits from the operation of aircraft in international traffic shall be taxable only in the Contracting State in which the place of effective management of the enterprise is situated.

2.   Profits from the operation of ships in international traffic shall be taxable only in the Contracting State in which the place of effective management of the enterprise is situated unless the shipping activities arising from such operation in the other Contracting State are more than casual. If such activities are more than casual, such profits may be taxed in that other State. The profits to be taxed in that other State shall be determined on the basis of an appropriate allocation of

the overall net profits derived by the enterprise from its shipping operations. The tax computed in accordance with such allocation shall then be reduced by ___ per cent. (The percentage is to be established through bilateral negotiations.)

3.   Profits from the operation of boats engaged in inland waterways transport shall be taxable only in the Contracting State in which the place of effective management of the enterprise is situated.

4.   If the place of effective management of a shipping enterprise or of an inland waterways transport enterprise is aboard a ship or boat, then it shall be deemed to be situated in the Contracting State in which the home harbour of the ship or boat is situated, or if there is no such home harbour, in the Contracting State of which the operator of the ship or boat is a resident.

5.   The provisions of paragraphs 1 and 2 shall also apply to profits from the participation in a pool, a joint business or an international operating agency.

Article 9
ASSOCIATED ENTERPRISES

1.   Where:

(*a*)   an enterprise of a Contracting State participates directly or indirectly in the management, control or capital of an enterprise of the other Contracting State, or

(*b*)   the same persons participate directly or indirectly in the management, control or capital of an enterprise of a Contracting State and an enterprise of the other Contracting State,

and in either case conditions are made or imposed between the two enterprises in their commercial or financial relations which differ from those which would be made between independent enterprises, then any profits which would, but for those conditions, have accrued to one of the enterprises, but, by reason of those conditions, have not so accrued, may be included in the profits of that enterprise and taxed accordingly.

2.　　Where a Contracting State includes in the profits of an enterprise of that State—and taxes accordingly—profits on which an enterprise of the other Contracting State has been charged to tax in that other State and the profits so included are profits which would have accrued to the enterprise of the first-mentioned State if the conditions made between the two enterprises had been those which would have been made between independent enterprises, then that other State shall make an appropriate adjustment to the amount of the tax charged therein on those profits. In determining such adjustment, due regard shall be had to the other provisions of the Convention and the competent authorities of the Contracting States shall, if necessary, consult each other.

3.　　The provisions of paragraph 2 shall not apply where judicial, administrative or other legal proceedings have resulted in a final ruling that by actions giving rise to an adjustment of profits under paragraph 1, one of the enterprises concerned is liable to penalty with respect to fraud, gross negligence or wilful default.

Article 10

DIVIDENDS

1.　　Dividends paid by a company which is a resident of a Contracting State to a resident of the other Contracting State may be taxed in that other State.

2.　　However, such dividends may also be taxed in the Contracting State of which the company paying the dividends is a resident and according to the laws of that State, but if the beneficial owner of the dividends is a resident of the other Contracting State, the tax so charged shall not exceed:

>   (*a*)　　＿＿ per cent (the percentage is to be established through bilateral negotiations) of the gross amount of the dividends if

the beneficial owner is a company (other than a partnership) which holds directly at least 10 per cent of the capital of the company paying the dividends;

(b) ____ per cent (the percentage is to be established through bilateral negotiations) of the gross amount of the dividends in all other cases.

The competent authorities of the Contracting States shall by mutual agreement settle the mode of application of these limitations.

This paragraph shall not affect the taxation of the company in respect of the profits out of which the dividends are paid.

3.   The term "dividends" as used in this article means income from shares, "jouissance" shares or "jouissance" rights, mining shares, founders' shares or other rights, not being debt claims, participating in profits, as well as income from other corporate rights which is subjected to the same taxation treatment as income from shares by the laws of the State of which the company making the distribution is a resident.

4.   The provisions of paragraphs 1 and 2 shall not apply if the beneficial owner of the dividends, being a resident of a Contracting State, carries on business in the other Contracting State of which the company paying the dividends is a resident, through a permanent establishment situated therein, or performs in that other State independent personal services from a fixed base situated therein, and the holding in respect of which the dividends are paid is effectively connected with such permanent establishment or fixed base. In such case the provisions of article 7 or article 14, as the case may be, shall apply.

5.   Where a company which is a resident of a Contracting State derives profits or income from the other Contracting State, that other State may not impose any tax on the dividends paid by the company, except in so far as such dividends are paid to a resident of that other State or in so far as the holding in respect of which the dividends are paid is effectively connected with a permanent establishment or a

fixed base situated in that other State, nor subject the company's un-distributed profits to a tax on the company's undistributed profits, even if the dividends paid or the undistributed profits consist wholly or partly of profits or income arising in such other State.

Article 11

INTEREST

1.   Interest arising in a Contracting State and paid to a resident of the other Contracting State may be taxed in that other State.

2.   However, such interest may also be taxed in the Contracting State in which it arises and according to the laws of that State, but if the beneficial owner of the interest is a resident of the other Con-tracting State, the tax so charged shall not exceed ___ per cent (the percentage is to be established through bilateral negotiations) of the gross amount of the interest. The competent authorities of the Con-tracting States shall by mutual agreement settle the mode of applica-tion of this limitation.

3.   The term "interest" as used in this article means income from debt claims of every kind, whether or not secured by mortgage and whether or not carrying a right to participate in the debtor's profits, and in particular, income from government securities and income from bonds or debentures, including premiums and prizes attaching to such securities, bonds or debentures. Penalty charges for late pay-ment shall not be regarded as interest for the purpose of this article.

4.   The provisions of paragraphs 1 and 2 shall not apply if the ben-eficial owner of the interest, being a resident of a Contracting State, carries on business in the other Contracting State in which the inter-est arises, through a permanent establishment situated therein, or per-forms in that other State independent personal services from a fixed base situated therein, and the debt claim in respect of which the inter-est is paid is effectively connected with (*a*) such permanent establish-ment or fixed base, or with (*b*) business activities referred to in (*c*) of

paragraph 1 of article 7. In such cases the provisions of article 7 or article 14, as the case may be, shall apply.

5.   Interest shall be deemed to arise in a Contracting State when the payer is a resident of that State. Where, however, the person paying the interest, whether he is a resident of a Contracting State or not, has in a Contracting State a permanent establishment or a fixed base in connection with which the indebtedness on which the interest is paid was incurred, and such interest is borne by such permanent establishment or fixed base, then such interest shall be deemed to arise in the State in which the permanent establishment or fixed base is situated.

6.   Where, by reason of a special relationship between the payer and the beneficial owner or between both of them and some other person, the amount of the interest, having regard to the debt claim for which it is paid, exceeds the amount which would have been agreed upon by the payer and the beneficial owner in the absence of such relationship, the provisions of this article shall apply only to the last-mentioned amount. In such case, the excess part of the payments shall remain taxable according to the laws of each Contracting State, due regard being had to the other provisions of this Convention.

Article 12

ROYALTIES

1.   Royalties arising in a Contracting State and paid to a resident of the other Contracting State may be taxed in that other State.

2.   However, such royalties may also be taxed in the Contracting State in which they arise and according to the laws of that State, but if the beneficial owner of the royalties is a resident of the other Contracting State, the tax so charged shall not exceed ___ per cent (the percentage is to be established through bilateral negotiations) of the gross amount of the royalties. The competent authorities of the Con-

tracting States shall by mutual agreement settle the mode of application of this limitation.

3.   The term "royalties" as used in this article means payments of any kind received as a consideration for the use of, or the right to use, any copyright of literary, artistic or scientific work including cinematograph films, or films or tapes used for radio or television broadcasting, any patent, trademark, design or model, plan, secret formula or process, or for the use of, or the right to use, industrial, commercial or scientific equipment or for information concerning industrial, commercial or scientific experience.

4.   The provisions of paragraphs 1 and 2 shall not apply if the beneficial owner of the royalties, being a resident of a Contracting State, carries on business in the other Contracting State in which the royalties arise, through a permanent establishment situated therein, or performs in that other State independent personal services from a fixed base situated therein, and the right or property in respect of which the royalties are paid is effectively connected with (a) such permanent establishment or fixed base, or with (b) business activities referred to in (c) of paragraph 1 of article 7. In such cases the provisions of article 7 or article 14, as the case may be, shall apply.

5.   Royalties shall be deemed to arise in a Contracting State when the payer is a resident of that State. Where, however, the person paying the royalties, whether he is a resident of a Contracting State or not, has in a Contracting State a permanent establishment or a fixed base in connection with which the liability to pay the royalties was incurred, and such royalties are borne by such permanent establishment or fixed base, then such royalties shall be deemed to arise in the State in which the permanent establishment or fixed base is situated.

6.   Where by reason of a special relationship between the payer and the beneficial owner or between both of them and some other person, the amount of the royalties, having regard to the use, right or information for which they are paid, exceeds the amount which would have been agreed upon by the payer and the beneficial owner in the absence of such relationship, the provisions of this article shall

apply only to the last-mentioned amount. In such case, the excess part of the payments shall remain taxable according to the laws of each Contracting State, due regard being had to the other provisions of this Convention.

Article 13

CAPITAL GAINS

1.　Gains derived by a resident of a Contracting State from the alienation of immovable property referred to in article 6 and situated in the other Contracting State may be taxed in that other State.

2.　Gains from the alienation of movable property forming part of the business property of a permanent establishment which an enterprise of a Contracting State has in the other Contracting State or of movable property pertaining to a fixed base available to a resident of a Contracting State in the other Contracting State for the purpose of performing independent personal services, including such gains from the alienation of such a permanent establishment (alone or with the whole enterprise) or of such fixed base, may be taxed in that other State.

3.　Gains from the alienation of ships or aircraft operated in international traffic, boats engaged in inland waterways transport or movable property pertaining to the operation of such ships, aircraft or boats, shall be taxable only in the Contracting State in which the place of effective management of the enterprise is situated.

4.　Gains from the alienation of shares of the capital stock of a company, or of an interest in a partnership, trust or estate, the property of which consists directly or indirectly principally of immovable property situated in a Contracting State may be taxed in that State. In particular:

(1) Nothing contained in this paragraph shall apply to a company, partnership, trust or estate, other than a company, partnership, trust or estate engaged in the business of management of im-

movable properties, the property of which consists directly or indirectly principally of immovable property used by such company, partnership, trust or estate in its business activities.

(2) For the purposes of this paragraph, "principally" in relation to ownership of immovable property means the value of such immovable property exceeding 50 per cent of the aggregate value of all assets owned by the company, partnership, trust or estate.

5. Gains from the alienation of shares other than those mentioned in paragraph 4 representing a participation of ___ per cent (the percentage is to be established through bilateral negotiations) in a company which is a resident of a Contracting State may be taxed in that State.

6. Gains from the alienation of any property other than that referred to in paragraphs 1, 2, 3, 4 and 5 shall be taxable only in the Contracting State of which the alienator is a resident.

Article 14

INDEPENDENT PERSONAL SERVICES

1. Income derived by a resident of a Contracting State in respect of professional services or other activities of an independent character shall be taxable only in that State except in the following circumstances, when such income may also be taxed in the other Contracting State:

(*a*) If he has a fixed base regularly available to him in the other Contracting State for the purpose of performing his activities; in that case, only so much of the income as is attributable to that fixed base may be taxed in that other Contracting State; or

(*b*) If his stay in the other Contracting State is for a period or periods amounting to or exceeding in the aggregate 183 days in any twelve-month period commencing or ending in the fiscal year concerned; in that case, only so much of the income as is derived from his activities performed in that other State may be taxed in that other State.

2.   The term "professional services" includes especially independent scientific, literary, artistic, educational or teaching activities as well as the independent activities of physicians, lawyers, engineers, architects, dentists and accountants.

Article 15
DEPENDENT PERSONAL SERVICES

1.   Subject to the provisions of articles 16, 18 and 19, salaries, wages and other similar remuneration derived by a resident of a Contracting State in respect of an employment shall be taxable only in that State unless the employment is exercised in the other Contracting State. If the employment is so exercised, such remuneration as is derived therefrom may be taxed in that other State.

2.   Notwithstanding the provisions of paragraph 1, remuneration derived by a resident of a Contracting State in respect of an employment exercised in the other Contracting State shall be taxable only in the first-mentioned State if:

   (*a*)   The recipient is present in the other State for a period or periods not exceeding in the aggregate 183 days in any twelve-month period commencing or ending in the fiscal year concerned; and

   (*b*)   The remuneration is paid by, or on behalf of, an employer who is not a resident of the other State; and

   (*c*)   The remuneration is not borne by a permanent establishment or a fixed base which the employer has in the other State.

3.   Notwithstanding the preceding provisions of this article, remuneration derived in respect of an employment exercised aboard a ship or aircraft operated in international traffic, or aboard a boat engaged in inland waterways transport, may be taxed in the Contracting

State in which the place of effective management of the enterprise is situated.

Article 16

DIRECTORS' FEES AND REMUNERATION OF TOP-LEVEL MANAGERIAL OFFICIALS

1.   Directors' fees and other similar payments derived by a resident of a Contracting State in his capacity as a member of the Board of Directors of a company which is a resident of the other Contracting State may be taxed in that other State.

2.   Salaries, wages and other similar remuneration derived by a resident of a Contracting State in his capacity as an official in a top-level managerial position of a company which is a resident of the other Contracting State may be taxed in that other State.

Article 17

ARTISTES AND SPORTSPERSONS

1.   Notwithstanding the provisions of articles 14 and 15, income derived by a resident of a Contracting State as an entertainer, such as a theatre, motion picture, radio or television artiste, or a musician, or as a sportsperson, from his personal activities as such exercised in the other Contracting State, may be taxed in that other State.

2.   Where income in respect of personal activities exercised by an entertainer or a sportsperson in his capacity as such accrues not to the entertainer or sportsperson himself but to another person, that income may, notwithstanding the provisions of articles 7, 14 and 15, be taxed in the Contracting State in which the activities of the entertainer or sportsperson are exercised.

Article 18

PENSIONS AND SOCIAL SECURITY PAYMENTS

Article 18 *(alternative A)*

1.   Subject to the provisions of paragraph 2 of article 19, pensions and other similar remuneration paid to a resident of a Contracting State in consideration of past employment shall be taxable only in that State.

2.   Notwithstanding the provisions of paragraph 1, pensions paid and other payments made under a public scheme which is part of the social security system of a Contracting State or a political subdivision or a local authority thereof shall be taxable only in that State.

Article 18 *(alternative B)*

1.   Subject to the provisions of paragraph 2 of article 19, pensions and other similar remuneration paid to a resident of a Contracting State in consideration of past employment may be taxed in that State.

2.   However, such pensions and other similar remuneration may also be taxed in the other Contracting State if the payment is made by a resident of that other State or a permanent establishment situated therein.

3.   Notwithstanding the provisions of paragraphs 1 and 2, pensions paid and other payments made under a public scheme which is part of the social security system of a Contracting State or a political subdivision or a local authority thereof shall be taxable only in that State.

Article 19

GOVERNMENT SERVICE

1. (*a*) Salaries, wages and other similar remuneration, other than a pension, paid by a Contracting State or a political subdivision or a local authority thereof to an individual in respect of services rendered to that State or subdivision or authority shall be taxable only in that State.

   (*b*) However, such salaries, wages and other similar remuneration shall be taxable only in the other Contracting State if the services are rendered in that other State and the individual is a resident of that State who:

   (i) Is a national of that State; or

   (ii) Did not become a resident of that State solely for the purpose of rendering the services.

2. (*a*) Any pension paid by, or out of funds created by, a Contracting State or a political subdivision or a local authority thereof to an individual in respect of services rendered to that State or subdivision or authority shall be taxable only in that State.

   (*b*) However, such pension shall be taxable only in the other Contracting State if the individual is a resident of, and a national of, that other State.

3. The provisions of articles 15, 16, 17 and 18 shall apply to salaries, wages and other similar remuneration, and to pensions, in respect of services rendered in connection with a business carried on by a Contracting State or a political subdivision or a local authority thereof.

Article 20

STUDENTS

Payments which a student or business trainee or apprentice who is or was immediately before visiting a Contracting State a resident of the other Contracting State and who is present in the first-mentioned State solely for the purpose of his education or training receives for the purpose of his maintenance, education or training shall not be taxed in that State, provided that such payments arise from sources outside that State.

Article 21

OTHER INCOME

1.   Items of income of a resident of a Contracting State, wherever arising, not dealt with in the foregoing articles of this Convention shall be taxable only in that State.

2.   The provisions of paragraph 1 shall not apply to income, other than income from immovable property as defined in paragraph 2 of article 6, if the recipient of such income, being a resident of a Contracting State, carries on business in the other Contracting State through a permanent establishment situated therein, or performs in that other State independent personal services from a fixed base situated therein, and the right or property in respect of which the income is paid is effectively connected with such permanent establishment or fixed base. In such case the provisions of article 7 or article 14, as the case may be, shall apply.

3.   Notwithstanding the provisions of paragraphs 1 and 2, items of income of a resident of a Contracting State not dealt with in the foregoing articles of this Convention and arising in the other Contracting State may also be taxed in that other State.

Chapter IV

TAXATION OF CAPITAL

Article 22

CAPITAL

1.   Capital represented by immovable property referred to in article 6, owned by a resident of a Contracting State and situated in the other Contracting State, may be taxed in that other State.

2.   Capital represented by movable property forming part of the business property of a permanent establishment which an enterprise of a Contracting State has in the other Contracting State or by movable property pertaining to a fixed base available to a resident of a Contracting State in the other Contracting State for the purpose of performing independent personal services may be taxed in that other State.

3.   Capital represented by ships and aircraft operated in international traffic and by boats engaged in inland waterways transport, and by movable property pertaining to the operation of such ships, aircraft and boats, shall be taxable only in the Contracting State in which the place of effective management of the enterprise is situated.

[4.   All other elements of capital of a resident of a Contracting State shall be taxable only in that State.]

(The Group decided to leave to bilateral negotiations the question of the taxation of the capital represented by immovable property and movable property and of all other elements of capital of a resident of a Contracting State. Should the negotiating parties decide to include in the Convention an article on the taxation of capital, they will have to determine whether to use the wording of paragraph 4 as shown or wording that leaves taxation to the State in which the capital is located.)

Chapter V

METHODS FOR THE ELIMINATION OF DOUBLE TAXATION

Article 23 A

EXEMPTION METHOD

1.   Where a resident of a Contracting State derives income or owns capital which, in accordance with the provisions of this Convention, may be taxed in the other Contracting State, the first-mentioned State shall, subject to the provisions of paragraphs 2 and 3, exempt such income or capital from tax.

2.   Where a resident of a Contracting State derives items of income which, in accordance with the provisions of articles 10, 11 and 12, may be taxed in the other Contracting State, the first-mentioned State shall allow as a deduction from the tax on the income of that resident an amount equal to the tax paid in that other State. Such deduction shall not, however, exceed that part of the tax, as computed before the deduction is given, which is attributable to such items of income derived from that other State.

3.   Where in accordance with any provision of this Convention income derived or capital owned by a resident of a Contracting State is exempt from tax in that State, such State may nevertheless, in calculating the amount of tax on the remaining income or capital of such resident, take into account the exempted income or capital.

Article 23 B

CREDIT METHOD

1.   Where a resident of a Contracting State derives income or owns capital which, in accordance with the provisions of this Con-

vention, may be taxed in the other Contracting State, the first-mentioned State shall allow as a deduction from the tax on the income of that resident an amount equal to the income tax paid in that other State; and as a deduction from the tax on the capital of that resident, an amount equal to the capital tax paid in that other State. Such deduction in either case shall not, however, exceed that part of the income tax or capital tax, as computed before the deduction is given, which is attributable, as the case may be, to the income or the capital which may be taxed in that other State.

2.   Where, in accordance with any provision of this Convention, income derived or capital owned by a resident of a Contracting State is exempt from tax in that State, such State may nevertheless, in calculating the amount of tax on the remaining income or capital of such resident, take into account the exempted income or capital.

Chapter VI

SPECIAL PROVISIONS

Article 24

NON-DISCRIMINATION

1.   Nationals of a Contracting State shall not be subjected in the other Contracting State to any taxation or any requirement connected therewith which is other or more burdensome than the taxation and connected requirements to which nationals of that other State in the same circumstances, in particular with respect to residence, are or may be subjected. This provision shall, notwithstanding the provisions of article 1, also apply to persons who are not residents of one or both of the Contracting States.

2.   Stateless persons who are residents of a Contracting State shall not be subjected in either Contracting State to any taxation or any requirement connected therewith which is other or more burdensome than the taxation and connected requirements to which nationals of the State concerned in the same circumstances, in particular with respect to residence, are or may be subjected.

3.   The taxation on a permanent establishment which an enterprise of a Contracting State has in the other Contracting State shall not be less favourably levied in that other State than the taxation levied on enterprises of that other State carrying on the same activities. This provision shall not be construed as obliging a Contracting State to grant to residents of the other Contracting State any personal allowances, reliefs and reductions for taxation purposes on account of civil status or family responsibilities which it grants to its own residents.

4.   Except where the provisions of paragraph 1 of article 9, paragraph 6 of article 11, or paragraph 6 of article 12 apply, interest, royalties and other disbursements paid by an enterprise of a Contracting

State to a resident of the other Contracting State shall, for the purpose of determining the taxable profits of such enterprise, be deductible under the same conditions as if they had been paid to a resident of the first-mentioned State. Similarly, any debts of an enterprise of a Contracting State to a resident of the other Contracting State shall, for the purpose of determining the taxable capital of such enterprise, be deductible under the same conditions as if they had been contracted to a resident of the first-mentioned State.

5.   Enterprises of a Contracting State, the capital of which is wholly or partly owned or controlled, directly or indirectly, by one or more residents of the other Contracting State, shall not be subjected in the first-mentioned State to any taxation or any requirement connected therewith which is other or more burdensome than the taxation and connected requirements to which other similar enterprises of the first-mentioned State are or may be subjected.

6.   The provisions of this article shall, notwithstanding the provisions of article 2, apply to taxes of every kind and description.

Article 25
MUTUAL AGREEMENT PROCEDURE

1.   Where a person considers that the actions of one or both of the Contracting States result or will result for him in taxation not in accordance with the provisions of this Convention, he may, irrespective of the remedies provided by the domestic law of those States, present his case to the competent authority of the Contracting State of which he is a resident or, if his case comes under paragraph 1 of article 24, to that of the Contracting State of which he is a national. The case must be presented within three years from the first notification of the action resulting in taxation not in accordance with the provisions of the Convention.

2.   The competent authority shall endeavour, if the objection appears to it to be justified and if it is not itself able to arrive at a satis-

factory solution, to resolve the case by mutual agreement with the competent authority of the other Contracting State, with a view to the avoidance of taxation which is not in accordance with this Convention. Any agreement reached shall be implemented notwithstanding any time limits in the domestic law of the Contracting States.

3.   The competent authorities of the Contracting States shall endeavour to resolve by mutual agreement any difficulties or doubts arising as to the interpretation or application of the Convention. They may also consult together for the elimination of double taxation in cases not provided for in the Convention.

4.   The competent authorities of the Contracting States may communicate with each other directly, including through a joint commission consisting of themselves or their representatives, for the purpose of reaching an agreement in the sense of the preceding paragraphs. The competent authorities, through consultations, shall develop appropriate bilateral procedures, conditions, methods and techniques for the implementation of the mutual agreement procedure provided for in this article. In addition, a competent authority may devise appropriate unilateral procedures, conditions, methods and techniques to facilitate the above-mentioned bilateral actions and the implementation of the mutual agreement procedure.

Article 26

EXCHANGE OF INFORMATION

1.   The competent authorities of the Contracting States shall exchange such information as is necessary for carrying out the provisions of this Convention or of the domestic laws of the Contracting States concerning taxes covered by the Convention, in so far as the taxation thereunder is not contrary to the Convention, in particular for the prevention of fraud or evasion of such taxes. The exchange of information is not restricted by article 1. Any information received by a Contracting State shall be treated as secret in the same manner as information obtained under the domestic laws of that State. How-

ever, if the information is originally regarded as secret in the transmitting State it shall be disclosed only to persons or authorities (including courts and administrative bodies) concerned with the assessment or collection of, the enforcement or prosecution in respect of, or the determination of appeals in relation to the taxes which are the subject of the Convention. Such persons or authorities shall use the information only for such purposes but may disclose the information in public court proceedings or in judicial decisions. The competent authorities shall, through consultation, develop appropriate conditions, methods and techniques concerning the matters in respect of which such exchanges of information shall be made, including, where appropriate, exchanges of information regarding tax avoidance.

2.   In no case shall the provisions of paragraph 1 be construed so as to impose on a Contracting State the obligation:

   (*a*)   To carry out administrative measures at variance with the laws and administrative practice of that or of the other Contracting State;

   (*b*)   To supply information which is not obtainable under the laws or in the normal course of the administration of that or of the other Contracting State;

   (*c*)   To supply information which would disclose any trade, business, industrial, commercial or professional secret or trade process, or information, the disclosure of which would be contrary to public policy (*ordre public*).

Article 27
MEMBERS OF DIPLOMATIC MISSIONS AND CONSULAR POSTS

Nothing in this Convention shall affect the fiscal privileges of members of diplomatic missions or consular posts under the general rules of international law or under the provisions of special agreements.

Chapter VII

FINAL PROVISIONS

Article 28

ENTRY INTO FORCE

1.   This Convention shall be ratified and the instruments of ratification shall be exchanged at _____ as soon as possible.

2.   The Convention shall enter into force upon the exchange of instruments of ratification and its provisions shall have effect:
   (*a*) (In State A): ....
   (*b*) (In State B): ....

Article 29

TERMINATION

This Convention shall remain in force until terminated by a Contracting State. Either Contracting State may terminate the Convention, through diplomatic channels, by giving notice of termination at least six months before the end of any calendar year after the year ____. In such event, the Convention shall cease to have effect:
   (*a*) (In State A): ....
   (*b*) (In State B): ....

TERMINAL CLAUSE

NOTE: The provisions relating to the entry into force and termination and the terminal clause concerning the signing of the Convention shall be drafted in accordance with the constitutional procedure of both Contracting States.

Part Two

COMMENTARIES ON THE ARTICLES OF THE UNITED NATIONS MODEL DOUBLE TAXATION CONVENTION BETWEEN DEVELOPED AND DEVELOPING COUNTRIES

[References to paragraphs from the OECD Model Convention Commentary are indicated at the end of each paragraph in square brackets.]

Commentary on chapter I

SCOPE OF THE CONVENTION

Article 1

PERSONS COVERED

A. GENERAL CONSIDERATIONS

1.   Article 1 of the United Nations Model Convention reproduces Article 1 of the OECD Model Convention.

2.   The title of article 1 has been changed in 1999 from "Personal scope" to "Persons covered". The first article of the Convention should normally specify the types of persons or taxpayers to whom the Convention applies. The title "Personal scope" did not convey the scope of application of the Convention. Hence, the title of article 1 has been appropriately changed to "Persons covered" to convey the correct scope of the Convention.

3.   Like the OECD Model Convention, the United Nations Model Convention applies to persons who are "residents of one or both of the Contracting States". The personal scope of most of the earliest conventions was more restrictive, in that it encompassed "citizens" of the Contracting States. However, in some early conventions that scope was wider, covering "taxpayers" of the Contracting States, that is persons who, although not residing in either State, are nevertheless liable to tax on part of their income or capital in each of them. In some articles there are exceptions to this rule, for example in articles 24, paragraph 1, 25, paragraph 1, and 26, paragraph 1.

4.   The United Nations Model Convention does not contain special provisions relating to partnerships. The Contracting States are therefore left free to examine the problems concerning partnerships in bilateral negotiations and to agree upon such special provisions as they may find necessary and appropriate. The OECD Committee on

Fiscal Affairs has adopted on 20 January 1999 the report of the Working Group entitled "The Application of the OECD Model Tax Convention to Partnerships". The report deals with the application of the provisions of the OECD Model Tax Convention, and indirectly of bilateral tax conventions based on that Model, to partnerships. The Committee recognizes, however, that many of the principles discussed in that report may also apply, *mutatis mutandis*, to other non-corporate entities. In this report, references to "partnerships" cover entities which qualify as such under civil or commercial law as opposed to tax law. The wide differences in the views of the OECD member countries stem from the fact that their domestic laws treat partnerships in different ways. In some OECD countries, partnerships are treated as taxable units and sometimes even as companies, while other OECD countries do not tax the partnership as such and only tax individual partners on their shares of partnership income. Similar differences in the tax treatment of partnerships exist in the developing countries.

5.   An important question is whether a partnership should itself be allowed the benefits of the Convention. If, under the laws of a Contracting State, partnerships are taxable entities, a partnership may qualify as a resident of that Contracting State under paragraph 1 of article 4 and therefore be entitled to benefits of the Convention. However, if a partnership is a conduit and only partners are taxed on partnership income, the partnership may also be disregarded under the Convention, at least in the absence of special rules in the Convention providing otherwise.

6.   The application of the Convention to partners may also depend on the laws of the Contracting States. The laws of the Contracting States also determine the treatment under the Convention of a disposition of a partnership interest.

7.   If the Contracting States differ in their treatments of partnerships, different articles of the Convention can apply to the same transaction in the two States, which may result in double taxation or non-taxation in both States.

8.   With respect to the improper use of the convention, the OECD Commentary observes as under:

"Improper use of the Convention

The purpose of double taxation conventions is to promote, by eliminating international double taxation, exchange of goods and services, and the movement of capital and persons; they should not, however, help tax avoidance or evasion. True, taxpayers have the possibility, irrespective of double taxation conventions, to exploit differences in tax levels between States and the tax advantages provided by various countries' taxation laws, but it is for the States concerned to adopt provisions in their domestic laws to counter such manoeuvres. Such States will then wish, in their bilateral double taxation conventions, to preserve the application of provisions of this kind contained in their domestic laws." [para. 7]

"Moreover, the extension of the network of double taxation conventions still reinforces the impact of such manoeuvres by making it possible, using artificial legal constructions, to benefit both from the tax advantages available under domestic laws and the tax relief provided for in double taxation conventions." [para. 8]

"This would be the case, for example, if a person (whether or not a resident of a Contracting State), acts through a legal entity created in a State essentially to obtain treaty benefits that would not be available directly. Another case would be an individual who has in a Contracting State both his permanent home and all his economic interests, including a substantial share holding in a company of that State, and who, essentially in order to sell the shares and escape taxation in that State on the capital gains from the alienation (by virtue of paragraph [6] of Article 13), transfers his permanent home to the other Contracting State, where such gains are subject to little or no tax." [para. 9]

"Some of these situations are dealt with in the Convention, e.g., by the introduction of the concept of 'beneficial owner' (in Articles 10, 11 and 12) and of special provisions, for so-called artiste-companies (paragraph 2 of Article 17). Such problems are also mentioned in the Commentaries on Article 10 (paragraphs 17 and 22), Article 11 (paragraph 12), and Article 12 (paragraph 7). It may be appropriate for Contracting States to agree in bilateral negotiations that any relief from tax should not apply in certain cases, or to agree that the application of the provisions of domestic laws against tax avoidance should not be affected by the Convention." [para. 10]

9.   The OECD Commentary sets forth a useful inventory of approaches to address the problem of improper uses of the Convention, many of them involving conduit companies, as follows:

"A solution to the problem of conduit companies would be to disallow treaty benefits to a company not owned, directly or indirectly, by residents of the State of which the company is a resident. For example, such a 'look through' provision might have the following wording:

'A company that is a resident of a Contracting State shall not be entitled to relief from taxation under this Convention with respect to any item of income, gains or profit if it is owned or controlled directly or through one or more companies, wherever resident, by persons who are not residents of a Contracting State.'

Contracting States wishing to adopt such a provision may also want, in their bilateral negotiations, to determine the criteria according to which a company would be considered as owned or controlled by non-residents." [para. 13]

"Conduit situations can be created by the use of tax-exempt (or nearly tax-exempt) companies that may be distinguished by special legal characteristics. The improper use of tax treaties may then be avoided by denying the tax treaty benefits to these companies (the exclusion approach). The main cases are specific types of companies enjoying tax privileges in their State of residence giving them in fact a status similar to that of a non-resident. As such privileges are granted mostly to specific types of companies as defined in the commercial law or the tax law of a country, the most radical solution would be to exclude such companies from the scope of the treaty. Another solution would be to insert a safeguarding clause such as the following:

> 'No provision of the Convention conferring an exemption from, or reduction of, tax shall apply to income received or paid by a company as defined under Section . . . of the . . . Act, or under any similar provision enacted by . . . after the signature of the Convention.'

The scope of this provision could be limited by referring only to specific types of income, such as, dividends, interest, capital gains or director's fees. Under such provisions companies of the type concerned would remain entitled to the protection offered under Article 24 (Non-discrimination) and to the benefits of Article 25 (Mutual agreement procedure) and they would be subject to the provisions of Article 26 (Exchange of information)." [para. 15]

"General subject-to-tax provisions provide that the treaty benefits to the State of source are granted only if the income in question is subject to tax in the State of residence. This corresponds to the aim of tax treaties, namely, to avoid double taxation. For a number of reasons, however, the Model Convention does not recommend such a general provision. While this seems adequate with respect to normal international relationship, a subject-to-tax approach might well be adopted in a typical conduit situation. A safeguarding provision of this kind could have the following wording:

> "Where income arising in a Contracting State is received by a company resident of the other Contracting State and one or more persons not resident in that other Contracting State
>
> (*a*) have directly or indirectly or through one or more companies, wherever resident, a substantial interest in such company, in the form of participation or otherwise, or

(*b*) exercise directly or indirectly, alone or together, the management or control of such company,

any provision of this Convention conferring an exemption from, or a reduction of, tax shall apply only to income that is subject to tax in the last-mentioned State under the ordinary rules of its tax law."

The concept of 'substantial interest' may be further specified when drafting a bilateral convention. Contracting States may express it, for instance, as a percentage of the capital or of the voting rights of the company." [para. 17]

10. The OECD Commentary cautions:

"The solutions described above are of a general nature and they need to be accompanied by specific provisions to ensure that treaty benefits will be granted in bona fide cases. Such provisions could have the following wording:

(*a*) *General bona fide provision*

The foregoing provisions shall not apply where the company establishes that the principal purpose of the company, the conduct of its business and the acquisition or maintenance by it of the share holding or other property from which the income in question is derived, are motivated by sound business reasons and thus do not have as primary purpose the obtaining of any benefit under this Convention.

(*b*) *Activity provision*

The foregoing provisions shall not apply where the company is engaged in substantive business operations in the Contracting State of which it is a resident and the relief from taxation claimed from the other Contracting State is with respect to income which is connected with such operations.

(*c*) *Amount of tax provision*

The foregoing provisions shall not apply where the reduction of tax claimed is not greater than the tax actually imposed by the Contracting State of which the company is a resident.

(*d*) *Stock exchange provision*

The foregoing provisions shall not apply to a company which is a resident of a Contracting State if the principal class of its shares is registered on an approved stock exchange in a Contracting State or if such company is wholly owned—directly or through one or more companies each of which is a resident of the first-mentioned State—by a company which is a resident of the first-mentioned State and the principal class of whose shares is so registered.

(*e*) *Alternative relief provision*

In cases where an anti-abuse clause refers to non-residents of a Contracting State, it could be provided that such expression 'shall not be deemed to include residents of third States that have income tax conventions in force with the Contracting State from which relief from taxation is claimed and such conventions provide relief from taxation not less than the relief from taxation claimed under this Convention'.

These provisions illustrate possible approaches. The specific wording of the provisions to be included in a particular treaty depends on the general approach taken in that treaty and should be determined on a bilateral basis. Also, where the competent authorities of the Contracting States have the power to apply discretionary provisions, it may be considered appropriate to include an additional rule that would give the competent authority of the source country the discretion to allow the benefits of the Convention to a resident of the other State even if the resident failed to pass any of the tests described above." [para. 21]

11.   In this connection, the OECD Commentary observes:

"Other forms of abuse of tax treaties (e.g., the use of a base company) and of possible ways to deal with them such as 'substance-over-form' rules and 'sub-part F type' provisions have also been analysed." [para. 22]

"The large majority of OECD Member countries consider that such measures are part of the basic domestic rules set by national tax law for determining which facts give rise to a tax liability. These rules are not addressed in tax treaties and are therefore not affected by them. One could invoke the spirit of the Convention, which would be violated only if a company, which is a person within the meaning of the Convention, ended up with no or almost no activity or income being attributed to it, and the Contracting States took divergent views on the subject, with economic double taxation resulting therefrom, the same income being taxed twice in the hands of two different taxpayers (cf. paragraph 2 of Article 9). A dissenting view, on the other hand, holds that such rules are subject to general provisions of tax treaties against double taxation, especially where the treaty itself contains provisions aimed at counteracting its improper use." [para. 23]

"It is not easy to reconcile these divergent opinions, either in theory or in mutual agreement procedures on specific cases. The main problem seems to be whether or not general principles such as "substance-over-form" are inherent in treaty provisions, i.e., whether they can be applied in any case, or only to the extent they are expressly mentioned in bilateral conventions. The dissenting view argues that to give domestic rules preference over treaty rules as to who, for tax purposes, is regarded as the recipient of the income shifted to a base company, would erode the protection of taxpayers against double taxation (e.g., where by applying these rules, base company income is taxed in the country of the shareholders even though there is no permanent establishment of the base company there). However, it is the view of the wide majority that such rules, and the underlying principles, do not have to be confirmed in the text of the convention to be applicable." [para. 24]

"While these and the other counteracting measures described in the reports[12] [found in Volume II of the OECD Model Convention] are not inconsistent with the spirit of tax treaties, there is agreement that Member countries should carefully observe the specific obligations enshrined in tax treaties, as long as there is no clear evidence that the treaties are being improperly used. Furthermore, it seems desirable that counteracting measures comply with the spirit of tax treaties with a view to avoiding double taxation. Where the taxpayer complies with such counteracting measures, it might furthermore be appropriate to grant him the protection of the treaty network." [para. 25]

"The majority of Member countries accept counteracting measures as a necessary means of maintaining equity and neutrality of national tax laws in an international environment characterised by very different tax burdens, but believe that such measures should be used only for this purpose. It would be contrary to the general principles underlying the Model Convention and to the spirit of tax treaties in general if counteracting measures were to be extended to activities such as production, normal rendering of services or trading of companies engaged in real industrial or commercial activity, when they are clearly related to the economic environment of the country where they are resident in a situation where these activities are carried out in such a way that no tax avoidance could be suspected. Counteracting measures should not be applied to countries in which taxation is comparable to that of the country of residence of the taxpayer." [para. 26]

---

[12]The two reports from the Committee on Fiscal Affairs of the OECD entitled "Double Taxation Conventions and the Use of Base Companies" and "Double Taxation Conventions and the Use of Conduit Companies" may be seen in the OECD Model Convention Volume II at pages R(5)-I and R(6)-I.

Article 2

TAXES COVERED BY THE CONVENTION

A. GENERAL CONSIDERATIONS

1.   Article 2 of the United Nations Model Convention reproduces paragraphs 1, 2 and 3 of Article 2 of the OECD Model Convention, whereas paragraph 4 differs from paragraph 4 of the OECD Model Convention.

2.   This article is designed to clarify the terminology and nomenclature concerning the taxes to be covered by the convention. In this connection, it may be observed that the same income or capital may be subject in the same country to various taxes—either taxes which differ in nature or taxes of the same nature levied by different political subdivisions or local authorities. Hence double taxation cannot be wholly avoided unless the methods for the relief of double taxation applied in each Contracting State take into account all the taxes to which such income or capital is subject. Consequently, the terminology and nomenclature relating to the taxes covered by a treaty must be clear, precise and as comprehensive as possible. As noted in the OECD Commentary on Article 2 of the OECD Model Convention, this is necessary:

> "to ensure identification of the Contracting States' taxes covered by the Convention, to widen as much as possible the field of application of the Convention by including, as far as possible, and in harmony with the domestic laws of the Contracting States, the taxes imposed by their political subdivisions or local authorities, and to avoid the necessity of concluding a new convention whenever the Contracting States' domestic laws are modified, by means of the periodical exchange of lists and through a procedure for mutual consultation." [para. 1]

B.   COMMENTARY ON THE PARAGRAPHS OF ARTICLE 2

Paragraph 1

3.   This paragraph states that the Convention applies to taxes on income and on capital, irrespective of the authority on behalf of which such taxes are imposed (e.g., the State itself or its political sub-divisions or local authorities) and irrespective of the method by which the taxes are levied (e.g., by direct assessment or by deduction at the source, in the form of surtaxes or surcharges or as additional taxes).

Paragraph 2

4.   This paragraph defines taxes on income and on capital, as taxes on total income, on total capital or on elements of income or of capital, including taxes on gains from the alienation of movable or immovable property, taxes on capital appreciation and taxes on the total amounts of wages or salaries paid by enterprises. Practices re-garding the coverage of taxes on the total amount of wages and sala-ries paid by enterprises vary from country to country and this matter should be taken into account in bilateral negotiations. According to the Commentary on Article 2, paragraph 2, of the OECD Model Con-vention, the last-named taxes do not include "social security charges or any other charges paid where there is a direct connection between the levy and the individual benefits to be received". The OECD Com-mentary further observes:

> "Clearly a State possessing taxing powers—and it alone—may levy the taxes imposed by its legislation together with any duties or charges accessory to them: increases, costs, interest etc. It has not been considered necessary to specify this in the Article, as it is obvious that in the levying of the tax the accessory duties or charges depend on the same rule as the principal duty." [para. 4]

> "The Article does not mention 'ordinary taxes' or 'ex-traordinary taxes'. Normally, it might be considered justifi-

able to include extraordinary taxes in a Model Convention, but experience has shown that such taxes are generally imposed in very special circumstances. In addition, it would be difficult to define them. They may be extraordinary for various reasons; their imposition, the manner in which they are levied, their rates, their objects, etc. This being so, it seems preferable not to include extraordinary taxes in the Article. But, as it is not intended to exclude extraordinary taxes from all conventions, ordinary taxes have not been mentioned either. The Contracting States are thus free to restrict the convention's field of application to ordinary taxes, to extend it to extraordinary taxes, or even to establish special provisions." [para. 5]

Paragraph 3

5.   This paragraph provides the Contracting States an opportunity to enumerate the taxes to which the Convention is to apply. According to the Commentary on Article 2, paragraph 3, of the OECD Model Convention, the list "is not exhaustive", for "it serves to illustrate the preceding paragraphs of the article". In principle, however, it is expected to be "a complete list of taxes imposed in each State at the time of signature and covered by the Convention".

Paragraph 4

6.   This paragraph supplements paragraph 3 by stating that the Convention is to apply also to any identical or substantially similar taxes which are imposed after the date of signature of the Convention in addition to, or in place of, the existing taxes. According to the Commentary on Article 2, paragraph 4, of the OECD Model Convention, "this provision is necessary to prevent the Convention from becoming inoperative in the event of one of the States modifying its taxation laws". Prior to the amendment in 1999, the second sentence of paragraph 4 read as under:

    "At the end of each year, the competent authorities of the Contracting States shall notify each other of changes which have been made in their respective taxation laws."

It was considered that the scope of this provision was very wide since, in practice, most Contracting States do not communicate with each other on each change in their tax laws. Moreover, the requirement to exchange information on changes in tax laws should extend only to significant changes in law which affect the application of the Convention. Such a provision can be found in several bilateral tax treaties. Hence, it was decided to change the second sentence of paragraph 4 as under:

> "The competent authorities of the Contracting States shall notify each other of significant changes made to their tax law."

Commentary on chapter II

DEFINITIONS

Article 3

GENERAL DEFINITIONS

A. GENERAL CONSIDERATIONS

1.   Article 3 of the United Nations Model Convention reproduces Article 3 of the OECD Model Convention. Several general definitions are normally necessary for the understanding and application of a bilateral tax convention, although terms relating to more specialized concepts are usually defined or interpreted in special provisions. On the other hand, there are terms whose definitions are not included in the convention but are left to bilateral negotiations.

2.   Article 3 of the United Nations Model Convention, like Article 3 of the OECD Model Convention, sets forth a number of general definitions required for the interpretation of the terms used in the Convention. These terms are "person", "company", "enterprise of a Contracting State", "international traffic", "competent authority" and "national". Article 3 leaves space for the designation of the "competent authority" of each Contracting State. The terms "resident" and "permanent establishment" are defined in articles 4 and 5 respectively, while the interpretation of certain terms used in the articles on special categories of income (e.g., immovable property, dividends) is clarified in the articles concerned. The parties to a convention are left free to agree bilaterally on a definition of the terms "a Contracting State" and "the other Contracting State". They also may include in the definition of a Contracting State a reference to continental shelves.

B.   COMMENTARY ON THE PARAGRAPHS OF ARTICLE 3

Paragraph 1

(a)   The term "person"

3.   The term "person", which is defined in subparagraph (*a*) as including an individual, a company and any other body of persons, should be interpreted very broadly. According to the Commentary on Article 3 of the OECD Model Convention, the term also includes "any entity which, although itself not a body of persons, is treated as a body corporate for tax purposes [e.g., a foundation]".

(b)   The term "company"

4.   The definition of the term "company", like the corresponding definition in the OECD Model Convention, is formulated with special reference to article 10 on dividends. The definition is relevant to that article and to article 5, paragraph 8, and article 16, corresponding respectively to Article 5, paragraph 7, and Article 16 of the OECD Model Convention.

(c)   The term "enterprise of a Contracting State"

5.   Subparagraph (*c*) defines the terms "enterprise of a Contracting State" and "enterprise of the other Contracting State". It does not define the term "enterprise" *per se*, because, as noted in the Commentary on the OECD Model Convention, "the question whether an activity is performed within an enterprise or is deemed to constitute in itself an enterprise has always been interpreted according to the provisions of the domestic laws of the Contracting States".

(d)   The term "international traffic"

6.   The definition of the "international traffic" is based on the principle that the right to tax profits arising from the operation of ships or aircraft in international traffic resides only in the Contracting

State in which the place of effective management is situated. This principle is set forth in article 8 A, paragraph 1 (corresponding to Article 8, paragraph 1, of the OECD Model Convention), and in article 8 B, paragraph 1, and the first sentence of paragraph 2 (provided in the latter case that the shipping activities concerned are not more than casual). However, the Contracting States may agree on a bilateral basis to substitute a reference to residence in subparagraph (*d*) if appropriate to conform to the general tenor of the other articles relating to international traffic. In such cases, as noted in the Commentary on the OECD Model Convention, "the words 'an enterprise which has its place of effective management in a Contracting State' should be replaced by 'an enterprise of a Contracting State' or 'a resident of a Contracting State'".

7.　　As also noted in the OECD Commentary, the definition of the term "international traffic" is "broader than the term normally signifies [in order] to preserve for the State of the place of effective management the right to tax purely domestic traffic as well as international traffic between third States, and to allow the other Contracting State to tax traffic solely within its borders".

(*e*)　The term "competent authority"

8.　　As in the OECD Model Convention, the definition of the term "competent authority" is left to the Contracting States, which are free to designate one or more authorities as being competent for the purpose of applying the Convention. This approach is necessary because in some countries the implementation of double taxation conventions may not lie solely within the jurisdiction of the highest tax authorities in so far as some matters may be reserved to, or may fall within the competence of, other authorities.

(*f*)　The term "national"

9.　　Initially, the definition of the term "national" occurred in paragraph 2 of article 24 relating to "Non-discrimination". As a result, the definition of the term "national" would have restricted application only for the purposes of article 24. Since the term "national" has been referred to in other articles of the Convention as well, namely, article 4.2(*c*) and (*d*), article 19, article 24 and article 25, it was decided in 1999 to shift the definition of the term "national" from paragraph 2 of article 24 to subparagraph (*f*) of paragraph 1 of article 3. For natural persons, the definition merely states that the term applies to any individual possessing the nationality of a Contracting State. It has not been found necessary to introduce into the text of the Convention any considerations on the signification of the concept of nationality, any more than it seemed appropriate to make any special comment on the meaning and application of the word. In determining what is meant by "the nationals of a Contracting State" in relation to individuals, reference must be made to the sense in which the term is usually employed and each State's rules on the acquisition or loss of nationality.

10.   Subparagraph (*f*) is more specific as to legal persons, partnerships and associations. By declaring that any legal person, partnership or association deriving its status as such from the laws in force in a Contracting State is considered to be a national, the provision disposes of a difficulty which often arises in determining the nationality of companies. In defining the nationality of companies, some States have regard less to the law which governs the company than to the origin of the capital with which the company was formed or the nationality of the individuals or legal persons controlling it.

11.   Moreover, in view of the legal relationship created between the company and the State under whose laws it is constituted, which resembles the relationship of nationality for individuals, it seems appropriate not to deal with legal persons, partnerships and associations in a special provision, but to assimilate them with individuals under the term "national".

Paragraph 2

12.   Like article 3, paragraph 2, of the OECD Model Convention, this paragraph contains a general rule concerning the meaning of

terms used but not defined in the Convention. According to the OECD Commentary, it amended paragraph 2 in 1995 in order:

> ". . . to conform its text more closely to the general and consistent understanding of Member States. For purposes of paragraph 2, the meaning of any term not defined in the Convention may be ascertained by reference to the meaning it has for the purpose of any relevant provision of the domestic law of a Contracting State, whether or not a tax law. However, where a term is defined differently for the purposes of different laws of a Contracting State, the meaning given to that term for purposes of the laws imposing the taxes to which the Convention applies shall prevail over all others, including those given for the purposes of other tax laws. States that are able to enter into mutual agreements (under the provisions of Article 25 and, in particular, paragraph 3 thereof) that establish the meanings of terms not defined in the Convention should take those agreements into account in interpreting those terms." [para. 13.1]

When a conflict arises between the legislation in force when the Convention was signed and that in force when the tax is imposed, the latter interpretation prevails.

13. The OECD Commentary states:

> "However, paragraph 2 specifies that this applies only if the context does not require an alternative interpretation. The context is determined in particular by the intention of the Contracting States when signing the Convention as well as the meaning given to the term in question in the legislation of the other Contracting State (an implicit reference to the principle of reciprocity on which the Convention is based). The wording of the Article therefore allows the competent authorities some leeway." [para. 12]

> "Consequently, the wording of paragraph 2 provides a satisfactory balance between, on the one hand, the need to ensure the permanency of commitments entered into by States when signing a convention (since a State should not be allowed to make a convention partially inoperative by amending after-

wards in its domestic law the scope of terms not defined in the Convention) and, on the other hand, the need to be able to apply the Convention in a convenient and practical way over time (the need to refer to outdated concepts should be avoided)." [para. 13]

Article 4

RESIDENT

A. GENERAL CONSIDERATIONS

1.   Article 4 of the United Nations Model Convention reproduces Article 4 of the OECD Model Convention with one adjustment, namely, the addition in 1999 of the criterion "place of incorporation" to the list of criteria in paragraph 1 for taxation as a resident. According to the Commentary on Article 4 of the OECD Model Convention,

"The concept of 'resident of a Contracting State' has various functions and is of importance in three cases:

(*a*)   in determining a convention's personal scope of application;

(*b*)   in solving cases where double taxation arises in consequence of double residence;

(*c*)   in solving cases where double taxation arises as a consequence of taxation in the State of residence and in the State of source or situs." [para. 1]

2.   Like Article 4 of the OECD Model Convention, article 4 of the United Nations Model Convention defines the expression "resident of a Contracting State" and establishes rules for resolving cases of double residence. In the two typical cases of conflict between two residences and between residence and source or situs, the conflict arises because, under their domestic laws, one or both Contracting States claim that the person concerned is resident in their territory. In this connection the OECD Commentary provides the following clarification:

"Generally the domestic laws of the various States impose a comprehensive liability to tax—'full tax liability'—based on the taxpayers' personal attachment to the State concerned (the 'State of residence'). This liability to tax is not imposed only on persons who are 'domiciled' in a State in the sense in which 'domicile' is usually taken in the legislations (private law). The cases of full liability to tax are extended to comprise also, for instance, persons who stay continually, or maybe only for a certain period, in the territory of the State. Some legislations impose full liability to tax on individuals who perform services on board ships which have their home harbour in the State." [para. 3]

"Conventions for the avoidance of double taxation do not normally concern themselves with the domestic laws of the Contracting States laying down the conditions under which a person is to be treated fiscally as 'resident' and, consequently, is fully liable to tax in that State. They do not lay down standards which the provisions of the domestic laws on 'residence' have to fulfil in order that claims for full tax liability can be accepted between the Contracting States. In this respect the States take their stand entirely on the domestic laws." [para. 4]

"This manifests itself quite clearly in the cases where there is no conflict at all between two residences, but where the conflict exists only between residence and source or situs. But the same view applies in conflicts between two residences. The special point in these cases is only that no solution of the conflict can be arrived at by reference to the concept of residence adopted in the domestic laws of the States concerned. In these cases special provisions must be established in the Convention to determine which of the two concepts of residence is to be given preference." [para. 5]

B. COMMENTARY ON THE PARAGRAPHS OF ARTICLE 4

Paragraph 1

3. The Group decided to adopt as paragraph 1 of article 4, the paragraph 1 of article 4 of the OECD Model Convention, and had initially decided not to adopt the second sentence which reads: "This term [resident of a Contracting State], however, does not include any person who is liable to tax in that State in respect only of income from sources in that State or capital situated therein". The second sentence, which was included in the OECD Convention to deal, for example, with the special situation of foreign diplomats and consular staffs serving in a country which taxed residents on the basis of their worldwide income, who might be considered (under the domestic law of the country in which they are serving) as residents but, because of their special status, might nevertheless be taxable only on income from sources in that State, has been incorporated in 1999 in paragraph 1 of article 4 of the United Nations Model Convention as well.

4. The OECD Commentary observes: "In accordance with the provisions of the second sentence of paragraph 1, a person is not to be considered a 'resident of a Contracting State' in the sense of the Convention if, although not domiciled in that State, he is considered to be a resident according to the domestic laws but is subject only to a taxation limited to the income from sources in the State or to capital situated in that State. That situation exists in some States in relation to individuals, e.g., in the case of foreign diplomatic and consular staff serving in their territory. According to its wording and spirit the provision would also exclude from the definition of a resident of a Contracting State foreign-held companies exempted from tax on their foreign income by privileges tailored to attract conduit companies. This, however, has inherent difficulties and limitations. Thus it has to be interpreted restrictively because it might otherwise exclude from the scope of the Convention all residents of countries adopting a territorial principle in their taxation, a result which is clearly not intended. The exclusion of certain companies from the definition

would not, of course, prevent Contracting States from exchanging information about their activities. [cf. paragraph 2 of the OECD Commentary on article 26 (reproduced in paragraph 3 of the Commentary on article 26 below)]. Indeed, States may feel it appropriate to develop spontaneous exchanges of information about companies which seek to obtain treaty benefits unintended by the Model Convention." [para. 8]

5.   Paragraph 1, similar to the corresponding provision of the OECD Model Convention, refers to the concept of residence contained in the domestic laws of the Contracting States and lists the criteria for taxation as a resident: domicile, residence, place of management (to which the United Nations Model Convention adds "place of incorporation") or any other criterion of a similar nature. Thus formulated, the definition of the term "resident of a Contracting State" is, according to the OECD Commentary, aimed at covering, as far as individuals are concerned, "the various forms of personal attachment to a State which, in the domestic taxation laws, form the basis of a comprehensive taxation (full liability to tax)". [para. 8]

6.   The OECD Commentary observes as under:

"It has been the general understanding of most Member states that the government of each State, as well as any political sub-division or local authority thereof, is a resident of that State for purposes of the Convention. Before 1995, the Model did not explicitly state this; in 1995, Article 4 was amended to conform the text of the Model to this understanding." [para. 8.1]

It may be mentioned that in 1999, the United Nations Model Convention also adopted the same amendment.

Paragraph 2

7.   This paragraph, which reproduces Article 4, paragraph 2, of the OECD Model Convention, lists in decreasing order of relevance a number of subsidiary criteria to be applied when an individual is a resident of both Contracting States and the preceding criteria do not

provide a clear-cut determination of his status as regards residence. It may be noted that in 1999, the word "only" has been inserted in sub-paragraphs (*a*), (*b*) and (*c*) of paragraph 2, following the changes previously made to the OECD Model Convention. The OECD Commentary states:

> "This paragraph relates to the case where, under the provisions of paragraph 1, an individual is a resident of both Contracting States." [para. 9]

> "To solve this conflict special rules must be established which give the attachment to one State a preference over the attachment to the other State. As far as possible, the preference criterion must be of such a nature that there can be no question but that the person concerned will satisfy it in one State only, and at the same time it must reflect such an attachment that it is felt to be natural that the right to tax devolves upon that particular State. The facts to which the special rules will apply are those existing during the period when the residence of the taxpayer affects tax liability, which may be less than an entire taxable period. [Assume that] in one calendar year an individual is a resident of State A under that State's tax laws from 1 January to 31 March, then moves to State B. Because the individual resides in State B for more than 183 days, the individual is treated by the tax laws of State B as a State B resident for the entire year. Applying the special rules to the period 1 January to 31 March, the individual was a resident of State A. Therefore, both State A and State B should treat the individual as a State A resident for that period, and as a State B resident from 1 April to 31 December." [para. 10]

> "The Article gives preference to the Contracting State in which the individual has a permanent home available to him. This criterion will frequently be sufficient to solve the conflict, e.g., where the individual has a permanent home in one Contracting State and has only made a stay of some length in the other Contracting State." [para. 11]

> "Subparagraph (*a*) means, therefore, that in the application of the convention (that is, where there is a conflict be-

tween the laws of the two States) it is considered that the residence is that place where the individual owns or possesses a home; this home must be permanent, that is to say, the individual must have arranged and retained it for his permanent use as opposed to staying at a particular place under such conditions that it is evident that the stay is intended to be of short duration." [para. 12]

"As regards the concept of home, it should be observed that any form of home may be taken into account (house or apartment belonging to or rented by the individual, rented furnished room). But the permanence of the home is essential; this means that the individual has arranged to have the dwelling available to him at all times continuously, and not occasionally for the purpose of a stay which, owing to the reasons for it, is necessarily of short duration (travel for pleasure, business travel, educational travel, attending a course at a school etc.)." [para. 13]

"If the individual has a permanent home in both Contracting States, paragraph 2 gives preference to the State with which the personal and economic relations of the individual are closer, this being understood as the centre of vital interests. In the cases where the residence cannot be determined by reference to this rule, paragraph 2 provides as subsidiary criteria, first, habitual abode, and then nationality. If the individual is a national of both States or of neither of them, the question shall be solved by mutual agreement between the States concerned according to the procedure laid down in Article 25." [para. 14]

"If the individual has a permanent home in both Contracting States, it is necessary to look at the facts in order to ascertain with which of the two States his personal and economic relations are closer. Thus, regard will be had to his family and social relations, his occupations, his political, cultural or other activities, his place of business, the place from which he administers his property etc. The circumstances must be examined as a whole, but it is nevertheless obvious that considerations based on the personal acts of the individual must receive special attention. If a person who has a home in one State sets up a second in the other State while retaining the first, the fact that he retains the first in the environment where he has always lived, where he has worked, and where he has his family and possessions, can, together with other elements, go to demonstrate that he has retained his centre of vital interests in the first State." [para. 15]

"Subparagraph (*b*) establishes a secondary criterion for two quite distinct and different situations:

(*a*)   the case where the individual has a permanent home available to him in both Contracting States and it is not possible to determine in which one he has his centre of vital interests;

(*b*)   the case where the individual has a permanent home available to him in neither Contracting State.

Preference is given to the Contracting State where the individual has an habitual abode." [para. 16]

"In the first situation, the case where the individual has a permanent home available to him in both States, the fact of having an habitual abode in one State rather than in the other appears therefore as the circumstance which, in case of doubt as to where the individual has his centre of vital interests, tips the balance towards the State where he stays more frequently. For this purpose regard must be had to stays made by the individual not only at the permanent home in the State in question but also at any other place in the same State." [para. 17]

"The second situation is the case of an individual who has a permanent home available to him in neither Contracting State, as for example, a person going from one hotel to another. In this case also all stays made in a State must be considered without it being necessary to ascertain the reasons for them." [para. 18]

"In stipulating that in the two situations which it contemplates preference is given to the Contracting State where the individual has an habitual abode, subparagraph (*b*) does not specify over what length of time the comparison must be made. The comparison must cover a sufficient length of time for it to be possible to determine whether the residence in each of the two States is habitual and to determine also the intervals at which the stays take place." [para. 19]

"Where, in the two situations referred to in subparagraph (b) the individual has an habitual abode in both Contracting States or in neither, preference is given to the State of which he is a national. If, in these cases still, the individual is a national of both Contracting States or of neither of them the subparagraph (d) assigns to the competent authorities the duty of resolving the difficulty by mutual agreement according to the procedure established in Article 25." [para. 20]

Paragraph 3

8.　　Paragraph 3, which reproduces Article 4, paragraph 3, of the OECD Model Convention, deals with companies and other bodies of persons, irrespective of whether they are legal persons. The OECD Commentary indicates that "It may be rare in practice for a company etc., to be subject to tax as a resident in more than one State, but it is, of course, possible if, for instance, one State attaches importance to the registration and the other State to the place of effective management. So, in the case of companies, etc., also, special rules as to the preference must be established". [para. 21] According to the OECD Commentary, "It would not be an adequate solution to attach importance to a purely formal criterion like registration. Therefore paragraph 3 attaches importance to the place where the company, etc., is actually managed". [para. 22] It may be mentioned that, as in the case of the OECD Model Convention, the word "only" has been added in 1999 to the tie-breaker test for determining the residence of dual residents, other than individuals.

9.　　The OECD Commentary goes on to state:

"The formulation of the preference criterion in the case of persons other than individuals was considered in particular in connection with the taxation of income from shipping, inland waterways transport and air transport. A number of conventions for the avoidance of double taxation on such income accord the taxing power to the State in which the 'place of management' of the enterprise is situated; other conventions attach importance to its 'place of effective management', others again to the 'fiscal domicile of the operator'." [para. 23]

"As a result of these considerations, the 'place of effective management' has been adopted as the preference criterion for persons other than individuals." [para. 24]

10.   It is understood that when establishing the "place of effective management", circumstances which may, *inter alia*, be taken into account are the place where a company is actually managed and controlled, the place where the decision-making at the highest level on the important policies essential for the management of the company takes place, the place that plays a leading part in the management of a company from an economic and functional point of view and the place where the most important accounting books are kept.

11.   A particular issue, as regards a bilateral treaty between State A and State B, can arise in relation to a company which is under paragraph 1 of article 4, a resident of State A, and which is in receipt of, say, interest income, not directly, but instead, through a permanent establishment which it has in a third country, State C. Applying the Model treaty, as it stands, has the effect that such a company can claim the benefit of the terms on, say, withholding tax on interest in the treaty between State A and State B, in respect of interest that is paid to its permanent establishment in State C. This is one example of what is known as a "triangular case". Some concern has been expressed that treaties can be open to abuse where, in the example given, State C is a tax haven and State A exempts the profits of permanent establishments of its resident enterprises. The situation is discussed in depth in the OECD study on the subject: reprinted as "Triangular Cases" in Volume II of the OECD Model Convention. States which wish to protect themselves against potential abuse can take advantage of the possible solutions suggested there, by adopting additional treaty provisions.

Article 5

PERMANENT ESTABLISHMENT

A.   GENERAL CONSIDERATIONS

1.   Article 5 of the United Nations Model Convention incorporates several provisions of article 5 of the OECD Model Convention (either unchanged or substantially amended) and some new provisions. Details on the amendments and new provisions are provided in the Commentary on the paragraphs of the article.

2.   The concept of permanent establishment is used in bilateral tax treaties principally for the purpose of determining the right of a Contracting State to tax the profits of an enterprise of the other Contracting State. According to that concept, the profits of an enterprise of one Contracting State are taxable in the other only if the enterprise maintains a permanent establishment in the latter State and only to the extent that the profits are attributable to the permanent establishment. The concept of permanent establishment is to be found in the early model conventions including the 1928 model conventions of the League of Nations. The Model Convention reaffirms the concept and supplements it with the new concept of a "fixed base", to be used in the case of professional services or other activities of an independent character.

B.   COMMENTARY ON THE PARAGRAPHS OF ARTICLE 5

Paragraph 1

3.   This paragraph, which reproduces Article 5, paragraph 1, of the OECD Model Convention, defines the term "permanent establishment", emphasizing its essential nature as a "fixed place of business" with a specific "situs". According to the OECD Commentary, this definition contains the following conditions:

> "—the existence of a 'place of business', i.e., a facility such as premises or, in certain instances, machinery or equipment;

—this place of business must be 'fixed', i.e., it must be established at a distinct place with a certain degree of permanence;

—the carrying on of the business of the enterprise through this fixed place of business. This means usually that persons who, in one way or another, are dependent on the enterprise (personnel) conduct the business of the enterprise in the State in which the fixed place is situated." [para. 2]

The OECD Commentary goes on to observe:

"It could perhaps be argued that in the general definition some mention should also be made of the other characteristic of a permanent establishment to which some importance has sometimes been attached in the past, namely that the establishment must have a productive character—i.e., contribute to the profits of the enterprise. In the present definition this course has not been taken. Within the framework of a well-run business organization it is surely axiomatic to assume that each part contributes to the productivity of the whole. It does not, of course, follow in every case that because in the wider context of the whole organization a particular establishment has 'a productive character' it is consequently a permanent establishment to which profits can properly be attributed for the purpose of tax in a particular territory." [para. 3]

"The term 'place of business' covers any premises, facilities or installations used for carrying on the business of the enterprise whether or not they are used exclusively for that purpose. A place of business may also exist where no premises are available or required for carrying on the business of the enterprise and it simply has a certain amount of space at its disposal. It is immaterial whether the premises, facilities or installations are owned or rented by or are otherwise at the disposal of the enterprise. A place of business may thus be constituted by a pitch in a market place, or by a certain permanently used area in a Customs depot (e.g., for the storage of dutiable goods). Again the place of business may be situated in the business facilities of another enterprise. This may be the case, for instance, where the foreign enterprise has at its constant disposal certain premises or a part thereof owned by the other enterprise." [para. 4]

"According to the definition, the place of business has to be a 'fixed' one. Thus in the normal way there has to be a link between the place of business and a specific geographical point. It is immaterial how long an enterprise of a Contracting State operates in the other Contracting State if it does not do so at a distinct place, but this does not mean that the equipment constituting the place of business has to be actually fixed to the soil on which it stands. It is enough that the equipment remains on a particular site." [para. 5]

"Since the place of business must be fixed, it also follows that a permanent establishment can be deemed to exist only if the place of business has a certain degree of permanency, i.e., if it is not of a purely temporary nature. If the place of business was not set up merely for a temporary purpose, it can constitute a permanent establishment, even though it existed, in practice, only for a very short period of time because of the special nature of the activity of the enterprise or because, as a consequence of special circumstances (e.g., death of the tax-payer, investment failure), it was prematurely liquidated. Where a place of business which was, at the outset, designed for a short temporary purpose only, is maintained for such a period that it cannot be considered as a temporary one, it becomes a fixed place of business and thus—retrospectively—a permanent establishment." [para. 6]

"For a place of business to constitute a permanent establishment the enterprise using it must carry on its business wholly or partly through it. As stated . . . above, the activity need not be of a productive character. Furthermore, the activity need not be permanent in the sense that there is no interruption of operation, but operations must be carried out on a regular basis." [para. 7]

"Where tangible property such as facilities, industrial, commercial or scientific (ICS) equipment, buildings, or intangible property such as patents, procedures and similar property, are let or leased to third parties through a fixed place of business maintained by an enterprise of a Contracting State in the other State, this activity will, in general, render the place of business a permanent establishment. The same applies if capital is made available through a fixed place of business. If an enterprise of a State lets or leases facilities, ICS equipment, buildings or intangible property to an enterprise of the other State without maintaining for such letting or leasing activity a fixed place of business in the other State, the leased facility, ICS equipment, building or intangible property, as such, will not constitute a permanent establishment of the lessor provided the contract is limited to the mere leasing of the ICS equipment etc. This remains the case even when, for example, the lessor supplies personnel after installation to operate the equipment provided that their responsibility is limited solely to the operation or maintenance of the ICS equipment under the direction, responsibility and control of the lessee. If the personnel have wider responsibilities, for example participation in the decisions regarding the work for which the equipment is used, or if they operate, service, inspect and maintain the equipment under the responsibility and control of the lessor, the activity of the lessor may go beyond the mere leasing of ICS equipment and may constitute an entrepreneurial activity. In such a case a permanent establishment could be deemed to exist if the criterion of permanency is met. When such activity is connected with, or is similar in character to, those mentioned in paragraph 3, the time limit of [six] months applies. Other cases have to be determined according to the circumstances." [para. 8]

"The business of an enterprise is carried on mainly by the entrepreneur or persons who are in a paid-employment relationship with the enterprise (personnel). This personnel includes employees and other persons receiving instructions from the enterprise (e.g., dependent agents). The powers of such personnel in its relationship with third parties are irrelevant. It makes no difference whether or not the dependent agent is authorized to conclude contracts if he works at the fixed place of business. But a permanent establishment may nevertheless exist if the business of the enterprise is carried on mainly through automatic equipment, the activities of the personnel being restricted to setting up, operating, controlling and maintaining such equipment. Whether or not gaming and vending machines and the like set up by an enterprise of a State in the other State constitute a permanent establishment thus depends on whether or not the enterprise carries on a business activity besides the initial setting up of the machines. A permanent establishment does not exist if the enterprise merely sets up the machines and then leases the machines to other enterprises. A permanent establishment may exist, however, if the enterprise which sets up the machines also operates and maintains them for its own account. This also applies if the machines are operated and maintained by an agent dependent on the enterprise." [para. 10]

"A permanent establishment begins to exist as soon as the enterprise commences to carry on its business through a fixed place of business. This is the case once the enterprise prepares, at the place of business, the activity for which the place of business is to serve permanently. The period of time during which the fixed place of business itself is being set up by the enterprise should not be counted, provided that this activity differs substantially from the activity for which the place of business is to serve permanently. The permanent establishment ceases to exist with the disposal of the fixed place of business or with the cessation of any activity through it, that is when all acts and measures connected with the former activities of the permanent establishment are terminated (winding up current business transactions, maintenance and repair of facilities). A temporary interruption of operations, however, cannot be regarded as closure. If the fixed place of business is leased to another enterprise, it will normally only serve the activities of that enterprise instead of the lessor's; in general, the lessor's permanent establishment ceases to exist, except where he continues carrying on a business activity of his own through the fixed place of business." [para. 11]

Paragraph 2

4.   Paragraph 2, which reproduces article 5, paragraph 2, of the OECD Model Convention, singles out several examples of what can be regarded, *prima facie*, as being permanent establishments. Developing countries often wish to broaden as much as possible the scope of the term "permanent establishment" and suggest that a warehouse should be included among the specific examples. However, the Group agreed not to expand the list of examples in view of the fact that the deletion of "delivery" from the excluded activities described in subparagraphs (*a*) and (*b*) of paragraph 4 meant that a "warehouse" used for that purpose is a permanent establishment. A "commercial warehouse", where for example space is rented to other concerns, is covered as a permanent establishment. According to the OECD Commentary, it is assumed that the Contracting States interpret the terms listed "in such a way that such places of business constitute permanent establishments only if they meet the requirements of paragraph 1". The OECD Commentary points out that the term "place of management" is mentioned separately because it is not necessarily an "office" and that "where the laws of the two Contracting States do not contain the concept of a 'place of management' as distinct from an office, there will be no need to refer to the former term in their bilateral convention". [para. 13]

5.   In connection with subparagraph (*f*), which provides that the term "permanent establishment" includes mines, oil or gas wells, quarries or any other place of extraction of natural resources, the OECD Commentary states that "the term 'any other place of extraction of natural resources' should be interpreted broadly" to include, for example, all places of extraction of hydrocarbons whether on or off-shore. Because subparagraph (*f*) does not mention exploration for natural resources, whether on or off-shore, paragraph 1 governs

whether exploration activities are carried on through a permanent establishment. The OECD Commentary states:

> "Since, however, it has not been possible to arrive at a common view on the basic questions of the attribution of taxation rights and of the qualification of the income from exploration activities, the Contracting States may agree upon the insertion of specific provisions. They may agree, for instance, that an enterprise of a Contracting State, as regards its activities of exploration of natural resources in a place or area in the other Contracting State:
>
> (*a*) shall be deemed not to have a permanent establishment in that other State; or
>
> (*b*) shall be deemed to carry on such activities through a permanent establishment in that other State; or
>
> (*c*) shall be deemed to carry on such activities through a permanent establishment in that other State if such activities last longer than a specified period of time.
>
> The Contracting States may moreover agree to submit the income from such activities to any other rule." [para. 15]

6.   As mentioned above, in subparagraph (*f*) the expression "any other place of extraction of natural resources" should be interpreted broadly. Some members from developing countries argued that for this purpose, "fishing vessels" could be treated as the place of extraction or exploitation of natural resources, since "fish" constitutes natural resources. In their analysis, although it is true that all places or apparatus designated as "permanent establishment" in subparagraphs (*a*) to (*e*) in paragraph 2 have a certain degree of permanence or constitute "immovable property", yet fishing vessels can be considered as a place used for extraction of natural resources, which may not necessarily mean only minerals which are embedded in the earth. In fact, fishing vessels can be compared with the movable drilling platform which is used in off-shore drilling operations for gaining access to mineral oil or petrol. Where such fishing vessels are used in the territorial waters or the exclusive economic zone of the coastal state, the activities of such vessels would constitute a permanent es-

tablishment, situated in that State. However, some other members took the view that such an interpretation was open to objection that it constituted too broad a reading of the term "permanent establishment" and of the natural language of the subparagraph, and that, accordingly, in their opinion, any treaty partner countries which sought to advance such a proposition in respect of fishing activities, should make that explicit by adopting it as a new and separate category in the list in this article. Accordingly, the interpretation on the nature of this activity would be left to negotiations between Contracting States.

Paragraph 3

7.   This paragraph covers a broader range of activities than Article 5, paragraph 3, of the OECD Model Convention, which states, "A building site or construction or installation project constitutes a permanent establishment only if it lasts more than twelve months". In addition to the term "installation project" used in the OECD Model Convention, subparagraph 3(*a*) of the United Nations Model Convention includes an "assembly project" as well as "supervisory activities" in connection with "a building site, a construction, installation or assembly project". Another difference is that while the OECD Model Convention provides that a site or project is a permanent establishment only if it lasts more than twelve months, the United Nations Model Convention reduces the minimum duration to six months. In special cases, this six-month period could be reduced in bilateral negotiations to not less than three months.

8.   Some developing countries have supported a more elaborate version of subparagraph 3(*a*), which would extend the provision to encompass a situation:

> "where such project or activity, being incidental to the sale of machinery or equipment, continues for a period not exceeding six months and the charges payable for the project or activities exceed 10 per cent of the sale price of the machinery or equipment".

Other members of the Group believe that such a provision would not be appropriate, particularly if the machinery was installed by an enterprise other than the one doing the construction work.

9.   Article 5, paragraph 3, subparagraph (*b*), deals with the furnishing of services, including consultancy services, which are not covered specifically in the OECD Model Convention in connection with the concept of permanent establishment. It is believed that management and consultancy services should be covered because the provision of such services in developing countries by corporations of industrialized countries often involves very large sums of money.

10.   Concerning the six-month threshold in paragraph 3, subparagraphs (*a*) and (*b*), of article 5 of the United Nations Model Convention, some developing countries would prefer to remove the time limit altogether for two main reasons: first, because construction, assembly and similar activities could as a result of modern technology be of very short duration and still result in a considerable profit for the enterprise carrying on those activities; and second, because the period during which the foreign personnel involved in the activities remained in the source country was irrelevant to the right of developing countries to tax the income. Other members from developing countries feel that any time limit should be removed because such a limitation was apt to be used by enterprises of capital-exporting countries to evade taxation in the source country. The view has been expressed that there is no reason why a construction project should not be treated in the same manner as persons covered by Article 17 of the OECD Model Convention, who are taxed at the place where their activities are performed irrespective of the duration of those activities. Nevertheless, the goal of the treaty is to promote international trade and development, and the idea behind the time limit is that business enterprises of one Contracting State should be encouraged to initiate preparatory or ancillary operations in the other Contracting State without becoming immediately subject to the tax of the latter State, so as to facilitate a more permanent and larger commitment at a later stage.

11.   In this connection, the OECD Commentary observes:

"The [six] month test applies to each individual site or project. In determining how long the site or project has existed, no account should be taken of the time previously spent by the contractor concerned on other sites or projects which are totally unconnected with it. A building site should be regarded as a single unit, even if it is based on several contracts, provided that it forms a coherent whole commercially and geographically. Subject to this proviso, a building site forms a single unit even if the orders have been placed by several persons (e.g., for a row of houses). The [six] month threshold has given rise to abuses; it has sometimes been found that enterprises (mainly contractors or sub-contractors working on the continental shelf or engaged in activities connected with the exploration and exploitation of the continental shelf) divided their contracts up into several parts, each covering a period less than [six] months and attributed to a different company, which was, however, owned by the same group. Apart from the fact that such abuses may, depending on the circumstances, fall under the application of legislative or judicial anti-avoidance rules, countries concerned with this issue can adopt solutions in the framework of bilateral negotiations." [para. 18]

"A site exists from the date on which the contractor begins his work, including any preparatory work, in the country where the construction is to be established, e.g., if he installs a planning office for the construction. In general, it continues to exist until the work is completed or permanently abandoned. A site should not be regarded as ceasing to exist when work is temporarily discontinued. Seasonal or other temporary interruptions should be included in determining the life of a site. Seasonal interruptions include interruptions due to bad weather. Temporary interruption could be caused, for example, by shortage of material or labour difficulties. Thus, for example, if a contractor started work on a road on 1st May, stopped on 1st [August] because of bad weather conditions or a lack of materials but resumed work on 1st [October], completing the road on 1st [January] the following year, his construction project should be regarded as a permanent establishment because [eight] months elapsed between the date he commenced work (1st May) and the date he finally finished (1st [January] of the following year). If an enterprise (general contractor) which has undertaken the performance of a comprehensive project, subcontracts parts of such a project to other enterprises (subcontractors), the period spent by a subcontractor working on the building site must be considered as being spent by the general contractor on the building project. The subcontractor himself has a permanent establishment at the site if his activities there last more than [six] months." [para. 19]

"The very nature of a construction or installation project may be such that the contractor's activity has to be relocated continuously or at least from time to time, as the project progresses. This would be the case for instance where roads or canals were being constructed, waterways dredged, or pipelines laid. In such a case, the fact that the work force is not present for [six] months in one particular place is immaterial. The activities performed at each particular spot are part of a single project, and that project must be regarded as a permanent establishment if, as a whole, it lasts for more than [six] months." [para. 20]

12.   Subparagraph (b) encompasses service activities only if they "continue (for the same or a connected project) within a Contracting State for a period or periods aggregating more than six months within any twelve-month period". The words "for the same or a connected project" are included because it is not appropriate to add together unrelated projects in view of the uncertainty which that step involves and the undesirable distinction it creates between an enterprise with, for example, one project of three months' duration and another with two unrelated projects, each of three months' duration, one following the other. However, some members find the injection of a "project" limitation either too easy to manipulate or too narrow in that it might

preclude taxation in the case of a continuous number of separate projects, each of four or five months' duration.

13.   Some members from developing countries expressed the view that in bilateral negotiations a clause could be inserted in paragraph 3 stipulating that if an enterprise of one Contracting State operates fishing ships in the territorial waters of the other Contracting State, the ships could be considered permanent establishments in the latter State. This clause might apply only if the ships exceed a threshold stated in terms of fish caught or some other criterion.

14.   If a service activity is a permanent establishment under paragraph 3, only profits attributable to the permanent establishment are taxable in the source country.

15.   The following passages of the Commentary on of the OECD Model Convention are relevant to article 5, paragraph 3(a), of the United Nations Model Convention:

> "This paragraph provides expressly that a building site or construction or installation project constitutes a permanent establishment only if it lasts more than [six] months. Any of those items which does not meet this condition does not of itself constitute a permanent establishment, even if there is within it an installation, for instance an office or a workshop within the meaning of paragraph 2, associated with the construction activity." [para. 16]

> "The term 'building site or construction or installation project' includes not only the construction of buildings but also the construction of roads, bridges or canals, the laying of pipe-lines and excavating and dredging. Planning and supervision of the erection of a building are covered by this term, if carried out by the building contractor. However, planning and supervision is not included if carried out by another enterprise whose activities in connection with the construction concerned are restricted to planning and supervising the work. If that other enterprise has an office which it uses only for planning or supervision activities relating to a site or project which

does not constitute a permanent establishment, such office does not constitute a fixed place of business within the meaning of paragraph 1, because its existence has not a certain degree of permanence." [para. 17]

Paragraph 4

16.   This paragraph reproduces article 5, paragraph 4 of the OECD Model Convention with two substantive amendments: the deletion of "delivery" in subparagraphs (*a*) and (*b*). The deletion of the word "delivery" means that a "warehouse" used for that purpose is a permanent establishment. A "commercial warehouse", where space is rented to other concerns, is also a permanent establishment under paragraph 2.

17.   The word "delivery" is deleted because the presence of a stock of goods for prompt delivery facilitates sales of the product and thereby the earning of profit in the host country by the enterprise having the facility. A continuous connection and hence the existence of such a supply of goods should be a permanent establishment, leaving as a separate matter the determination of the amount of income properly attributable to the permanent establishment. Some members from developed countries disagree with this conclusion, believing that since only a small amount of income would normally be allocated to a permanent establishment whose only activity is delivery, this variance from the OECD Model Convention serves no purpose.

18.   The question whether the use of facilities for the "delivery of goods" could be incorporated in subparagraphs 4(*a*) and (*b*) as an activity that would not give rise to a permanent establishment has engaged the attention of the Group of Experts for a long time, primarily because the phrase "delivery of goods" is included in subparagraphs 4(*a*) and (*b*) of Article 5 of the OECD Model Convention. It has been observed that many developing countries had agreed to raise the threshold of permanent establishment and that almost 75 per cent of the bilateral tax treaties entered into by developing countries have included the "delivery of goods" in subparagraphs 4(*a*) and (*b*) in their treaties as revealed in a study in 1997. It cannot be ignored that the

omission of "delivery of goods" in subparagraphs 4(*a*) and (*b*) of article 5 in the United Nations Model Convention is one of the important features which distinguish it from the OECD Model Convention. On the other hand, it is contended that even if the delivery of goods is treated as an activity which gives rise to a permanent establishment, very little income per se could be attributed to this activity. On the other hand, if such activity of "delivery of goods" is considered as giving rise to a permanent establishment, there would be a tendency on the part of tax authorities to try to attribute income to this activity, whether in reality income actually arose or not. This may lead to fruitless and prolonged litigation. The Group of Experts did not reach a consensus to amend the provisions of subparagraphs 4(*a*) and (*b*) of article 5 to include "delivery of goods" as an activity which may not constitute a permanent establishment. Hence, the Contracting States may consider both these divergent points of view while entering into bilateral tax treaties.

19.   Subparagraph (*f*) was added to paragraph 4 of article 5 in 1999. Subparagraph (*f*) of the OECD Model Convention provides that "the maintenance of a fixed place of business solely for any combination of activities mentioned in subparagraphs (*a*) to (*e*)" is not a permanent establishment if "the overall activity of the fixed place of business resulting from this combination is of a preparatory or auxiliary character". The question of inclusion of subparagraph 4(*f*) was further re-examined at the instance of a member from a developed country. Some members responded that it is administratively difficult to allocate income to the activities specified in paragraph 4 and that, since none of the activities described in subparagraphs (*a*) to (*e*) separately constitute a permanent establishment, it was difficult to see how adding them together resulted in a permanent establishment.

20.   The relevant portion of the Commentary on subparagraph (*f*) of paragraph 4 of the OECD text is as follows:

> ". . . subparagraph (*f*) provides that combinations of activities mentioned in subparagraphs (*a*) to (*e*) in the same fixed place of business shall be deemed not to be a permanent establishment, provided that the overall activity of the fixed place of

business resulting from this combination is of a preparatory or auxiliary character. Thus, the provisions of paragraph 4 are designed to prevent an enterprise of one State being taxed in the other State if it carries on in the other State, activities of a purely preparatory or auxiliary character." [para. 21]

"As already mentioned in paragraph 21 above, paragraph 4 is designed to provide for exceptions to the general definition of paragraph 1 in respect of fixed places of business which are engaged in activities having a preparatory or auxiliary character. Therefore, according to subparagraph (*f*) of paragraph 4, the fact that one fixed place of business combines any of the activities mentioned in subparagraphs (*a*) to (*e*) of paragraph 4 does not mean of itself that a permanent establishment exists. As long as the combined activity of such a place of business is merely preparatory or auxiliary, a permanent establishment should be deemed not to exist. Such combinations should not be viewed on rigid lines, but should be considered in the light of particular circumstances. The criterion 'preparatory or auxiliary character' is to be interpreted in the same way as is set out for the same criterion of subparagraph (*e*). Subparagraph (*f*) is of no importance in a case where an enterprise maintains several fixed places of business within the meaning of subparagraphs (*a*) to (*e*) provided that they are separated from each other locally and organizationally, as in such a case each place of business has to be viewed separately and in isolation for deciding the question whether or not a permanent establishment exists. States which want to allow any combination of items mentioned in subparagraphs (*a*) to (*e*) disregarding whether or not the criterion of the preparatory or auxiliary character of such a combination is met, are free to do so by deleting the words "provided" to "character" in subparagraph (*f*)." [para. 27]

21. The Commentary on the OECD Model Convention states that the business activities listed in paragraph 4 are "treated as exceptions to the general definition laid down in paragraph 1" and that they "are not permanent establishments, even if the activity is carried on

through a fixed place of business". The OECD Commentary stresses that "the common feature of these activities is that they are in general preparatory or auxiliary activities" and that "the provisions of paragraph 4 are designed to prevent an enterprise of one State from being taxed in the other State, if it carries on in that other State activities of a purely preparatory or auxiliary character". The OECD Commentary states further:

> "Subparagraph (*a*) relates only to the case in which an enterprise acquires the use of facilities for storing [or] displaying . . . its own goods or merchandise. Subparagraph (*b*) relates to the stock of merchandise itself and provides that the stock, as such, shall not be treated as a permanent establishment if it is maintained for the purpose of storage [or] display . . . Subparagraph (*c*) covers the case in which a stock of goods or merchandise belonging to one enterprise is processed by a second enterprise, on behalf of, or for the account of, the first-mentioned enterprise. The reference to the collection of information in subparagraph (*d*) is intended to include the case of the newspaper bureau which has no purpose other than to act as one of many 'tentacles' of the parent body; to exempt such a bureau is to do no more than to extend the concept of 'mere purchase'." [para. 22]

> "Subparagraph (*e*) provides that a fixed place of business through which the enterprise exercises solely an activity which has for the enterprise a preparatory or auxiliary character, is deemed not to be a permanent establishment. The wording of this subparagraph makes it unnecessary to produce an exhaustive list of exceptions. Furthermore, this subparagraph provides a generalized exception to the general definition in paragraph 1 and, when read with that paragraph, provides a more selective test, by which to determine what constitutes a permanent establishment. To a considerable degree it limits that definition and excludes from its rather wide scope a number of forms of business organizations which, although they are carried on through a fixed place of business, should not be treated as permanent establishments. It is recognized that such

a place of business may well contribute to the productivity of the enterprise, but the services it performs are so remote from the actual realization of profits that it is difficult to allocate any profit to the fixed place of business in question. Examples are fixed places of business solely for the purpose of advertising or for the supply of information or for scientific research or for the servicing of a patent or a know-how contract, if such activities have a preparatory or auxiliary character." [para. 23]

"It is often difficult to distinguish between activities which have a preparatory or auxiliary character and those which have not. The decisive criterion is whether or not the activity of the fixed place of business in itself forms an essential and significant part of the activity of the enterprise as a whole. Each individual case will have to be examined on its own merits. In any case, a fixed place of business whose general purpose is one which is identical to the general purpose of the whole enterprise, does not exercise a preparatory or auxiliary activity. Where, for example, the servicing of patents and know-how is the purpose of an enterprise, a fixed place of business of such enterprise exercising such an activity cannot get the benefits of subparagraph (e). A fixed place of business which has the function of managing an enterprise or even only a part of an enterprise or of a group of the concern cannot be regarded as doing a preparatory or auxiliary activity, for such a managerial activity exceeds this level. If enterprises with international ramifications establish a so-called 'management office' in States in which they maintain subsidiaries, permanent establishments, agents or licensees, such office having supervisory and co-ordinating functions for all departments of the enterprise located within the region concerned, a permanent establishment will normally be deemed to exist, because the management office may be regarded as an office within the meaning of paragraph 2. Where a big international concern has delegated all management functions to its regional management offices so that the functions of the head office of the concern are restricted to general supervision (so-called polycentric enterprises), the regional management offices even have to be regarded as a 'place of management' within the meaning of subparagraph (*a*) of paragraph 2. The function of managing an enterprise, even if it only covers a certain area of the operations of the concern, constitutes an essential part of the business operations of the enterprise and therefore can in no way be regarded as an activity which has a preparatory or auxiliary character within the meaning of subparagraph (*e*) of paragraph 4." [para. 24]

"A permanent establishment could also be constituted if an enterprise maintains a fixed place of business in order to supply spare parts to customers for the machinery supplied to such customers, and to maintain or repair such machinery. Since these after-sale organisations perform an essential and significant part of the services of an enterprise vis-à-vis its customers, their activities are not merely auxiliary ones. Sub-paragraph (*e*) applies only if the activity of the fixed place of business is limited to a preparatory or auxiliary one. This would not be the case where, for example, the fixed place of business does not only give information but also furnishes plans etc., specially developed for the purposes of the individual customer. Nor would it be the case if a research establishment were to concern itself with manufacture." [para. 25]

"Moreover, subparagraph (*e*) makes it clear that the activities of the fixed place of business must be carried on for the enterprise. A fixed place of business which renders services not only to its enterprise but also directly to the other enterprises, for example to other companies of a group to which the company owning the fixed place belongs, would not fall within the scope of subparagraph (*e*)." [para. 26]

"The fixed places of business mentioned in paragraph 4 cannot be deemed to constitute permanent establishments so long as their activities are restricted to the functions which are the prerequisite for assuming that the fixed place of business is not a permanent establishment. This will be the case even if the contracts necessary for establishing and carrying on the business are concluded by those in charge of the places of business themselves. The employees of places of business within the meaning of paragraph 4 who are authorized to conclude such contracts should not be regarded as agents within the meaning of paragraph 5. A case in point would be a research institution the manager of which is authorized to conclude the contracts necessary for maintaining the institution and who exercises this authority within the framework of the functions of the institution. A permanent establishment, however, exists if the fixed place of business exercising any of the functions listed in paragraph 4 were to exercise them not only on behalf of the enterprise to which it belongs but also on behalf of other enterprises. If, for instance, an advertising agency maintained by an enterprise were also to engage in advertising for other enterprises, it would be regarded as a permanent establishment of the enterprise by which it is maintained." [para. 28]

"If a fixed place of business under paragraph 4 is deemed not to be a permanent establishment, this exception applies likewise to the disposal of movable property forming part of the business property of the place of business at the termination of the enterprise's activity in such installation . . . Since, for example, the display of merchandise is excepted under subparagraphs (a) and (b), the sale of the merchandise at the termination of a trade fair or convention is covered by this exception. The exception does not, of course, apply to sales of merchandise not actually displayed at the trade fair or convention." [para. 29]

"A fixed place of business used both for activities which rank as exceptions (paragraph 4) and for other activities would be regarded as a single permanent establishment and taxable as regards both types of activities. This would be the case, for instance, where a store maintained for the delivery of goods also engaged in sales." [para. 30]

Paragraph 5

22.   It is a generally accepted principle that an enterprise having a person acting for it in a State should, under certain conditions, be treated as having a permanent establishment in that State, even if the enterprise does not have a fixed place of business in that State within the meaning of paragraphs 1 and 2. Paragraph 5 gives that State the right to tax if the person acting for the enterprise is a dependent agent and various other requirements are met. Dependent agents, who may be individuals or companies, generally are a permanent establishment of the enterprise if they carry out on behalf of such enterprise one of the activities that would constitute a permanent establishment under this Model if such enterprise carried out such activity itself.

23.   A dependent agent is a "permanent establishment" only if the agent's authority is used repeatedly and not merely in isolated cases. The OECD Commentary states further:

> ". . . Also, the phrase 'authority to conclude contracts in the name of the enterprise' does not confine the application of the paragraph to an agent who enters into contracts literally in the name of the enterprise; the paragraph applies equally to an agent who concludes contracts which are binding on the enterprise even if those contracts are not actually in the name of the enterprise. The authority to conclude contracts must cover contracts relating to operations which constitute the business proper of the enterprise. It would be irrelevant, for instance, if the person had authority to engage employees for the enterprise to assist that person's activity for the enterprise or if the person were authorized to conclude in the name of the enterprise, similar contracts relating to internal operations only. Moreover the authority has to be habitually exercised in the other State; whether or not this is the case should be determined on the basis of the commercial realities of the situation. A person who is authorized to negotiate all elements and details of a contract in a way binding on the enterprise can be said to exercise this authority 'in that State', even if the contract is signed by another person in the State in which the enterprise is

situated. Since, by virtue of paragraph 4, the maintenance of a fixed place of business solely for purposes listed in that paragraph is deemed not to constitute a permanent establishment, a person whose activities are restricted to such purposes does not create a permanent establishment either." [paras. 32 and 33]

24.   With the addition of subparagraph 5(*b*), this paragraph departs substantially from and is considerably broader in scope than Article 5, paragraph 5, of the OECD Model Convention, which the Group considered to be too narrow in scope because it restricted the type of agent who would be deemed to create a permanent establishment of a non-resident enterprise, exposing it to taxation in the source country. Some members from developing countries pointed out that a narrow formula might encourage tax evasion by permitting an agent who was in fact dependent to represent himself as acting on his own behalf. It was the understanding of the Group that the phrase "authority to conclude contracts on behalf of " in subparagraph 5(*a*) of article 5 means that the agent had legal authority to bind the enterprise for business purposes and not only for administrative purposes (e.g., conclusion of lease or electricity and manpower contracts).

25.   The Group of Experts understood that the subparagraph 5(*b*) was to be interpreted such that if all the sales-related activities take place outside the host State and only delivery, by an agent, takes place there, such a situation would not lead to a permanent establishment. However, if sales-related activities (e.g., advertising or promotion) are also conducted in that State on behalf of the resident (whether or not by the enterprise itself or by its dependent agents) and have contributed to the sale of such goods or merchandise, a permanent establishment may exist.

Paragraph 6

26.   This paragraph does not correspond to any provision of the OECD Model Convention. It was included because it was the common feeling of the Group that the OECD definition of permanent establishment was not adequate to deal with certain aspects of the

insurance business. Members from developing countries pointed out that if an insurance agent was independent, the profits would not be taxable in accordance with the provisions suggested in article 5, paragraph 7, of the United Nations Model Convention (based on Article 5, paragraph 6, of the OECD Model Convention); and if the agent was dependent, no tax could be imposed because insurance agents normally had no authority to conclude contracts as would be required under the provisions suggested in subparagraph 5(a) (based on Article 5, paragraph 5, of the OECD Model Convention). Those members expressed the view that taxation of insurance profits in the country where the premiums were being paid was desirable and should take place independently of the status of the agent. However, such taxation is based on the assumption that the person (employee or representative) through whom premiums are collected and risk insured is present in the country where the risk is located.

27.   Once agreement had been reached on the principle of including a special provision on insurance, the discussion in the Group focused mainly on cases involving representation through "an independent agent". Members from developing countries felt it would be desirable to provide that a permanent establishment existed in such cases because of the nature of the insurance business, the fact that the risks were situated within the country claiming tax jurisdiction, and the facility with which persons could, on a part-time basis, represent insurance companies on the basis of an "independent status", making it difficult to distinguish between dependent and independent insurance agents. Members from developed countries, on the other hand, stressed that in cases involving independent agents, insurance business should not be treated differently from such activities as the sale of tangible commodities. Those members also drew attention to the difficulties involved in ascertaining the total amount of business done when the insurance was handled by several independent agents within the same country. In view of the difference in approach, the Group agreed that the case of representation through independent agents should be left to bilateral negotiations, which could take account of the methods used to sell insurance and other features of the insurance business in the countries concerned.

Paragraph 7

28.   The first sentence of this paragraph reproduces Article 5, paragraph 6, of the OECD Model Convention in its entirety, with a few minor drafting changes. The relevant portions of the Commentary on the OECD text are as follows:

> "Where an enterprise of a Contracting State carries on business dealings through a broker, general commission agent or any other agent of an independent status, it cannot be taxed in the other Contracting State in respect of those dealings if the agent is acting in the ordinary course of his business . . . Although it stands to reason that such an agent, representing a separate enterprise, cannot constitute a permanent establishment of the foreign enterprise, paragraph [7] has been inserted in the article for the sake of clarity and emphasis." [para. 36]

> "A person will come within the scope of paragraph [7]—i.e., he will not constitute a permanent establishment of the enterprise on whose behalf he acts—only if
>
> (a)   he is independent of the enterprise both legally and economically,
>
> (b)   he acts in the ordinary course of his business when acting on behalf of the enterprise." [para. 37]

> "Whether a person is independent of the enterprise represented depends on the extent of the obligations which this person has vis-à-vis the enterprise. Where the person's commercial activities for the enterprise are subject to detailed instructions or to comprehensive control by it, such person cannot be regarded as independent of the enterprise. Another important criterion will be whether the entrepreneurial risk has to be borne by the person or by the enterprise the person represents. A subsidiary is not to be considered dependent on its parent company solely because of the parent's ownership of the share capital. Persons cannot be said to act in the ordinary course of their own business if, in place of the enterprise, such persons perform activities which, economically, belong to the sphere of the enterprise rather than to that of their own busi-

ness operations. Where, for example, a commission agent not only sells the goods or merchandise of the enterprise in his own name but also habitually acts, in relation to that enterprise, as a permanent agent having an authority to conclude contracts, he would be deemed in respect of this particular activity to be a permanent establishment, since he is thus acting outside the ordinary course of his own trade or business (namely that of a commission agent), unless his activities are limited to those mentioned at the end of paragraph 5." [para. 38]

29.   In the 1980 edition of the United Nations Model Convention, the second sentence of paragraph 7 read as under:

"However, when the activities of such an agent are devoted wholly or almost wholly on behalf of the enterprise, he will not be considered an agent of an independent status within the meaning of this paragraph." (This sentence is an addition to the corresponding paragraph in the OECD Model Convention.)

30.   It was considered that this sentence, as worded, gave rise to anomalous situations. There was reason to believe that, as worded, whenever the number of enterprises for which an agent of an independent status was working was reduced to one, such an agent's status was changed to "agent of dependent status". In 1999, it was considered necessary to remove this anomaly and doubt by rephrasing the second sentence as under:

"However, when the activities of such an agent are devoted wholly or almost wholly on behalf of that enterprise, and conditions are made or imposed between that enterprise and the agent in their commercial and financial relations which differ from those which would have been made between independent enterprises, he will not be considered as an agent of an independent status within the meaning of this paragraph."

31.   As redrafted, it has been made clear that to determine the status of an agent as not being of "an independent status", it would be necessary to take into account the entirety of the commercial and fi-

nancial relations between the enterprise and the agent which will show that they differ from those expected between independent enterprises at arm's length. Hence, as worded, the mere fact that the number of enterprises for which an agent acted as an agent of an independent status fell to one will not change his status from being an agent of independent status to that of a dependent status.

Paragraph 8

32.   This paragraph reproduces Article 5, paragraph 7, of the OECD Model Convention. The Commentary on the OECD text is as follows:

> "It is generally accepted that the existence of a subsidiary company does not, of itself, constitute that subsidiary company a permanent establishment of its parent company. This follows from the principle that, for the purpose of taxation, such a subsidiary company constitutes an independent legal entity. Even the fact that the trade or business carried on by the subsidiary company is managed by the parent company does not constitute the subsidiary company a permanent establishment of the parent company." [para. 40]

> "However, a subsidiary company will constitute a permanent establishment for its parent company under the same conditions stipulated in paragraph 5 as are valid for any other unrelated company, i.e., if it cannot be regarded as an independent agent in the meaning of paragraph [7], and if it has and habitually exercises an authority to conclude contracts in the name of the parent company. And the effects would be the same as for any other unrelated company to which paragraph 5 applies." [para. 41]

> "The same rules should apply to activities which one subsidiary carries on for any other subsidiary of the same company." [para. 42]

Commentary on chapter III

TAXATION OF INCOME

Article 6

INCOME FROM IMMOVABLE PROPERTY

A. GENERAL CONSIDERATIONS

1.   Article 6 of the United Nations Model Convention reproduces Article 6 of the OECD Model Convention.

2.   In taxing income from immovable property, the object should be the taxation of profits rather than of gross income; the expenses incurred in earning income from real property or from agriculture or forestry should therefore be taken into account. This objective should not, however, preclude the use of a withholding tax on rents from real property, based on gross income; in such cases the rate should take into account the fact that expenses have been incurred. On the other hand, if a withholding tax on gross rents is used, it will be just as satisfactory if the owner of the real property can elect to have the income from the property taxed on a net basis under the regular income tax. Article 6 is not intended to prevent a country which taxes income from agriculture or other immovable property on an estimated or similar basis from continuing to use that method.

3.   Some members from developing countries were of the view that the distribution of dividends by a company referred to in article 13, paragraph 4, should be treated as income from immovable property and, therefore, as covered by article 6. However, this view was not shared by most other members.

4.   It was noted that in some countries, a person may receive income (typically rental income) from immovable property in circumstances where that person instead of owning the immovable property owns shares of a company owning that property and that such shares entitle that person to the use or enjoyment of the property. Con-

tracting States are free to expand the scope of the article to cover such income. They may also expand the scope of article 22 to allow source taxation of shares of such companies.

B.   COMMENTARY ON THE PARAGRAPHS OF ARTICLE 6

Paragraph 1

5.   This paragraph grants the right to tax income from immovable property (including income from agriculture or forestry) to the State of source, that is, the State where the property in question is situated. In the words of the Commentary on the OECD Model Convention, this provision is based on "the fact that there is always a very close economic connection between the source of this income and the State of source".

6.   The OECD Commentary observes: "Although income from agriculture or forestry is included in Article 6, Contracting States are free to agree in their bilateral conventions to treat such income under Article 7. Article 6 deals only with income which a resident of a Contracting State derives from immovable property situated in the other Contracting States. It does not, therefore, apply to income from immovable property situated in the Contracting State of which the recipient is a resident within the meaning of Article 4 or situated in a third State; the provisions of paragraph 1 of Article 21 shall apply to such income." [para. 1]

Paragraph 2

7.   This paragraph, which gives the term "immovable property" the meaning that it has under the law of the Contracting State in which the property is situated, is intended to alleviate difficulties of interpretation with regard to whether an asset or a right is to be regarded as immovable property. In addition the paragraph lists a number of assets and rights which are in any case to be regarded as covered by the term. On the other hand, the paragraph provides that ships, boats and aircraft shall not be regarded as immovable property.

Like the OECD Model Convention, the United Nations Model Convention contains no special provision concerning income from indebtedness secured by immovable property, a matter which is dealt with under the article relating to interest.

Paragraph 3

8.   This paragraph provides that the general rule set forth in paragraph 1 shall apply regardless of the form in which immovable property is used.

Paragraph 4

9.   The Commentary on the OECD Model Convention observes that this paragraph "makes it clear that the provisions of paragraphs 1 and 3 apply also to income from immovable property, of industrial, commercial and other enterprises and to income from immovable property used for the performance of independent personal services". The OECD Commentary also observes that:

"the right to tax of the State of source has priority over the right to tax of the other State and applies also where in the case of an enterprise or of non-industrial and non-commercial activities, income is only indirectly derived from immovable property. This does not prevent income from immovable property, when derived through a permanent establishment, from being treated as income of an enterprise, but secures that income from immovable property will be taxed in the State in which the property is situated also in the case where such property is not part of a permanent establishment situated in that State. It should further be noted that the provisions of the article do not prejudge the application of domestic law as regards the manner in which income from immovable property is to be taxed". [para. 4]

Article 7

BUSINESS PROFITS

A. GENERAL CONSIDERATIONS

1.   Article 7 of the United Nations Model Convention consists of several provisions of article 7 of the OECD Model Convention, either unchanged or substantially amended, and some new provisions.

2.   There is general acceptance of the arm's length rule embodied in the OECD Model Convention, under which the profits attributable to a permanent establishment are those which would be earned by the establishment if it were a wholly independent entity dealing with its head office as if it were a distinct and separate enterprise operating under conditions and selling at prices prevailing in the regular market. The profits so attributable are normally the profits shown on the books of the establishment. Nevertheless, this rule permits the authorities of the country in which the permanent establishment is located to rectify the accounts of the enterprise, so as to reflect properly income which the establishment would have earned if it were an independent enterprise dealing with its head office at arm's length. The application of the arm's length rule to the allocation of profits between the home office and its permanent establishment presupposes for most countries that the domestic legislation authorizes a determination on the basis of the arm's length principle.

3.   The application of the arm's length rule is particularly important in connection with the difficult and complex problem of deductions to be allowed to the permanent establishment. It is also generally accepted that in calculating the profits of a permanent establishment, allowance should be made for expenses, wherever incurred, for the purpose of the business of the permanent establishment, including executive and general administrative expenses. Apart from what may be regarded as ordinary expenses, there are some classes of expenditure that give rise to special problems. These include interest and royalties etc. paid by the permanent establishment to its head office in return for money lent or patent rights li-

censed by the latter to the permanent establishment. They further include commission (except for reimbursement of actual expenses) for specific services or for the exercise of management services by the enterprise for the benefit of the establishment. In this case, it is considered that the payments should not be allowed as deductions in computing the profits of the permanent establishment. Conversely, such payments made to a permanent establishment by the head office should be excluded from the profits of the permanent establishment. On the other hand, an allocable share of such payments, e.g., interest and royalties, paid by the enterprise to third parties should be allowed. For a further consideration of this matter, a reference may be made to the OECD Commentaries reproduced in paragraph 19.

4.   Under the OECD Model Convention, only profits attributable to the permanent establishment may be taxed in the source country. The United Nations Model Convention amplifies this attribution principle by a force of attraction rule, which permits the enterprise, once it carries out business through a permanent establishment in the source country, to be taxed on some business profits in that country arising from transactions outside the permanent establishment. Where, owing to the force of attraction principle, the profits of an enterprise other than those attributable directly to the permanent establishment may be taxed in the State where the permanent establishment is situated, such profits should be determined in the same way as if they were attributable directly to the permanent establishment.

5.   The United Nations Model Convention does not contain paragraph 5 of Article 7 of the OECD Model Convention, which states, "No profits shall be attributed to a permanent establishment by reason of the mere purchase by that permanent establishment of goods or merchandise for the enterprise". The Group of Experts could not reach a consensus on whether profits should be attributed to a permanent establishment by reason of the mere purchase of goods and therefore decided to include in article 7 a note stating that this question should be settled in bilateral negotiations. Several members from developing countries believe that this provision could be in-

cluded if it were amended to include a statement that in the case of a permanent establishment engaged in purchasing and other activities, profits derived from purchasing activities should be attributed to the permanent establishment. Other members from developing countries felt that the provision should be omitted because, even where purchasing is the sole activity of an enterprise in the source country, a permanent establishment could exist in that country, the purchasing activity may contribute to the overall profit of the enterprise, and some portion of that profit thus may appropriately be taxed by that country. The members from developed countries generally favoured inclusion of OECD paragraph 5, without amendment.

6.　　The Commentary on OECD Model Convention contains the following preliminary remarks on Article 7:

> "This Article is in many respects a continuation of, and a corollary to, Article 5 on the definition of the concept of permanent establishment. The permanent establishment criterion is commonly used in international double taxation conventions to determine whether a particular kind of income shall or shall not be taxed in the country from which it originates but the criterion does not of itself provide a complete solution to the problem of the double taxation of business profits . . . [W]hen an enterprise of a Contracting State carries on business in the other Contracting State the authorities of that second State have to ask themselves two questions before they levy tax on the profits of the enterprise: the first question is whether the enterprise has a permanent establishment in their country; if the answer is in the affirmative the second question is what, if any, are the profits on which that permanent establishment should pay tax. It is with the rules to be used in determining the answer to this second question that Article 7 is concerned. Rules for ascertaining the profits of an enterprise of a Contracting State which is trading with an enterprise of the other Contracting State when both enterprises are members of the same group of enterprises or are under the same effective control are dealt with in Article 9". [para. 1]

" . . . The question of what criteria should be used in attributing profits to a permanent establishment, and of how to allocate profits from transactions between enterprises under common control, has had to be dealt with in a large number of double taxation conventions and it is fair to say that the solutions adopted have generally conformed to a standard pattern. It is generally recognized that the essential principles on which this standard pattern is based are well founded, and it has been thought sufficient to restate them with some slight amendments and modifications primarily aimed at producing greater clarity. The two Articles incorporate a number of directives. They do not, nor in the nature of things could they be expected to, lay down a series of precise rules for dealing with every kind of problem that may arise when an enterprise of one State makes profits in another. Modern commerce organizes itself in an infinite variety of ways, and it would be quite impossible within the fairly narrow limits of an article in a double taxation convention to specify an exhaustive set of rules for dealing with every kind of problem that may arise. However, since such problems may result in unrelieved double taxation or non-taxation of certain profits, it is more important for tax authorities to agree on mutually consistent methods of dealing with these problems, using, where appropriate, the mutual agreement procedure provided for in Article 25, than to adopt unilateral interpretations of basic principles to be adhered to despite differences of opinion with other States. In this respect, the methods for solving some of the problems most often encountered are discussed below." [para. 2]

B. COMMENTARY ON THE PARAGRAPHS OF ARTICLE 7

Paragraph 1

7.   This paragraph reproduces Article 7, paragraph 1, of the OECD Model Convention, with the addition of clauses (*b*) and (*c*). In the discussion preceding the adoption by the Group of Experts of this paragraph, several members from developing countries expressed

support for the force of attraction rule, although they would limit its application to business profits covered by Article 7 of the OECD Model Convention and not extend it to income from capital (dividends, interest and royalties) covered by other treaty provisions. They argued that neither sales through independent commission agents nor purchase activities would become taxable to the principal under that rule. Some members from developed countries pointed out that the force of attraction rule had been found unsatisfactory and abandoned in recent tax treaties concluded by them because of the undesirability of taxing income from an activity that was totally unrelated to the establishment and that was in itself not extensive enough to constitute a permanent establishment. They also stressed the uncertainty that such an approach would create for taxpayers. Members from developing countries pointed out that the force of attraction approach avoids some administrative problems because, under that approach, it is not necessary to determine whether particular activities are related to the permanent establishment or the income involved attributable to it. That was the case especially with respect to transactions conducted directly by the home office within the country, but similar in nature to those conducted by the permanent establishment. However, after discussion, it was proposed that the "force of attraction" rule should be limited so that it would apply to sales of goods or merchandise and other business activities in the following manner: If an enterprise has a permanent establishment in the other Contracting State for the purpose of selling goods or merchandise, sales of the same or a similar kind may be taxed in that State even if they are not conducted through the permanent establishment; a similar rule applies if the permanent establishment is used for other business activities and the same or similar activities are performed without any connection with the permanent establishment.

8.   Some members of the Group of Experts consider that the force of attraction rule shall not apply where an enterprise is able to demonstrate that the sales or business activities were carried out for reasons other than obtaining treaty benefits. This recognizes that an enterprise may have legitimate business reasons for choosing not

to carry out sales or business activities through its permanent establishment.

9.   The Commentary on the corresponding provision of the OECD Model Convention contains the following:

"This paragraph is concerned with two questions. First, it restates the generally accepted principle of double taxation conventions that an enterprise of one State shall not be taxed in the other State unless it carries on business in that other State through a permanent establishment situated therein. It . . . has come to be accepted in international fiscal matters that until an enterprise of one State sets up a permanent establishment in another State it should not properly be regarded as participating in the economic life of that other State to such an extent that it comes within the jurisdiction of that other State's taxing rights." [para. 3]

"The second and more important point [stated in the second sentence] is that . . . when an enterprise carries on business through a permanent establishment in another State that State may tax the profits of the enterprise but only so much of them as is attributable to the permanent establishment; in other words that the right to tax does not extend to profits that the enterprise may derive from that State otherwise than through the permanent establishment. This is a question on which there may be differences of view. Some countries have taken the view that when a foreign enterprise has set up a permanent establishment within their territory it has brought itself within their fiscal jurisdiction to such a degree that they can properly tax all profits that the enterprise derives from their territory, whether the profits come from the permanent establishment or from other activities in that territory. But it is thought that it is preferable to adopt the principle contained in the second sentence of paragraph 1, namely that the test that business profits should not be taxed unless there is a permanent establishment is one that should properly be applied not to the enterprise itself but to its profits. To put the matter another way, the principle laid down in the second sentence of paragraph 1 is based on the view that in taxing the profits that a foreign enterprise derives from a particular country, the fiscal authorities of that country should look at the separate sources of profit that the enterprise derives from their country and should apply to each the permanent establishment test. This is of course without prejudice to other articles." [para. 5]

"On this matter, naturally, there is room for differences of view, and since it is an important question it may be useful to set out the arguments for each point of view." [para. 6]

"Apart from the background question of fiscal jurisdiction, the main argument commonly put forward against the solution advocated above is that there is a risk that it might facilitate avoidance of tax. This solution, the argument runs, might leave it open to an enterprise to set up in a particular country a permanent establishment which made no profits, was never intended to make profits, but existed solely to supervise a trade, perhaps of an extensive nature, that the enterprise carried on in that country through independent agents and the like. Moreover, the argument goes, although the whole of this trade might be directed and arranged by the permanent establishment, it might be difficult in practice to prove that was the case. If the rates of tax are higher in that country than they are in the country in which the head office is situated, then the enterprise has a strong incentive to see that it pays as little tax as possible in the other territory; the main criticism of the solution advocated above is that it might conceivably provide the enterprise with a means of ensuring that result." [para. 7]

"Apart again from the question of the proper extent of fiscal jurisdiction, the main argument in favour of the proposed solution is that it is conducive to simple and efficient administration, and that it is more closely adapted to the way in which business is commonly transacted. The organization of modern business is highly complex. In OECD Member countries, there are a considerable number of companies each of which is engaged in a wide diversity of activities and is carrying on business extensively in many countries. It may be that such a company may have set up a permanent establishment in a second country and may be transacting a considerable amount of business through that permanent establishment in one particular kind of manufacture; that a different part of the same company may be selling quite different goods or manufactures in that second country through independent agents; and that the company may have perfectly genuine reasons for taking this course—reasons based on, for example, either on the historical pattern of its business or on commercial convenience. Is it desirable that the fiscal authorities should go so far as to insist on trying to search out the profit element of each of the transactions carried on through independent agents, with a view to aggregating that profit with the profits of the permanent establishment? Such an article might interfere seriously with ordinary commercial processes, and so be out of keeping with the aims of the Convention." [para. 8]

"It is no doubt true that evasion of tax could be practised by undisclosed channelling of profits away from a permanent establishment and that this may sometimes need to be watched, but it is necessary in considering this point to preserve a sense of proportion and to bear in mind what is said above. It is not, of course, sought in any way to sanction any such malpractice, or to shelter any concern thus evading tax from the consequences that would follow from detection by the fiscal authorities concerned. It is fully recognized that Contracting States should be free to use all methods at their disposal to fight fiscal evasion." [para. 9]

"For the reasons given above, it is thought that the argument that the solution advocated might lead to increased avoidance of tax by foreign enterprises should not be given undue weight. Much more importance is attached to the desirability of interfering as little as possible with existing business organizations and of refraining from inflicting demands for information on foreign enterprises which are unnecessarily onerous." [para. 10]

Paragraph 2

10.   This paragraph reproduces Article 7, paragraph 2, of the OECD Model Convention. In the discussion relating to that paragraph, a member from a developed country pointed out that his country was having some problems with inconsistent determination of the profits properly attributable to a permanent establishment, especially with regard to "turnkey" contracts. Under a turnkey contract a contractor agrees to construct a factory or similar facility and make it ready for operation; when the facility is ready for operation, it is handed over to the purchaser, who can then begin operations. The international tax problems occur when the facility is to be constructed in one country by a contractor resident in another country. The actual construction activities carried on in one country clearly constitute a permanent establishment within that country if of sufficiently long duration. Turnkey contracts, however, often involve components other than normal construction activities, including the purchase of capital goods, the performance of architectural and engineering services and the provision of technical assistance. Those latter items, it was explained, are sometimes completed before construction activities actually start (and hence, before the creation of a permanent establishment at the construction site) and often outside the country in which the construction site/permanent establishment is situated.

11.   The question thus arose how much of the total profits of the turnkey contract is properly attributable to the permanent establishment and thus taxable in the country in which it is situated. A member from a developed country said that he knew of instances in which countries had sought to attribute the entire profits of the contract to the permanent establishment. It was his view, however, that only the profits attributable to activities carried on by the permanent establishment should be taxed in the country in which the permanent establishment was situated, unless the profits included items of income dealt with separately in other articles of the Convention and were taxable in that country accordingly.

12.   The Group recognized that the problem was a complex and potentially controversial one involving many interrelated issues,

such as source of income rules and the definitions of permanent establishment and profits of an enterprise. The Group acknowledged that the problem might be considered in the course of bilateral negotiations, but it agreed upon no amendment to address it.

13.   Some members of the Group of Experts were of the view that the last part of paragraph 2 was too narrow, as they consider that it refers only to transactions between the permanent establishment and the home office, and does not take into account transactions between the permanent establishment and, for example, other permanent establishments of the same enterprise. For this purpose, Contracting States may consider the alternative clarification as under:

> "There shall in each Contracting State be attributed to that permanent establishment the profits that it might be expected to make if it were a distinct and independent enterprise engaged in the same or similar activities under the same or similar conditions."

14.   Although the point in controversy relating to the allocation of profits between different permanent establishments as opposed to allocation between a permanent establishment and its head office was not in doubt, it was generally accepted that the concern of the Group of Experts should be clearly brought out.

15.   As observed in paragraph 11 of the OECD Commentaries, paragraph 2 as presently worded contains the central directive on which the allocation of profits to a permanent establishment was intended to be based. This paragraph incorporates the view that was generally contained in bilateral conventions, that the profits to be attributed to a permanent establishment were those which that permanent establishment would have made if, instead of dealing with its head office, it had been dealing with an entirely separate enterprise under conditions and at prices prevailing in the ordinary market. This corresponds to the "arm's length" principle discussed in the Commentary on article 9. Normally, the profits so determined would be the same profits that one would expect to be determined by the ordinary processes of business accountancy. Since the arm's length prin-

ciple also extends to the allocation of profits which the permanent establishment may derive from transactions with other permanent establishments of the enterprise, the existing paragraph 2 should be construed to specifically make it applicable to such situations. As interpreted, where an enterprise of a Contracting State carries on its business activities in the other Contracting State through a permanent establishment situated therein, it would be necessary to allocate to such permanent establishment the profits which it could be in a position to make if it were a distinct enterprise engaged in the same or similar activities under the same or similar conditions and operating at arm's length, and dealing wholly independently with the enterprise of which it is a permanent establishment or the other permanent establishments of that enterprise.

16.   Relevant portions of the OECD Commentary on this paragraph are as follows:

"... The arm's length principle also extends to the allocation of profits which the permanent establishment may derive from transactions with other permanent establishments of the enterprise; but Contracting States which consider that the existing paragraph does not in fact cover these more general transactions may in their bilateral negotiations, agree upon more detailed provisions or amend paragraph 2 to read as follows:

'Subject to the provisions of paragraph 3, where an enterprise of a Contracting State carries on business in the other Contracting State through a permanent establishment situated therein, there shall in each Contracting State be attributed to that permanent establishment the profits which it might be expected to make if it were a distinct and independent enterprise engaged in the same or similar activities under the same or similar conditions.' " [para. 11]

"In the great majority of cases, trading accounts of the permanent establishment which are commonly available if only because a well-run business organization is normally concerned to know what is the profitability of its various branches will be used by the taxation authorities concerned to ascertain the profit properly attributable to that establishment. Exceptionally there may be no separate accounts . . . But where there are such accounts they will naturally form the starting point for any processes of adjustment in case adjustment is required to produce the amount of properly attributable profits. It should perhaps be emphasized that the directive contained in paragraph 2 is no justification for tax administrations to construct hypothetical profit figures in vacuo; it is always necessary to start with the real facts of the situation as they appear from the business records of the permanent establishment and to adjust as may be shown to be necessary the profit figures which those facts produce." [para. 12]

"This raises the question as to what extent such accounts should be relied upon when they are based on agreements between the head office and its permanent establishments (or between the permanent establishments themselves). Clearly, such internal agreements cannot qualify as legally binding contracts. However, to the extent that the trading accounts of the head office and the permanent establishments are both prepared symmetrically on the basis of such agreements and that those agreements reflect the functions performed by the different parts of the enterprise, these trading accounts could be accepted by tax authorities. In that respect, accounts could not be regarded as prepared symmetrically unless the values of transactions or the methods of attributing profits or expenses in the books of the permanent establishment corresponded exactly to the values or methods of attribution in the books of the head office in terms of the national currency or functional currency in which the enterprise recorded its transactions. However, where trading accounts are based on internal agreements that reflect purely artificial arrangements instead of the real economic functions of the different parts of the enterprise, these agreements should simply be ignored and the accounts corrected accordingly. This would be the case if, for example, a permanent establishment involved in sales were, under such an internal agreement, given the role of principal (accepting all the risks and entitled to all the profits from the sales) when in fact the permanent establishment concerned was nothing more than an intermediary or agent (incurring limited risks and entitled to receive only a limited share of the resulting income) or, conversely, were given the role of intermediary or agent when in reality it was a principal." [para. 12.1]

"In this respect, it should also be noted that the principle set out in paragraph 2 is subject to the provisions contained in paragraph 3, especially as regards the treatment of payments which, under the name of interest, royalties etc. are made by a permanent establishment to its head office in return for money loaned, or patent rights conceded by the latter to the permanent establishment . . ." [para. 12.2]

"Even where a permanent establishment is able to produce detailed accounts which purport to show the profits arising from its activities, it may still be necessary for the taxation authorities of the country concerned to rectify those accounts in accordance with the arm's length principle . . . Adjustment of this kind may be necessary, for example, because goods have been invoiced from the head office to the permanent establishment at prices which are not consistent with this principle, and profits have thus been diverted from the permanent establishment to the head office, or vice versa." [para. 13]

"In such cases, it will usually be appropriate to substitute for the prices used ordinary market prices for the same or similar goods supplied on the same or similar conditions. Clearly the price at which goods can be bought on open market terms varies with the quantity required and the period over which they will be supplied; such factors would have to be taken into account in deciding the open market price to be used. It is perhaps only necessary to mention at this point that there may sometimes be perfectly good commercial reasons for an enterprise invoicing its goods at prices less than those prevailing in the ordinary market; this may, for example, be a perfectly normal commercial method of establishing a competitive position in a new market and should not then be taken as evidence of an attempt to divert profits from one country to another. Difficulties may also occur in the case of proprietary goods produced by an enterprise, all of which are sold through its permanent establishments; if in such circumstances there is no open market price, and it is thought that the figures in the accounts are unsatisfactory, it may be necessary to calculate the permanent establishment's profits by other methods, for example, by applying an average ratio of gross profit to the turnover of the permanent establishment and then deducting from the figures so obtained the proper amount of expenses incurred. Clearly many special problems of this kind may arise in individual cases but the general rule should always be that the profits attributed to a permanent establishment should be based on that establishment's accounts in so far as accounts are available which represent the real facts of the situation. If available accounts do not represent the real facts then new accounts will have to be constructed, or the original ones rewritten, and for this purpose the figures to be used will be those prevailing in the open market." [para. 14]

"Many States consider that there is a realization of a taxable profit when an asset, whether or not trading stock, forming part of the business property of a permanent establishment situated within their territory is transferred to a permanent establishment or the head office of the same enterprise situated in another State. Article 7 allows such States to tax profits deemed to arise in connection with such a transfer. Such profits may be determined as indicated below. In cases where such transfer takes place, whether or not it is a permanent one, the question arises as to when taxable profits are realized. In practice, where such property has a substantial market value and is likely to appear on the balance sheet of the importing permanent establishment or other part of the enterprise after the taxation year during that in which the transfer occurred, the realization of the taxable profits will not, so far as the enterprise as a whole is concerned, necessarily take place in the taxation year of the transfer under consideration. However, the mere fact that the property leaves the purview of a tax jurisdiction may trigger the taxation of the accrued gains attributable to that property as the concept of realization depends on each country's domestic law." [para. 15]

"Where the countries in which the permanent establishments operate levy tax on the profits accruing from an internal transfer as soon as it is made, even when these profits are not actually realized until a subsequent commercial year, there will be inevitably a time lag between the moment when tax is paid abroad and the moment it can be taken into account in the country where the enterprise's head office is located. A serious problem is inherent in the time lag, especially when a permanent establishment transfers fixed assets or—in the event that it is wound up—its entire operating equipment stock, to some other part of the enterprise of which it forms part. In such cases, it is up to the head office country to seek, on a case by case basis, a bilateral solution with the outward country where there is serious risk of overtaxation . . ." [para. 15.1]

"Another significant problem concerning the transfer of assets, such as—bad loans, arises in relation to international banking. Debts may be transferred, for supervisory and financing purposes, from branch to head office or from branch to branch within a single bank. Such transfers should not be recognized where it cannot be reasonably considered that they take place for valid commercial reasons or that they would have taken place between independent enterprises, for instance where they are undertaken solely for tax purposes with the aim of maximizing the tax relief available to the bank. In such cases, the transfers would not have been expected to take place between wholly independent enterprises and therefore—would not have affected the amount of profits which such an independent enterprise might have been expected to make in independent dealing with the enterprise of which it is a permanent establishment." [para. 15.2]

"However, there may exist a commercial market for the transfer of such loans from one bank to another and the circumstances of an internal transfer may be similar to those which might be expected to have taken place between independent banks. An instance of such a transfer may be a case where a bank closed down a particular foreign branch and had therefore to transfer the debts concerned either back to its head office or to another branch. Another example might be the opening of a new branch in a given country and the subsequent transfer to it, solely for commercial reasons, of all loans previously granted to residents of that country by the head office or other branches. Any such transfer should be treated (to the extent it is recognized for tax purposes at all) as taking place at the open market value of the debt at the date of the transfer. Some relief has to be taken into account in computing the profits of the permanent establishment since, between separate entities, the value of the debt at the date of the transfer would have been taken into account in deciding on the price to be charged and principles of sound accounting require that the book value of the asset should be varied to take into account market values. (This question is further discussed in the report of the Committee on Fiscal Affairs entitled 'Attribution of . Income to Permanent Establishments'.) [para. 15.3] [Reproduced in Volume II of the OECD Model Convention at page R(13)-1.]

"Where loans which have gone bad are transferred, in order that full, but not excessive, relief for such a loss be granted, it is important that the two jurisdictions concerned reach an agreement for a mutually consistent basis for granting relief. In such cases, account should be taken of whether the transfer value, at the date of internal transfer, was the result of mistaken judgement as to the debtor's solvency or whether the value at that date reflected an appropriate judgement of the debtor's position at that time. In the former case, it may be appropriate for the country of the transferring branch to limit relief to the actual loss suffered by the bank as a whole and for the receiving country not to tax the subsequent apparent gain. Where, however, the loan was transferred for commercial reasons, from one part of the bank to another and did, after a certain time, improve in value, then the transferring branch should normally be given relief on the basis of the actual value at the time of the transfer. The position is somewhat different where the receiving entity is the head office of a bank in a credit country because normally the credit country will tax the bank on its worldwide profits and will therefore give relief by reference to the total loss suffered in respect of the loan between the time the loan was made and the time it was finally disposed of. In such a case, the transferring branch should receive relief for the period during which the loan was in the hands of that branch by reference to the principles above. The country of the head office will then give relief from double taxation by granting a credit for the tax borne by the branch in the host country." [para. 15.4]

Paragraph 3

17.   The first sentence of paragraph 3 of article 7 reproduces the entire text of Article 7, paragraph 3, of the OECD Model Convention. The rest of the paragraph consists of new provisions formulated by the Group of Experts. These provisions stem from a proposal by members from developing countries, who felt that it would be helpful to include all the necessary definitions and clarifications in the text, with a view, in particular, to assisting developing countries not represented in the Group. Some of those members also felt that provisions prohibiting the deduction of certain expenses should be included in the text of a bilateral tax treaty to make it clear that taxpayers were fully informed about their fiscal obligations. In the course of the discussion it was pointed out that the additions to the OECD text would ensure that the permanent establishment would be able to deduct interest, royalties and other expenses incurred by the head office on behalf of the establishment. The Group agreed that if billings by the head office included the full costs, both direct and indirect, then there should not be a further allocation of the executive and administrative

expenses of the head office, since that would produce a duplication of such charges on the transfer between the head office and the permanent establishment. It was pointed out that it was important to determine how the price was fixed and what elements of cost it included. Where an international wholesale price was used, it would normally include indirect costs. There was general agreement within the Group that any duplication of costs and expenses should be prevented.

18.   The business profits of an enterprise of a Contracting State are exigible to tax in that State alone unless the enterprise carries on business in the other Contracting State through a permanent establishment situated therein. The profits and gains of the business would be worked out by deducting all expenses relatable to the business activity, other than the capital expenditure which are currently not deductible or expenses of a personal or non-business nature which cannot be attributed to the business of the enterprise. Normally, many countries while considering the question of deductibility of business expenses apply the criteria of such expenditure being wholly, exclusively and necessarily for the purposes of the business. The basic objective in this behalf is to ensure that the expenditure claimed as deduction in determining the taxable profits is that such expenditure is relevant, referable and necessary for carrying out the business operations. There has to exist a nexus between the expenditure and the business activity so that the expenditure incurred is justified by business expediency, smooth running or facilitating character of the expenditure for business operations. After it has been determined that an item is deductible under the foregoing criteria, then it should be considered whether there are specific legislative provisions placing a monetary or other ceiling limits on the allowableness of business expenditure, otherwise claims for deductibility of expenditure will have to be considered in its entirety, without considering the reasonableness of the amount or its impact on the profitability of business operations.

19.   The OECD Commentary on Article 7, paragraph 3, is relevant:

"This paragraph clarifies, in relation to the expenses of a permanent establishment, the general directive laid down in paragraph 2. The paragraph specifically recognizes that in calculating the profits of a permanent establishment allowance is to be made for expenses, wherever incurred, that were incurred for the purposes of the permanent establishment. Clearly in some cases it will be necessary to estimate or to calculate by conventional means the amount of expenses to be taken into account. In the case, for example, of general administrative expenses incurred at the head office of the enterprise, it may be appropriate to take into account a proportionate part based on the ratio that the permanent establishment's turnover (or perhaps gross profits) bears to that of the enterprise as a whole. Subject to this, it is considered that the amount of expenses to be taken into account as incurred for the purposes of the permanent establishment should be the actual amount so incurred. The deduction allowable to the permanent establishment for any of the expenses of the enterprise attributed to it does not depend upon the actual reimbursement of such expenses by the permanent establishment." [para. 16]

"It has sometimes been suggested that the need to reconcile paragraphs 2 and 3 created practical difficulties as paragraph 2 required that prices between the permanent establishment and the head office be normally charged on an arm's length basis, giving to the transferring entity the type of profit which it might have been expected to make were it dealing with an independent enterprise, whilst the wording of paragraph 3 suggested that the deduction for expenses incurred for the purposes of permanent establishments should be the actual cost of those expenses, normally without adding any profit element. In fact, whilst the application of paragraph 3 may raise some practical difficulties, especially in relation to the separate enterprise and arm's length principles underlying paragraph 2, there is no difference of principle between the two paragraphs. Paragraph 3 indicates that in determining the profits of a permanent establishment, certain expenses must be allowed as deductions whilst paragraph 2 provides that the profits determined in accordance with the rule contained in paragraph 3 relating to the deduction of expenses must be those that a separate and distinct enterprise engaged in the same or similar activities under the same or similar conditions would have made. Thus, whilst paragraph 3 provides a rule applicable for the determination of the profits of the permanent establishment, paragraph 2 requires that the profits so determined correspond to the profits that a separate and independent enterprise would have made." [para. 17]

"In applying these principles to the practical determination of the profits of a permanent establishment, the question may arise as to whether a particular cost incurred by an enterprise can truly be considered as an expense incurred for the purposes of the permanent establishment, keeping in mind the separate and independent enterprise principles of paragraph 2. Whilst in general independent enterprises in their dealings with each other will seek to realize a profit and, when transferring property or providing services to each other, will charge such prices as the open market would bear, nevertheless, there are also circumstances where it cannot be considered that a particular property or service would have been obtainable from an independent enterprise or when independent enterprises may agree to share between them the costs of some activity which is pursued in common for their mutual benefit. In these particular circumstances, it may be appropriate to treat any relevant costs incurred by the enterprise as an expense incurred for the permanent establishment. The difficulty arises in making a distinction between these circumstances and the cases where a cost incurred by an enterprise should not be considered as an expense of the permanent establishment and the relevant property or service should be considered, on the basis of the separate and independent enterprises principle, to have been transferred between the head office and the permanent establishment at a price including an element of profit. The question must be whether the internal transfer of property and services, be it temporary or final, is of the same kind as those which the enterprise, in the normal course of business, would have charged to a third party at an arm's length price, i.e., by normally including in the sale price an appropriate profit." [para. 17.1]

"On the one hand, the answer to that question will be in the affirmative if the expense is initially incurred in performing a function the direct purpose of which is to make sales of a specific good or service and to realize a profit through a permanent establishment. On the other hand, the answer will be in the negative if, on the basis of the facts and circumstances of the specific case, it appears that the expense is initially incurred in performing a function the essential purpose of which is to rationalize the overall costs of the enterprise or to increase in a general way its sales." [para. 17.2]

"Where goods are supplied for resale whether in a finished state or as raw materials or semi-finished goods, it will normally be appropriate for the provisions of paragraph 2 to apply and for the supplying part of the enterprise to be allocated a profit, measured by reference to arm's length principles. But there may be exceptions even here. One example might be where goods are not supplied for resale but for temporary use in the trade so that it may be appropriate for the parts of the enterprise which share the use of the material to bear only their share of the cost of such material, e.g., in the case of machinery, the depreciation costs that relate to its use by each of these parts . . ." [para. 17.3]

"In the case of intangible rights, the rules concerning the relations between enterprises of the same group (e.g., payment of royalties or cost-sharing arrangements) cannot be applied in respect of the relations between parts of the same enterprise. Indeed, it may be extremely difficult to allocate 'ownership' of the intangible right solely to one part of the enterprise and to argue that this part of the enterprise should receive royalties from the other parts as if it were an independent enterprise. Since there is only one legal entity it is not possible to allocate legal ownership to any particular part of the enterprise and in practical terms it will often be difficult to allocate the costs of creation exclusively to one part of the enterprise. It may therefore be preferable for the costs of creation of intangible rights to be regarded as attributable to all parts of the enterprise which will make use of them and as incurred on behalf of the various parts of the enterprise to which they are relevant accordingly. In such circumstances it would be appropriate to allocate the actual costs of the creation of such intangible rights between the various parts of the enterprise without any mark-up for profit or royalty. In so doing, tax authorities must be aware of the fact that the possible adverse consequences deriving from any research and development activity (e.g., the responsibility related to the products and damages to the environment) shall also be allocated to the various parts of the enterprise, therefore giving rise, where appropriate, to a compensatory charge." [para. 17.4]

"The area of services is the one in which difficulties may arise in determining whether in a particular case a service should be charged between the various parts of a single enterprise at its actual cost or at that cost plus a mark-up to represent a profit to the part of the enterprise providing the service. The trade of the enterprise, or part of it, may consist of the provision of such services and there may be a standard charge for their provision. In such a case it will usually be appropriate to charge a service at the same rate as is charged to the outside customer." [para. 17.5]

"Where the main activity of a permanent establishment is to provide specific services to the enterprise to which it belongs and where these services provide a real advantage to the enterprise and their costs represent a significant part of the expenses of the enterprise, the host country may require that a profit margin be included in the amount of the costs. As far as possible, the host country should then try to avoid schematic solutions and rely on the value of these services in the given circumstances of each case." [para. 17.6]

"However, more commonly the provision of services is merely part of the general management activity of the company taken as a whole as where, for example, the enterprise conducts a common system of training and employees of each part of the enterprise benefit from it. In such a case it would usually be appropriate to treat the cost of providing the service as being part of the general administrative expenses of the enterprise as a whole which should be allocated on an actual cost basis to the various parts of the enterprise to the extent that the costs are incurred for the purposes of that part of the enterprise, without any mark-up to represent profit to another part of the enterprise." [para. 17.7]

"Special considerations apply to payments which, under the name of interest, are made to a head office by its permanent establishment with respect to loans made by the former to the latter. In that case, the main issue is not so much whether a debtor/creditor relationship should be recognized within the same legal entity as whether an arm's length interest rate should be charged. This is because:

—from the legal standpoint, the transfer of capital against payment of interest and an undertaking to repay in full at the due date is really a formal act incompatible with the true legal nature of a permanent establishment;

—from the economic standpoint, internal debts and receivables may prove to be non-existent, since if an enterprise is solely or predominantly equity-funded it ought not to be allowed to deduct interest charges that is has manifestly not had to pay. While, admittedly, symmetrical charges and returns will not distort the enterprise's overall profits, partial results may well be arbitrarily changed." [para. 18]

"If debts incurred by the head office of an enterprise were used solely to finance its activity or clearly and exclusively the activity of a particular permanent establishment, the problem would be reduced to one of thin capitalization of the actual user of such loans. In fact, loans contracted by an enterprise's head office usually serve its own needs only to a certain extent, the rest of the money borrowed providing basic capital for its permanent establishments." [para. 18.1]

"The approach previously suggested in this Commentary, namely the direct and indirect apportionment of actual debt charges, did not prove to be a practical solution, notably since it was unlikely to be applied in a uniform manner. Also, it is well known that the indirect apportionment of total interest payment charges, or of the part of interest that remains after certain direct allocations, comes up against practical difficulties. It is also well known that direct apportionment of total interest expense may not accurately reflect the cost of financing the permanent establishment because the taxpayer may be able to control where loans are booked and adjustments may need to be made to reflect economic reality." [para. 18.2]

"Consequently, . . . it would be preferable to look for a practicable solution that would take into account a capital structure appropriate to both the organization and the functions performed. For that reason, the ban on deductions for internal debts and receivables should continue to apply generally, subject to the special problems of banks mentioned below." [para. 18.3] (This question is further discussed in the reports of the Committee entitled "Attributes of Income to Permanent Establishment" and "Thin Capitalization".[13])

"It is, however, recognized that special considerations apply to payments of interest made by different parts of a financial enterprise (e.g., a bank) to each other on advances etc. (as distinct from capital allotted to them), in view of the fact that making and receiving advances is closely related to the ordinary business of such enterprises . . ." [para. 19]

"Another . . . question [is] whether any part of the total profits of an enterprise should be deemed to arise from the exercise of good management. Consider the case of a company

---

[13]These two reports are reproduced in Volume II of the OECD Model Convention at pages R(13)-1 and R(4)-1, respectively.

that has its head office in one country but carries on all its business through a permanent establishment situated in another country. In the extreme case it might well be that only the directors' meetings were held at the head office and that all other activities of the company, apart from purely formal legal activities were carried on in the permanent establishment. In such a case there is something to be said for the view that at least part of the profits of the whole enterprise arose from the skilful management and business acumen of the directors and that part of the profits of the enterprise ought, therefore, to be attributed to the country in which the head office was situated. If the company has been managed by a managing agency, then that agency would doubtless have charged a fee for its services and the fee might well have been a simple percentage participation in the profits of the enterprise. But, once again, whatever the theoretical merits of such a course, practical considerations weigh heavily against it. In the kind of case quoted the expenses of management would, of course, be set against the profits of the permanent establishment in accordance with the provisions of paragraph 3, but when the matter is looked at as a whole, it is thought that it would not be right to go further by deducting and taking into account some notional figure for 'profits of management'. In cases identical to the extreme case mentioned above, no account should therefore be taken in determining taxable profits of the permanent establishment of any notional figure such as profits of management." [para. 21]

"It may be, of course, that countries where it has been customary to allocate some proportion of the total profits of an enterprise to the head office of the enterprise to represent the profits of good management will wish to continue to make such an allocation. Nothing in the article is designed to prevent this. Nevertheless, it follows from what is said in paragraph 21 above that a country in which a permanent establishment is situated is in no way required to deduct when calculating the profits attributable to that permanent establishment an amount intended to represent a proportionate part of the profits of management attributable to the head office." [para. 22]

"It might well be that if the country in which the head office of an enterprise is situated allocates to the head office some percentage of the profits of the enterprise only in respect of good management, while the country in which the permanent establishment is situated does not, the resulting total of the amounts charged to tax in the two countries would be greater than it should be. In any such case the country in which the head office of the enterprise is situated should take the initiative in arranging for such adjustments to be made in computing the taxation liability in that country as may be necessary to ensure that any double taxation is eliminated." [para. 23]

"It is usually found that there are, or there can be constructed, adequate accounts for each part or section of an enterprise so that profits and expenses, adjusted as may be necessary, can be allocated to a particular part of the enterprise with a considerable degree of precision. This method of allocation is, it is thought, to be preferred in general wherever it is reasonably practicable to adopt it. There are, however, circumstances in which this may not be the case and paragraphs 2 and 3 are in no way intended to imply that other methods cannot properly be adopted where appropriate in order to arrive at the profits of a permanent establishment on a 'separate enterprise' footing. It may well be, for example, that profits of insurance enterprises can most conveniently be ascertained by special methods of computation, e.g., by applying appropriate coefficients to gross premiums received from policyholders in the country concerned. Again, in the case of a relatively small enterprise operating on both sides of the border between two countries, there may be no proper accounts for the permanent establishment nor means of constructing them. There may, too, be other cases where the affairs of the permanent establishment are so closely bound up with those of the head office that it would be impossible to disentangle them on any strict basis of branch accounts. Where it has been customary in such cases to estimate the arm's length profit of a permanent establishment by reference to suitable criteria, it may well be reasonable that that method should continue to be followed notwithstanding that the estimate thus made may not achieve as high a degree of accurate measurement of the profit as adequate accounts. Even where such a course has not been customary, it may, exceptionally, be necessary for practical reasons to estimate the arm's length profits." [para. 24]

20.   Some countries may wish to point out that they allow only those deductions that are permitted by their domestic laws.

21.   The question of making a specific provision in article 7, similar to that in paragraph 5 of Article 7 of the OECD Model Convention, regarding non-attribution of profits to a permanent establishment for "mere purchase" by that permanent establishment of goods or merchandise for the enterprise has been engaging the attention of the Group of Experts for some time. It has been considered that since under article 5 an office or facility maintained by an enterprise in a Contracting State in the other Contracting State for mere purchase of goods or merchandise does not constitute a permanent establishment, there would be very few cases where an enterprise having a permanent establishment dealing with other business would also have a purchasing facility for the enterprise. However, it has not been considered necessary to make any change in the existing provisions and the matter may be looked into during bilateral negotiations.

Paragraph 4

22.   This paragraph reproduces Article 7, paragraph 4, of the OECD Model Convention. The OECD Commentary on the paragraph is as follows:

"It has in some cases been the practice to determine the profits to be attributed to a permanent establishment not on the basis of separate accounts or by making an estimate of arm's length profit, but simply by apportioning the total profits of the enterprise by reference to various formulae. Such a method differs from those envisaged in paragraph 2, since it contemplates not an attribution of profits on a separate enterprise footing, but an apportionment of total profits; and indeed it might produce a result in figures which would differ from that which would be arrived at by a computation based on separate accounts. Paragraph 4 makes it clear that such a method may continue to be employed by a Contracting State if it has been customary in that State to adopt it, even though the figure arrived at may at times differ to some extent from that which would be obtained from separate accounts, provided that the result can fairly be said to be in accordance with the principles contained in the Article. It is emphasized, however, that in general the profits to be attributed to a permanent establishment should be determined by reference to the establishment's accounts if these reflect the real facts. It is considered that a method of allocation which is based on apportioning total profits is generally not as appropriate as a method which has regard only to the activities of the permanent establishment and should be used only where exceptionally it has as a matter of history been customary in the past and is accepted in the country concerned both by the taxation authorities and taxpayers generally there as being satisfactory. It is understood that paragraph 4 may be deleted where neither State uses such a method. Where, however, Contracting States wish to be able to use a method which has not been customary in the past the paragraph should be amended during the bilateral negotiations to make this clear." [para. 25]

"The essential character of a method [for apportioning] total profits is that a proportionate part of the profits of the whole enterprise is allocated to a part thereof, all parts of the enterprise being assumed to have contributed on the basis of the criterion or criteria adopted to the profitability of the whole. The difference between one such method and another arises for the most part from the varying criteria used to determine what is the correct proportion of the total profits. . . . [T]he criteria commonly used can be grouped into three main categories, namely those which are based on the receipts of the enterprise, its expenses or its capital structure. The first category covers allocation methods based on turnover or on commission, the second on wages and the third on the proportion of the total working capital of the enterprise allocated to each branch or part. It is not, of course, possible to say in vacuo that any of these methods is intrinsically more accurate than the others; the appropriateness of any particular method will depend on the circumstances to which it is applied. In some enterprises, such as those providing services or producing proprietary articles with a high profit margin, net profits will depend very much on turnover. For insurance enterprises it may be appropriate to make an apportionment of total profits by reference to premiums received from policyholders in each of the countries concerned. In the case of an enterprise manufacturing goods with a high-cost raw material or labour content, profits may be found to be related more closely to expenses. In the case of banking and financial concerns the proportion of total working capital may be the most relevant criterion. . . . [T]he general aim of any method [for apportioning] total profits ought to be to produce figures of taxable profit that approximate as closely as possible to the figures that would have been produced on a separate accounts basis, and it would not be desirable to attempt in this connection to lay down any specific directive other than that it should be the responsibility of the taxation authority, in consultation with the authorities of other countries concerned, to use the method which in the light of all the known facts seems most likely to produce that result." [para. 27]

"The use of any method which allocates to a part of an enterprise a proportion of the total profits of the whole does, of course, raise the question of the method to be used in computing the total profits of the enterprise. This may well be a matter which will be treated differently under the laws of different countries. This is not a problem which it would seem practicable to attempt to resolve by laying down any rigid rule. It is scarcely to be expected that it would be accepted that the profits to be apportioned should be the profits as they are computed under the laws of one particular country; each country concerned would have to be given the right to compute the profits according to the provisions of its own laws." [para. 28]

Paragraph 5

23.　This paragraph reproduces Article 7, paragraph 6, of the OECD Model Convention. In the words of the OECD Commentary, the paragraph "is intended to lay down clearly that a method of allocation once used should not be changed merely because in a particular year some other method produces more favourable results. One of the purposes of a double taxation convention is to give an enterprise of a Contracting State some degree of certainty about the tax treatment that will be accorded to its permanent establishment in the other Contracting State as well as to the part of it in its home State which is dealing with the permanent establishment; [this] paragraph [thus] gives an assurance of continuous and consistent tax treatment." [para. 31]

Paragraph 6

24.　This paragraph reproduces Article 7, paragraph 7, of the OECD Model Convention. The OECD Commentary on that paragraph is as follows:

"Although it has not been found necessary in the Convention to define the term 'profits', it should nevertheless be understood that the term when used in this Article and elsewhere in the Convention has a broad meaning including all income derived in carrying on an enterprise. Such a broad meaning corresponds to the use of the term made in the tax laws of most OECD Member countries." [para. 32]

"This interpretation of the term 'profits', however, may give rise to some uncertainty as to the application of the Convention. If the profits of an enterprise include categories of income which are treated separately in other Articles of the Convention, e.g., dividends, it may be asked whether the taxation of those profits is governed by the special Article on dividends etc. or by the provisions of this Article." [para. 33]

"To the extent that an application of this Article and the special Article concerned would result in the same tax treatment, there is little practical significance to this question. Further, . . . some of the special Articles contain specific provisions giving priority to a specific Article (cf. paragraph 4 of Article 6, paragraph 4 of Articles 10 and 11, paragraph [4] of Article 12 and paragraph 2 of Article 21)." [para. 34]

"It has seemed desirable, however, to lay down a rule of interpretation in order to clarify the field of application of the present Article in relation to the other Articles dealing with a specific category of income. In conformity with the practice generally adhered to in existing bilateral conventions, paragraph 7 gives first preference to the special Articles on dividends, interest etc. It follows from the rule that this article will be applicable to industrial and commercial income which does not belong to categories of income covered by the special articles, and, in addition, to dividends, interest etc. which under paragraph 4 of Articles 10 and 11, paragraph [4] of Article 12 and paragraph 2 of Article 21 fall within this Article . . . It is understood that the items of income covered by the special Articles may, subject to the provisions of the Convention, be taxed either separately, or as industrial and commercial profits, in conformity with the tax laws of the Contracting States." [para. 35]

"It is open to Contracting States to agree bilaterally upon special explanations or definitions concerning the term 'profits' with a view to clarifying the distinction between this term and, e.g., the concept of dividends. It may in particular be found appropriate to do so where in a convention under negotiation a deviation has been made from the definitions in the special Articles on dividends, interest and royalties. It may also be deemed desirable if the Contracting States wish to place on notice that, in agreement with the domestic tax laws of one or both of the States, the term 'profits' includes special classes of receipts such as income from the alienation or the letting of a business or of movable property used in a business. In this connection it may have to be considered whether it would be useful to include also additional rules for the allocation of such special profits." [para. 36]

"It should also be noted that, whilst the definition of 'royalties' in paragraph 2 of Article 12 of the 1963 Draft Convention and 1977 Model Convention included payments 'for the use of, or the right to use, industrial, commercial, or scientific equipment', the reference to these payments was subsequently deleted from that definition in order to ensure that income from the leasing of industrial, commercial or scientific equipment, including the income from the leasing of containers, falls under the provisions of Article 7 rather than those of Article 12, a result that the Committee on Fiscal Affairs considers to be appropriate given the nature of such income." [para. 37]

25.   With respect to the last quoted paragraph from the OECD Model Convention Commentary, it is important to note that in the revised United Nations Model Convention, payments "for the use of, or the right to use, industrial, commercial or scientific equipment" are treated differently. They remain within the definition of "royalties" in paragraph 3 of article 12 and accordingly by reason of paragraph 6 of article 7 continue to fall under the provisions of article 12, rather than those of article 7.

Article 8

SHIPPING, INLAND WATERWAYS TRANSPORT AND AIR TRANSPORT

A.   GENERAL CONSIDERATIONS

1.   Two alternative versions are given for article 8 of the United Nations Model Convention, namely article 8 (alternative A) and article 8 (alternative B). Article 8 (alternative A) reproduces Article 8 of the OECD Model Convention. Article 8 (alternative B) makes major substantive changes to Article 8 of the OECD Model Convention, dealing separately with profits from the operation of aircraft and profits from the operation of ships in paragraphs 1 and 2, respectively. The remaining paragraphs (3, 4 and 5) reproduce paragraphs 2, 3 and 4 of Article 8 of the OECD Model Convention with a minor adjustment in paragraph 5.

2.   With regard to the taxation of profits from the operation of ships in international traffic, several members of the Group from developed countries supported the position taken in Article 8 of the OECD Model Convention. In their view, shipping enterprises should not be exposed to the tax laws of the numerous countries to which their operations extended; taxation at the place of effective management was also preferable from the viewpoint of the various tax administrations. They argued that if every country taxed a portion of the profits of a shipping line, computed according to its own rules, the sum of those portions might well exceed the total income of the enterprise. According to them, that would constitute a serious problem, especially because taxes in the developing countries were often excessively high, and the total profits of shipping enterprises were frequently quite modest.

3.   Most members from developing countries asserted that those countries were not in a position to forgo even the limited revenue to be derived from taxing foreign shipping enterprises as long as their own shipping industries were not more fully developed. They recognized, however, that considerable difficulties were involved in deter-

mining a taxable profit in such a situation and allocating the profit to the various countries concerned.

4.   While some members from developed countries found taxation of shipping profits at the source acceptable, a large number of members from developed countries said they preferred the principle of exclusive taxation by the State in which the place of effective management of the enterprise was situated. Since no consensus could be reached on a provision concerning the taxation of shipping profits, the Group agreed that the question of such taxation should be left to bilateral negotiations.

5.   Although the texts of article 8 (alternatives A and B) both refer to the "place of effective management of the enterprise", some countries may wish to refer instead to the "country of residence of the enterprise".

6.   There was a consensus within the Group to recommend articles 8 (alternatives A and B) as alternatives. However, some members who could not agree to article 8 (alternative A) also could not agree to article 8 (alternative B) because of the phrase "more than casual". They argued that some countries might wish to tax either all shipping profits or all airline profits, and acceptance of article 8 (alternative B) might thus lead to revenue losses, considering the limited number of shipping companies or airlines whose effective management was situated in those countries. The group agreed that in such cases taxation should be left to bilateral negotiations.

7.   A member from a developing country suggested that the provisions of article 8 may be extended to cover rail or road transport. Since there were few cases of rail or road transport involving double taxation, Contracting States may, if considered necessary, refer to rail or road transport during bilateral negotiations.

8.   Some members from developing countries considered that the activity of transport carried out in inland waters, by definition, cannot be considered international transport and, by virtue of that, the fiscal or tax power should be attributed exclusively to the source

country in which the activities are carried out. Since article 8 deals with "Shipping, inland waterways transport and air transport", obviously all three modes of transport dealt with in this article involve problems of double taxation. Income derived from inland waterways transport is also subject to double taxation if a river or lake used for commercial transportation flows from more than one country with the headquarters of the establishment in one country and traffic originating in more than one country. Hence, it is possible that inland waterways transport would give rise to problems of double taxation.

B.   COMMENTARY ON THE PARAGRAPHS OF ARTICLE 8 (ALTERNATIVES A AND B)

Paragraph 1 of article 8 (alternative A)

9.   This paragraph, which reproduces Article 8, paragraph 1, of the OECD Model Convention, has the objective of ensuring that profits from the operation of ships or aircraft in international traffic will be taxed in one State alone. The paragraph's effect is that these profits are wholly exempt from tax at source and are taxed exclusively in the State in which is situated the place of effective management of the enterprise engaged in international traffic. The exemption from tax in the source country is predicated largely on the premise that the income of these enterprises is earned on the high seas, that exposure to the tax laws of numerous countries is likely to result in double taxation or at best in difficult allocation problems, and that exemption in places other than the home country ensures that the enterprises will not be taxed in foreign countries if their overall operations turn out to be unprofitable. Considerations relating to international air traffic are similar. Since many developing countries with water boundaries do not have resident shipping companies but do have ports used to a significant extent by ships from other countries, they have traditionally disagreed with the principle of such an exemption of shipping profits.

10.   The Commentary on the OECD Model Convention notes that the place of effective management may be situated in a country dif-

ferent from the country of residence of an enterprise operating ships or aircraft and that "some States therefore prefer to confer the exclusive taxing right on the State of residence". The Commentary suggests that States may, in bilateral negotiations, substitute a rule on the following lines: "Profits of an enterprise of a Contracting State from the operation of ships or aircraft in international traffic shall be taxable only in that State." The Commentary continues:

"Some other States, on the other hand, prefer to use a combination of the residence criterion and the place of effective management criterion by giving the primary right to tax to the State in which the place of effective management is situated while the State of residence eliminates double taxation in accordance with Article 23, so long as the former State is able to tax the total profits of the enterprise, and by giving the primary right to tax to the State of residence when the State of effective management is not able to tax total profits. States wishing to follow that principle are free to substitute a rule on the following lines:

'Profits of an enterprise of a Contracting State from the operation of ships or aircraft, other than those from transport by ships or aircraft operated solely between places in the other Contracting State, shall be taxable only in the first-mentioned State. However, where the place of effective management of the enterprise is situated in the other State and that other State imposes tax on the whole of the profits of the enterprise from the operation of ships or aircraft, the profits from the operation of ships or aircraft, other than those from transport by ships or aircraft operated solely between places in the first-mentioned State, may be taxed in that other State.'" [para. 3]

"The profits covered consist in the first place of the profits obtained by the enterprise from the carriage of passengers or cargo. With this definition, however, the provision would be unduly restrictive, in view of the development of shipping and air transport, and for practical considerations also. The provision therefore covers other classes of profits as well, i.e., those which by reason of their nature or their close relationship with the profits directly obtained from transport may all be placed in a single category. Some of these classes of profits are mentioned in the following paragraphs." [para. 4]

"Profits obtained by leasing a ship or aircraft on charter fully equipped, manned and supplied must be treated like the profits from the carriage of passengers or cargo. Otherwise, a great deal of business of shipping or air transport would not come within the scope of the provision. However, Article [12], and not Article 8, applies to profits from leasing a ship or aircraft on a bare boat charter basis except when it is an occasional source of income for an enterprise engaged in the international operation of ships or aircraft." [para. 5]

"The principle that the taxing right should be left to one Contracting State alone makes it unnecessary to devise detailed rules, e.g., for defining the profits covered, this being rather a question of applying general principles of interpretation." [para. 6]

"Shipping and air transport enterprises—particularly the latter—often engage in additional activities more or less closely connected with the direct operation of ships and aircraft. Although it would be out of the question to list here all the auxiliary activities which could properly be brought under the provision, nevertheless a few examples may usefully be given." [para. 7]

"The provision applies, inter alia, to the following activities:

(*a*)   the sale of passage tickets on behalf of other enterprises;

(*b*)   the operation of a bus service connecting a town with its airport;

(*c*)   advertising and commercial propaganda;

(*d*)   transportation of goods by truck connecting a depot with a port or airport." [para. 8]

"If an enterprise engaged in international transport undertakes to see to it that, in connection with such transport, goods are delivered directly to the consignee in the other Contracting State, such inland transportation is considered to fall within the scope of the international operation of ships or aircraft and, therefore, is covered by the provisions of this Article." [para. 9]

"Recently, 'containerization' has come to play an increasing role in the field of international transport. Such containers frequently are also used in inland transport. Profits derived by an enterprise engaged in international transport from the lease of containers which is supplementary or incidental to its international operation of ships or aircraft fall within the scope of this Article." [para. 10]

"On the other hand, the provision does not cover a clearly separate activity, such as the keeping of a hotel as a separate business; the profits from such an establishment are in any case easily determinable. In certain cases, however, circumstances are such that the provision must apply even to a hotel business, e.g., the keeping of a hotel for no other purpose than to provide transit passengers with night accommodation, the cost of such a service being included in the price of the passage ticket. In such a case, the hotel can be regarded as a kind of waiting room." [para. 11]

"There is another activity which is excluded from the field of application of the provision, namely, a shipbuilding yard operated in one country by a shipping enterprise having its place of effective management in another country." [para. 12]

"It may be agreed bilaterally that profits from the operation of a vessel engaged in fishing, dredging or hauling activities on the high seas be treated as income falling under this article." [para. 13]

"Investment income of shipping, inland waterways or air transport enterprises (e.g., income from stocks, bonds, shares or loans) is to be subjected to the treatment ordinarily applied to this class of income." [para. 14]

Paragraph 1 *of article* 8 *(alternative B)*

11. This paragraph reproduces Article 8, paragraph 1, of the OECD Model Convention, with the deletion of the words "ships or". Thus the paragraph does not apply to the taxation of profits from the operation of ships in international traffic but does apply to the taxation of profits from the operation of aircraft in international traffic. Hence the Commentary on article 8 A, paragraph 1, is relevant in so far as aircraft are concerned.

12. However, during the discussion by the Group of Experts, several members from developing countries, although agreeing to the consensus, pointed out, in connection with the taxation of profits from the operation of aircraft in international traffic, that no consideration had been given to the very substantial expenditure that developing countries incurred in the construction of airports. They considered that it would appear more reasonable to situate the geographical source of profits from international transportation at the place where passengers or freight were booked.

Paragraph 2 *of article* 8 *(alternative B)*

13. This paragraph allows profits from the operation of ships in international traffic to be taxed in the source country if operations in that country are "more than casual". It provides an independent operative rule for the shipping business and is not qualified by articles 5 and 7 relating to business profits governed by the permanent establishment rule. It thus covers both regular or frequent shipping visits and irregular or isolated visits, provided the latter were planned and not merely fortuitous. The phrase "more than casual" means a scheduled or planned visit of a ship to a particular country to pick up freight or passengers.

14. The overall net profits should, in general, be determined by the authorities of the country in which the place of effective management of the enterprise is situated (or country of residence). The final conditions of the determination might be decided in bilateral negotiations. In the course of such negotiations, it might be specified, for example,

whether the net profits were to be determined before the deduction of special allowances or incentives which could not be assimilated to depreciation allowances but could be considered rather as subsidies to the enterprise. It might also be specified in the course of the bilateral negotiations that direct subsidies paid to the enterprise by a Government should be included in net profits. The method for the recognition of any losses incurred during prior years, for the purpose of the determination of net profits, might also be worked out in the negotiations. In order to implement that approach, the country of residence would furnish a certificate indicating the net shipping profits of the enterprise and the amounts of any special items, including prior-year losses, which in accordance with the decisions reached in the negotiations were to be included in, or excluded from, the determination of the net profits to be apportioned or otherwise specially treated in that determination. The allocation of profits to be taxed might be based on some proportional factor specified in the bilateral negotiations, preferably the factor of outgoing freight receipts (determined on a uniform basis with or without the deduction of commissions). The percentage reduction in the tax computed on the basis of the allocated profits was intended to achieve a sharing of revenues that would reflect the managerial and capital inputs originating in the country of residence.

Paragraph 2 of article 8 (alternative A) and
paragraph 3 of article 8 (alternative B)

15.   Each of these paragraphs reproduces Article 8, paragraph 2, of the OECD Model Convention. The paragraphs apply not only to inland waterways transport between two or more countries but also to inland waterways transport effected by an enterprise of one country between two points in another country. They do not preclude the settlement through bilateral negotiations of any specific tax problem which may occur with regard to inland waterways transport, particularly between adjacent countries.

16.   With regard to enterprises not exclusively engaged in shipping, inland waterways transport or air transport, the Commentary on Article 8, paragraph 2, of the OECD Model Convention observes:

"If such an enterprise has in a foreign country permanent establishments exclusively concerned with the operation of its ships or aircraft, there is no reason to treat such establishments differently from the permanent establishments of enterprises engaged exclusively in shipping, inland waterways transport or air transport." [para. 19]

"Nor does any difficulty arise in applying the provisions of paragraphs 1 and 2 if the enterprise has in another State a permanent establishment which is not exclusively engaged in shipping, inland waterways transport or air transport. If its goods are carried in its own ships to a permanent establishment belonging to it in a foreign country, . . . none of the profit obtained by the enterprise through acting as its own carrier can properly be attributed to the permanent establishment. The same must be true even if the permanent establishment maintains installations for operating the ships or aircraft (e.g., consignment wharves) or incurs other costs in connection with the carriage of the enterprise's goods (e.g., staff costs). In this case, the permanent establishment's expenditure in respect of the operation of the ships, boats or aircraft should be attributed not to the permanent establishment but to the enterprise itself, since none of the profit obtained through the carrying benefits the permanent establishment." [para. 20]

"Where the enterprise's ships or aircraft are operated by a permanent establishment which is not the place of effective management of the whole enterprise (e.g., ships or aircraft put into service by the permanent establishment and figuring on its balance sheet), then the effective management for the purposes of paragraphs 1 and 2 must be considered, as regards the operation of the ships or aircraft as being in the Contracting State in which the permanent establishment is situated." [para. 21]

*Paragraph 3 of article 8 (alternative A) and
paragraph 4 of article 8 (alternative B)*

17.   Each of these paragraphs, which reproduce Article 8, paragraph 3, of the OECD Model Convention, refers to the case in which the place of effective management of the enterprise concerned is aboard a ship or a boat. As noted in the Commentary on the OECD Model Convention, "In this case tax will only be charged by the State where the home harbour of the ship or boat is situated. It is provided that if the home harbour cannot be determined, tax will be charged only in the Contracting State of which the operator of the ship or boat is a resident." [para. 22]

*Paragraph 4 of article 8 (alternative A) and
paragraph 5 of article 8 (alternative B)*

18.   Paragraph 4 of article 8 (alternative A) reproduces Article 8, paragraph 4, of the OECD Model Convention. Paragraph 5 of article 8 (alternative B) also reproduces the latter paragraph, with one adjustment, namely, the replacement of the phrase "paragraph 1" by the words "paragraphs 1 and 2". As the Commentary on the OECD Model Convention observes:

> "Various forms of international cooperation exist in shipping or air transport. In this field, international cooperation is secured through pooling agreements or other conventions of a similar kind which lay down certain rules for apportioning the receipts (or profits) from the joint business." [para. 23]

> "In order to clarify the taxation position of the participant in a pool, joint business or in an international operating agency and to cope with any difficulties which may arise, the Contracting States may bilaterally add the following, if they find it necessary:

>> 'but only to so much of the profits so derived as is attributable to the participant in proportion to its share in the joint operation'." [para. 24]

Article 9

ASSOCIATED ENTERPRISES

A.   GENERAL CONSIDERATIONS

1.   Article 9 of the United Nations Model Convention reproduces Article 9 of the OECD Model Convention, except for a new paragraph 3. As noted in the OECD Commentaries, "[t]his Article deals with adjustments to profits that may be made for tax purposes where transactions have been entered into between associated enterprises (parent and subsidiary companies and companies under common control) on other than arm's length terms" [para. 1]. It should be considered in conjunction with article 25 on mutual agreement procedure and article 26 on exchange of information.

2.   The application of the arm's length rule to the allocation of profits between the associated enterprises presupposes for most countries that the domestic legislation authorizes a determination on the basis of the arm's length principle.

3.   With regard to transfer pricing of goods, technology, trademarks and services between associated enterprises and the methodologies which may be applied for determining correct prices where transfers have been made on other than arm's length terms, the Contracting States will follow the OECD principles which are set out in the OECD Transfer Pricing Guidelines. These conclusions represent internationally agreed principles and the Group of Experts recommend that the Guidelines should be followed for the application of the arm's length principle which underlies the article.

B.   COMMENTARY ON THE PARAGRAPHS OF ARTICLE 9

Paragraph 1

4.   Paragraph 1 provides that in cases involving associated enterprises, the tax authorities of a Contracting State may for the purpose of calculating tax liabilities rewrite the accounts of the enterprises if as a result of the special relations between the enterprises the ac-

counts do not show the true taxable profits arising in that State. It is evidently appropriate that adjustment should be sanctioned in such circumstances, and this paragraph calls for little comment. The provision applies only if special conditions have been made or imposed between the two enterprises. "No rewriting of the accounts of associated enterprises is authorized if the transactions between such enterprises have taken place on normal open market commercial terms (on an arm's length basis)." [para. 2]

5.   The Group of Experts have made an amendment in 1999 of a drafting nature in paragraph 1 bringing the language of the main portion in line with that in the OECD Model Convention. Prior to the amendment, it read:

"... then any profits which would, but for those conditions, have not so accrued ..."

This portion of paragraph 1 has been modified in 1999 as under:

"... then any profits which would, but for those conditions, have accrued to one of the enterprises, but, by reason of those conditions, have not so accrued ..."

6.   As discussed in the Committee on Fiscal Affairs' Report on Thin Capitalization,[14] there is an interplay between tax treaties and domestic rules on thin capitalization relevant to the scope of the article. As noted in the Commentary on the OECD Model Convention:

"(*a*)   The Article does not prevent the application of national rules on thin capitalization in so far as their effect is to assimilate the profits of the borrower to an amount corresponding to the profits which would have accrued in an arm's length situation;

(*b*)   The Article is relevant not only in determining whether the rate of interest provided for in a loan contract is an arm's

---

[14]Adopted by the Council of the OECD on 26 November 1986 and reproduced in volume II of the loose-leaf version of the OECD Model Tax Convention at page R(4)-1.

length rate, but also whether a prima facie loan can be regarded as a loan or should be regarded as some other kind of payment, in particular a contribution to equity capital;

(*c*) The application of rules designed to deal with thin capitalization should normally not have the effect of increasing the taxable profits of the relevant domestic enterprise to more than the arm's length profit, and . . . this principle should be followed in applying existing tax treaties." [para. 3]

The OECD Commentary continues:

"The question arises as to whether special procedural rules which some countries have adopted for dealing with transactions between related parties are consistent with this Model. For instance, it may be asked whether the reversal of the burden of proof or presumptions of any kind which are sometimes found in domestic laws are consistent with the arm's length principle. A number of countries interpret the Article in such a way that it by no means bars the adjustment of profits under national law under conditions that differ from those of the Article and that it has the function of raising the arm's length principle at treaty level. Also, almost all Member countries consider that additional information requirements which would be more stringent than the normal requirements, or even a reversal of the burden of proof, would not constitute discrimination within the meaning of Article 24. However, in some cases the application of the national law of some countries may result in adjustments to profits at variance with the principles of the Article. Contracting States are enabled by the Article to deal with such situations by means of corresponding adjustments (see below) and under mutual agreement procedures." [para. 4]

Paragraph 2

7.   In the words of the OECD Commentary, "The rewriting of transactions between associated enterprises in the situation envisaged in paragraph 1 may give rise to economic double taxation (taxa-

tion of the same income in the hands of different persons), in so far as an enterprise of State A whose profits are revised upwards will be liable to tax on an amount of profit which has already been taxed in the hands of its associated enterprise in State B." The OECD Commentary observes that "paragraph 2 provides that in these circumstances, State B shall make an appropriate adjustment so as to relieve the double taxation". [para. 5]

However, according to the OECD Commentary,

" . . . an adjustment is not automatically to be made in State B simply because the profits in State A have been increased; the adjustment is due only if State B considers that the figure of adjusted profits correctly reflects what the profits would have been if the transactions had been at arm's length. In other words, the paragraph may not be invoked and should not be applied where the profits of one associated enterprise are increased to a level which exceeds what they would have been if they had been correctly computed on an arm's length basis. State B is therefore committed to make an adjustment of the profits of the affiliated company only if it considers that the adjustment made in State A is justified both in principle and as regards the amount." [para. 6]

"The paragraph does not specify the method by which an adjustment is to be made. OECD Member countries use different methods to provide relief in these circumstances and it is therefore left open for Contracting States to agree bilaterally on any specific rules which they wish to add to the Article. Some States, for example, would prefer the system under which, where the profits of enterprise X in State A are increased to what they would have been on an arm's length basis, the adjustment would be made by reopening the assessment on the associated enterprise Y in State B containing the doubly taxed profits in order to reduce the taxable profit by an appropriate amount. Some other States, on the other hand, would prefer to provide that, for the purposes of Article 23, the doubly taxed profits should be treated in the hands of enterprise Y of State B as if they may be taxed in State A; accordingly, the enterprise of State B is entitled to relief in State B, under Article 23, in respect of tax paid by its associate enterprise in State A." [para. 7]

"It is not the purpose of the paragraph to deal with what might be called 'secondary adjustments'. Suppose that an upward revision of taxable profits of enterprise X in State A has been made in accordance with the principle laid down in paragraph 1; and suppose also that an adjustment is made to the profits of enterprise Y in State B in accordance with the principle laid down in paragraph 2. The position has still not been restored exactly to what it would have been had the transactions taken place at arm's length prices because, as a matter of fact, the money representing the profits which are the subject of the adjustment is found in the hands of enterprise Y instead of in those of enterprise X. It can be argued that if arm's length pricing had operated and enterprise X had subsequently wished to transfer these profits to enterprise Y, it would have done so in the form of, for example, a dividend or a royalty (if enterprise Y were the parent of enterprise X) or in the form of, for example, a loan (if enterprise X were the parent of enterprise Y); and that in those circumstances there could have been other tax consequences (e.g., the operation of a withholding tax) depending upon the type of income concerned and the provisions of the article dealing with such income." [para. 8]

"These secondary adjustments, which would be required to establish the situation exactly as it would have been if transactions had been at arm's length, depend on the facts of the individual case . . . [N]othing in paragraph 2 prevents such secondary adjustments from being made where they are permitted under the domestic laws of Contracting States." [para. 9]

"The paragraph also leaves open the question whether there should be a period of time after the expiration of which State B would not be obliged to make an appropriate adjustment to the profits of enterprise Y following an upward revision of the profits of enterprise X in State A. Some States consider that State B's commitment should be open-ended—in other words, that however many years State A goes back to revise assessments, enterprise Y should in equity be assured of an appropriate adjustment in State B. Other States consider that an open-ended commitment of this sort is unreasonable as a matter of practical administration. In the circumstances, therefore, this problem has not been dealt with in the text of the Article; but Contracting States are left free in bilateral conventions to include, if they wish, provisions dealing with the length of time during which State B is to be under obligation to make an appropriate adjustment . . ." [para. 10]

"If there is a dispute between the parties concerned over the amount and character of the appropriate adjustment, the mutual agreement procedure provided for under Article 25 should be implemented; the Commentary on that Article contains a number of considerations applicable to adjustments of the profits of associated enterprises carried out on the basis of the present Article (following, in particular, adjustment of transfer prices) and to the corresponding adjustments which must then be made in pursuance of paragraph 2 thereof . . ." [para. 11]

8.   Some members of the Group of Experts had noted that a correlative adjustment under paragraph 2 could be very costly to a small country which may consider not including paragraph 2 in its treaties. Several members of the Group of Experts responded that they believed that paragraph 2 was an essential aspect of article 9. Failure to provide correlative adjustment will result in double taxation, which is contrary to the purpose of the Convention. However, a country could closely examine the primary adjustment under paragraph 1 before deciding what correlative adjustment was appropriate to reflect the primary adjustment. Another member suggested that it may be desirable to eliminate the obligation that a State may have to make a correlative adjustment when the other Contracting State has previously adjusted the transfer prices. He observed that it could be convenient to change the word "shall" to "may" and that Contracting States may, during bilateral negotiations, use the word that is convenient.

However, there was no consensus on this point and the language of paragraph 2 remains unchanged.

Paragraph 3

9.   The Group of Experts has made an amendment in 1999 to article 9 by inserting a new paragraph 3. Paragraph 2 of article 9 requires a country to make an "appropriate adjustment" (a correlative adjustment) to reflect a change in the transfer price made by a country under article 9, paragraph 1. The new paragraph 3 provides that the provisions of paragraph 2 shall not apply where the judicial, administrative or other legal proceedings have resulted in a final ruling that, by actions giving rise to an adjustment of profits under paragraph 1, one of the enterprises is liable to penalty with respect to fraud, gross negligence or wilful default. In other words, in case a final order has been passed in a judicial, administrative or other legal proceeding pointing out that in relation to the adjustment of profits under paragraph 1 one of the enterprises is visited with a penalty for fraud, gross negligence or wilful default, there would be no obligation to make the correlative adjustment under paragraph 2. This approach means that a taxpayer may be subject to non-tax and tax penalties. Member countries may consider such double penalties as too harsh. Some members pointed out that cases involving levy of such penalties are likely to be exceptional and there would be no application of this provision in a routine manner.

Article 10

DIVIDENDS

A.   General considerations

1.   Article 10 of the United Nations Model Convention reproduces the provisions of Article 10 of the OECD Model Convention with the exception of those of paragraph 2, which contains substantive differences. Article 10 deals with the taxation of dividends received by a resident of a Contracting State from sources in the other

Contracting State. Paragraph 1 provides that dividends may be taxed in the country of residence, and paragraph 2 provides that dividends may be taxed in the country of source, but at a limited tax rate. The term "dividends" is defined in paragraph 3 as generally including distributions of corporate profits to shareholders. As the OECD Commentary observes: "From the shareholders' standpoint, dividends are income from the capital which they have made available to the company as its shareholders." Paragraph 4 provides that paragraphs 1 and 2 do not apply to dividends that are attributable to a permanent establishment of the recipient in the source country, and paragraph 5 generally precludes a Contracting State from taxing dividends paid by a company resident in the other State unless the shareholder is a resident of the taxing State or the dividends are attributable to a permanent establishment of the recipient in that State.

B.   COMMENTARY ON THE PARAGRAPHS OF ARTICLE 10

Paragraph 1

2.   This paragraph, which reproduces Article 10, paragraph 1, of the OECD Model Convention, provides that dividends may be taxed in the State of the beneficiary's residence. It does not, however, provide that dividends may be taxed exclusively in that State and therefore leaves open the possibility of taxation by the State of which the company paying the dividends is a resident, that is, the State in which the dividends originate (source country). When the United Nations Model Convention was first considered, many members of the Group from developing countries felt that as a matter of principle dividends should be taxed only by the source country. According to them, if both the country of residence and the source country were given the right to tax, the country of residence should grant a full tax credit regardless of the amount of foreign tax to be absorbed and, in appropriate cases, a tax-sparing credit. One of those members emphasized that there was no necessity for a developing country to waive or reduce its withholding tax on dividends, especially if it offered tax incentives and other concessions. However, the Group reached a

consensus that dividends may be taxed by the State of the beneficiary's residence. Current practice in developing/developed country treaties generally reflects this consensus. Double taxation is eliminated or reduced through a combination of exemption or tax credit in the residence country and reduced withholding rates in the source country.

3.   According to the Commentary on Article 10, paragraph 1, of the OECD Model Convention,

". . . The term 'paid' has a very wide meaning, since the concept of payment means the fulfilment of the obligation to put funds at the disposal of the shareholder in the manner required by contract or by custom." [para. 7]

"The Article deals only with dividends paid by a company which is a resident of a Contracting State to a resident of the other Contracting State. It does not, therefore, apply to dividends paid by a company which is a resident of a third State or to dividends paid by a company which is a resident of a Contracting State which are attributable to a permanent establishment which an enterprise of that State has in the other Contracting State." [para. 8]

Paragraph 2

4.   This paragraph reproduces Article 10, paragraph 2, of the OECD Model Convention with certain changes which will be explained hereunder.

5.   The Group of Experts has amended the main provision of paragraph 2 in 1999 to bring it in line with that in the OECD Model Convention. Prior to the amendment, it was provided that such dividends could also be taxed in the Contracting State of which the company paying the dividends is a resident, but if the recipient is the beneficial owner of dividends, the tax was to be charged in the specified manner. This provision has been changed to provide that if the beneficial owner of the dividends is a resident of the other Contracting State, the tax would be charged in the specified manner. The

same change has been made in paragraph 2 of articles 11 and 12 relating to interest and royalties respectively. The purpose of this amendment is to allow the benefits of these articles (namely, 10, 11 and 12) to a beneficial owner residing in that other Contracting State regardless of the residence of any agent or other intermediary collecting the income on behalf of the beneficial owner, and while continuing to deny this benefit, when the beneficial owner was not a resident of that other Contracting State, even if the intermediary collecting the income was a resident. Although some members of the Group of Experts expressed doubts about the effects of this change on developing countries as also the countries that taxed dividends income on a remittance basis, even on re-examination it was considered that the amendment, as proposed, on the lines of the existing provision in the OECD Model Convention, did not require reconsideration. These remarks apply, mutatis mutandis, to similar amendments made to paragraph 2 of articles 11 (interest) and 12 (royalties).

6.   The OECD Model Convention restricts the tax in the source country to 5 per cent in subparagraph (*a*) for direct investment dividends and 15 per cent in subparagraph (*b*) for portfolio investment dividends, but the United Nations Model Convention leaves these percentages to be established through bilateral negotiations. Also, the minimum ownership necessary for direct investment dividends is reduced in subparagraph (*a*) from 25 per cent to 10 per cent. However, the 10 per cent threshold which determines the level of shareholding qualifying as a direct investment is illustrative only.

7.   The Group of Experts decided to replace "25 per cent" by "10 per cent" in subparagraph (*a*) as the minimum capital required for direct investment dividend status because in some developing countries non-residents are limited to a 50 per cent share ownership, and 10 per cent is a significant portion of such permitted ownership.

8.   The Group was unable to reach a consensus on the maximum tax rates to be permitted in the source country. Members from the developing countries, who basically preferred the principle of the taxation of dividends exclusively in the source country, considered that the rates prescribed by the OECD Model Convention would entail

too large a loss of revenue for the source country. Also, although they accepted the principle of taxation in the beneficiary's country of residence, they believed that any reduction in withholding taxes in the source country should benefit the foreign investor rather than the treasury of the beneficiary's country of residence, as may happen under the traditional tax-credit method if the reduction lowers the cumulative tax rate of the source country below the rate of the beneficiary's country of residence.

9.   The Group suggested some considerations that might guide countries in negotiations on the rates for source country taxation of direct investment dividends. If the developed (residence) country uses a credit system, treaty negotiations could appropriately seek a withholding tax rate at source that would, in combination with the basic corporate tax rate of the source country, produce a combined effective rate not exceeding the tax rate in the residence country. The parties' negotiating positions may also be affected by whether the residence country allows credit for taxes spared by the source country under tax incentive programmes. If the developed country uses an exemption system for double taxation relief, it could, in bilateral negotiations, seek a limitation on withholding rates on the grounds that (a) the exemption itself stresses the concept of not taxing intercorporate dividends, and a limitation of the withholding rate at source would be in keeping with that concept, and (b) the exemption and resulting departure from tax neutrality with domestic investment are of benefit to the international investor, and a limitation of the withholding rate at source, which would also benefit the investor, would be in keeping with this aspect of the exemption.

10.   Both the source country and the country of residence should be able to tax dividends on portfolio investment shares, although the relatively small amount of portfolio investment and its distinctly lesser importance compared with direct investment might make the issues concerning its tax treatment less intense in some cases. The Group decided not to recommend a maximum rate because source countries may have varying views on the importance of portfolio investment and on the figures to be inserted.

11.   In 1999, it was noted that recent developed/developing country treaty practice indicates a range of direct investment and portfolio investment withholding tax rates. Traditionally, dividend withholding rates in the developed/developing country treaties have been higher than those in treaties between developed countries. Thus, while the OECD direct and portfolio investment rates are 5 per cent and 15 per cent, developed/developing country treaty rates have traditionally ranged between 5 per cent and 15 per cent for direct investment dividends and 15 per cent and 25 per cent for portfolio dividends. Some developing countries have taken the position that short-term loss of revenue occasioned by low withholding rates is justified by the increased foreign investment in the medium and long terms. Thus, several modern developed/developing country treaties contain the OECD Model rates for direct investment, and a few treaties provide for even lower rates.

12.   Also, several special features in developed/developing country treaties have appeared: (*a*) the tax rates may not be the same for both countries, with higher rates allowed to the developing country; (*b*) tax rates may not be limited at all; (*c*) reduced rates may apply only to income from new investment; (*d*) the lowest rates or exemption may apply only to preferred types of investments (e.g., "industrial undertakings" or "pioneer investments"); and (*e*) dividends may qualify for reduced rates only if the shares have been held for a specified period. In treaties of countries that have adopted an imputation system of corporation taxation (i.e., integration of company tax into the shareholder's company tax or individual income tax) instead of the classical system of taxation (i.e., separate taxation of shareholder and corporation), specific provisions may ensure that the advanced credits and exemptions granted to domestic shareholders are extended to shareholders resident in the other Contracting State.

13.   Although the rates are fixed either partly or wholly for reasons connected with the general balance of the particular bilateral tax treaty, the following technical factors are often considered in fixing the rate:

(*a*) the corporate tax system of the country of source (e.g., the extent to which the country follows an integrated or classical system) and the total burden of tax on distributed corporate profits resulting from the system;

(*b*) the extent to which the country of residence can credit the tax on the dividends and the underlying profits against its own tax and the total tax burden imposed on the taxpayer, after relief in both countries;

(*c*) the extent to which matching credit is given in the country of residence for tax spared in the country of source;

(*d*) the achievement from the source country's point of view of a satisfactory balance between raising revenue and attracting foreign investment.

14.   The Commentary on the OECD Model Convention contains the following passages:

> "If a partnership is treated as a body corporate under the domestic laws applying to it, the two Contracting States may agree to modify subparagraph (*a*) of paragraph 2 in a way to give the benefits of the reduced rate provided for parent companies also to such partnership." [para. 11]

> "Under paragraph 2, the limitation of tax in the State of source is not available when an intermediary, such as agent or nominee, is interposed between the beneficiary and the payer, unless the beneficial owner is a resident of the other Contracting State . . . States which wish to make this more explicit are free to do so during bilateral negotiations . . ." [para. 12]

> "The tax rates fixed by the Article for the tax in the State of source are maximum rates. The States may agree, in bilateral negotiations, on lower rates or even on taxation exclusively in the State of the beneficiary's residence. The reduction of rates provided for in paragraph 2 refers solely to the taxation of dividends and not to the taxation of the profits of the company paying the dividends." [para. 13]

"The two Contracting States may also, during bilateral negotiations, agree to [lower the holding percentage required for direct investment dividends]. A lower percentage is, for instance, justified in cases where the state of residence of the parent company, in accordance with its domestic law, grants exemption to such a company for dividends derived from a holding of less than 25 per cent in a non-resident subsidiary." [para. 14]

"In subparagraph (*a*) of paragraph 2, the term 'capital' is used in [defining the minimum ownership required for direct investment dividends]. The use of this term in this context implies that, for the purposes of subparagraph (*a*), it should be used in the sense in which it is used for the purposes of distribution to the shareholder (in the particular case, the parent company).

(*a*) As a general rule, therefore, the term 'capital' in subparagraph (*a*) should be understood as it is understood in company law. Other elements, in particular the reserves, are not to be taken into account.

(*b*) Capital, as understood in company law, should be indicated in terms of par value of all shares which in the majority of cases will be shown as capital in the company's balance sheet.

(*c*) No account need be taken of differences due to the different classes of shares issued (ordinary shares, preference shares, plural voting shares, non-voting shares, bearer shares, registered shares etc.), as such differences relate more to the nature of the shareholder's right than to the extent of his ownership of the capital.

(*d*) When a loan or other contribution to the company does not, strictly speaking, come as capital under company law but when on the basis of internal law or practice ('thin capitalization', or assimilation of a loan to share capital), the income derived in respect thereof is treated as dividend under Article 10, the value of such loan or contribution is also to be taken as 'capital' within the meaning of subparagraph (*a*).

(*e*)   In the case of bodies which do not have capital within the meaning of company law, capital for the purpose of subparagraph (*a*) is to be taken as meaning the total of all contributions to the body which are taken into account for the purpose of distributing profits.

In bilateral negotiations, Contracting States may depart from the criterion of 'capital' used in subparagraph (*a*) of paragraph 2 and use instead the criterion of 'voting power'." [para. 15]

"Subparagraph (*a*) of paragraph 2 does not require that the company receiving the dividends must have owned at least [10] per cent of the capital for a relatively long time before the date of the distribution. This means that all that counts regarding the holding is the situation prevailing at the time material for the coming into existence of the liability to the tax to which paragraph 2 applies, i.e., in most cases the situation existing at the time when the dividends become legally available to the shareholders. The primary reason for this resides in the desire to have a provision which is applicable as broadly as possible. To require the parent company to have possessed the minimum holding for a certain time before the distribution of the profits could involve extensive inquiries. Internal laws of certain OECD Member countries provide for a minimum period during which the recipient company must have held the shares to qualify for exemption or relief in respect of dividends received. In view of this, Contracting States may include a similar condition in their conventions." [para. 16]

"The reduction envisaged in subparagraph (*a*) of paragraph 2 should not be granted in cases of abuse of this provision, for example, where a company with a holding of less than [10] per cent has, shortly before the dividends become payable, increased its holding primarily for the purpose of securing the benefits of the above-mentioned provision, or otherwise, where the qualifying holding was arranged primarily in order to obtain the reduction. To counteract such manoeuvres Contracting States may find it appropriate to add to subparagraph (*a*) a provision along the following lines:

'provided that this holding was not acquired primarily for the purpose of taking advantage of this provision'." [para. 17]

"Paragraph 2 lays down nothing about the mode of taxation in the State of source. It therefore leaves that State free to apply its own laws and, in particular, to levy the tax either by deduction at source or by individual assessment." [para. 18]

"The paragraph does not settle procedural questions. Each State should be able to use the procedure provided in its own laws. It can either forthwith limit its tax to the rates given in the article or tax in full and make a refund. Specific questions arise with triangular cases (see paragraph 53 of the Commentary on Article 24) [e.g., cases in which income arising in a Contracting State and beneficially owned by a resident of the other Contracting State is attributable to a permanent establishment in a third State]." [para. 19]

"It does not specify whether or not the relief in the State of source should be conditional upon the dividends being subject to tax in the State of residence. This question can be settled by bilateral negotiations." [para. 20]

"The Article contains no provisions as to how the State of the beneficiary's residence should make allowance for the taxation in the State of source of the dividends. This question is dealt with in Articles 23 A and 23 B." [para. 21]

"Attention is drawn generally to the following case: the beneficial owner of the dividends arising in a Contracting State is a company resident of the other Contracting State; all or part of its capital is held by shareholders resident outside that other State; its practice is not to distribute its profits in the form of dividends; and it enjoys preferential taxation treatment (private investment company, base company). The question may arise whether in the case of such a company it is justifiable to allow in the State of source of the dividends the limitation of tax which is provided in paragraph 2. It may be appropriate, when bilateral negotiations are being conducted, to agree upon special exceptions to the taxing rule laid down in this article, in order to define the treatment applicable to such companies." [para. 22]

Paragraph 3

15.　This paragraph reproduces Article 10, paragraph 3, of the OECD Model Convention, the Commentary on which reads as follows:

"In view of the great differences between the laws of OECD Member countries, it is impossible to define 'dividends' fully and exhaustively. Consequently, the definition merely mentions examples which are to be found in the majority of the Member countries' laws and which, in any case, are not treated differently in them. The enumeration is followed up by a general formula. In the course of the revision of the 1963 Draft Convention, a thorough study has been undertaken to find a solution which does not refer to domestic laws. This study has led to the conclusion that, in view of the still remaining dissimilarities between Member countries in the field of company law and taxation law, it did not appear to be possible to work out a definition of the concept of dividends that would be independent of domestic laws. It is open to the Contracting States, through bilateral negotiations, to make allowance for peculiarities of their laws and to agree to bring under the definition of 'dividends' other payments by companies falling under the article." [para. 23]

"The notion of dividends basically concerns distributions by companies within the meaning of subparagraph (*b*) of paragraph 1 of Article 3. Therefore the definition relates, in the first instance, to distributions of profits the title to which is constituted by shares, that is holdings in a company limited by shares (joint stock company). The definition assimilates to shares all securities issued by companies which carry a right to participate in the companies' profits without being debt claims; such are, for example, 'jouissance' shares or 'jouissance' rights, founders' shares or other rights participating in profits. In bilateral conventions, of course, this enumeration may be adapted to the legal situation in the Contracting States concerned. This may be necessary, in particular, as regards income from 'jouissance' shares and founders' shares. On the other hand, debt claims participating in profits do not come into this category . . . ; likewise interest on convertible debentures is not a dividend." [para. 24]

"Article 10 deals not only with dividends as such but also with interest on loans in so far as the lender effectively shares the risks run by the company, i.e., when repayment depends largely on the success or otherwise of the enterprise's business. Articles 10 and 11 do not therefore prevent the treatment of this type of interest as dividends under the national rules on thin capitalization applied in the borrower's country. The question whether the contributor of the loan shares the risks run by the enterprise must be determined in each individual case in the light of all the circumstances, as for example the following:

—the loan very heavily outweighs any other contribution to the enterprise's capital (or was taken out to replace a substantial portion of capital which has been lost) and is substantially unmatched by redeemable assets;

—the creditor will share in any profits of the company;

—the repayment of the loan is subordinated to claims of other creditors or to the payment of dividends;

—the level or payment of interest would depend on the profits of the company;

—the loan contract contains no final provisions for repayment by a definite date." [para. 25]

"The laws of many of the States put participations in a *Société à responsabilité limitée* (limited liability company) on the same footing as shares. Likewise, distributions of profits by cooperative societies are generally regarded as dividends." [para. 26]

"Distributions of profits by partnerships are not dividends within the meaning of the definition, unless the partnerships are subject, in the State where their place of effective management is situated, to a fiscal treatment substantially similar to that applied to companies limited by shares (for instance, in Belgium, Portugal and Spain, also in France as regards distributions to 'commanditaires' in the 'sociétés en commandite simple'). On the other hand, clarification in bilateral conventions may be necessary in cases where the taxation law of a Contracting State gives the owner of holdings in a company a right to opt, under certain conditions, for being taxed as a partner of a partnership, or, vice versa, gives the partner of a partnership the right to opt for taxation as the owner of holdings in a company." [para. 27]

"Payments regarded as dividends may include not only distributions of profits decided by annual general meetings of shareholders, but also other benefits in money or money's worth, such as bonus shares, bonuses, profits on a liquidation and disguised distributions of profits. The reliefs provided in the article apply so long as the State of which the paying company is a resident taxes such benefits as dividends. It is immaterial whether any such benefits are paid out of current profits made by the company or are derived, for example, from reserves, i.e., profits of previous financial years. Normally, distributions by a company which have the effect of reducing the membership rights, for instance, payments constituting a reimbursement of capital in any form whatever, are not regarded as dividends." [para. 28]

"The benefits to which a holding in a company confer entitlement are, as a general rule, available solely to the shareholders themselves. Should, however, certain of such benefits be made available to persons who are not shareholders within the meaning of company law, they may constitute dividends if:

—the legal relations between such persons and the company are assimilated to a holding in a company ('concealed holdings') and

—the persons receiving such benefits are closely connected with a shareholder; this is the case, for example, where the recipient is a relative of the shareholder or is a company belonging to the same group as the company owning the shares." [para. 29]

"When the shareholder and the person receiving such benefits are residents of two different States with which the State of source has concluded conventions, differences of views may arise as to which of these conventions is applicable. A similar problem may arise when the State of source has concluded a convention with one of the States but not with the other. This, however, is a conflict which may affect other types of income and the solution to it can be found only through an arrangement under the mutual agreement procedure." [para. 30]

Paragraph 4

16. This paragraph, which makes paragraphs 1 and 2 inapplicable to dividends on shares that are effectively connected with a permanent establishment or fixed base of the recipient in the source country, reproduces Article 10, paragraph 4, of the OECD Model Convention. The OECD Commentary notes that paragraph 4 does not adopt a force of attraction rule, allowing dividends to be taxed as business profits if the recipient has a permanent establishment or fixed base in the source country, regardless of whether the shareholding is connected with the permanent establishment. Rather, the paragraph only permits dividends to be taxed as business profits "if they are paid in respect of holdings forming part of the assets of the permanent establishment or otherwise effectively connected with that establishment". [para. 31]

Paragraph 5

17.   This paragraph, which bars a Contracting State from taxing dividends paid by a company resident in the other State merely because the company derives income or profits in the taxing State, reproduces Article 10, paragraph 5, of the OECD Model Convention, the Commentary on which reads as follows:

> "The Article deals only with dividends paid by a company which is a resident of a Contracting State to a resident of the other State. Certain States, however, tax not only dividends paid by companies resident therein—but even distributions by non-resident companies of profits arising within their territory. Each State, of course, is entitled to tax profits arising in its territory which are made by non-resident companies, to the extent provided in the Convention (in particular in Article 7). The shareholders of such companies should not be taxed as well at any rate, unless they are residents of the State and so naturally subject to its fiscal sovereignty." [para. 33]

> "Paragraph 5 rules out the extraterritorial taxation of dividends, i.e., the practice by which States tax dividends distributed by a non-resident company solely because the corporate profits from which the distributions are made originated in their territory (for example, realized through a permanent establishment situated therein). There is, of course, no question of extraterritorial taxation when the country of source of the corporate profits taxes the dividends because they are paid to a shareholder who is a resident of that State or to a permanent establishment or fixed base situated in that State." [para. 34]

> "Moreover, it can be argued that such a provision does not aim at, or cannot result in, preventing a State from subjecting the dividends to a withholding tax when distributed by foreign companies if they are cashed in its territory. Indeed, in such a case, the criterion for tax liability is the fact of the payment of the dividends, and not the origin of the corporate profits allotted for distribution. But if the person cashing the dividends in a Contracting State is a resident of the other Contracting

State (of which the distributing company is a resident), he may under Article 21 obtain exemption from, or refund of, the withholding tax of the first-mentioned State. Similarly, if the beneficiary of the dividends is a resident of a third State which had concluded a double taxation convention with the State where the dividends are cashed, he may, under Article 21 of that convention, obtain exemption from, or refund of, the withholding tax of the last-mentioned State." [para. 35]

"Paragraph 5 further provides that non-resident companies are not to be subjected to special taxes on undistributed profits." [para. 36]

"It might be argued that where the taxpayer's country of residence, pursuant to its counteracting measures (such as sub-part F legislation in the United States), seeks to tax profits which have not been distributed it is acting contrary to the provisions of paragraph 5. However, . . . the paragraph is confined to taxation at source and, thus, has no bearing on the taxation at residence under a counteracting legislation. In addition, the paragraph concerns only the taxation of the company and not that of the shareholder." [para. 37]

"The application of counteracting legislation may, however, pose some difficulties. If the income is attributed to the taxpayer then each item of the income would have to be treated under the relevant provisions of the Convention (business profits, interest, royalties). If the amount is treated as a deemed dividend then it is clearly derived from the base company thus constituting income from that company's country. Even then, it is by no means clear whether the taxable amount is to be regarded as a dividend within the meaning of Article 10 or as 'other income' within the meaning of Article 21. Under some counteracting measures the taxable amount is treated as a dividend with the result that an exemption provided for by a tax convention, e.g., an affiliation exemption, is also extended to it (for instance, in Germany). It is doubtful whether the Convention requires this to be done. If the country of residence considers that this is not the case, it may face the allegation that it is obstructing the normal operation of the affiliation exemption by taxing the dividend (in the form of 'deemed dividend') in advance." [para. 38]

"Where dividends are actually distributed by the base company, the provisions of a bilateral convention regarding dividends have to be applied in the normal way because there is dividend income within the meaning of the convention. Thus, the country of the base company may subject the dividend to a withholding tax. The country of residence of the shareholder will apply the normal methods for the elimination of double taxation (i.e., tax credit or tax exemption is granted). This implies that the withholding tax on the dividend should be credited in the shareholder's country of residence, even if the distributed profit (the dividend) has been taxed years before under counteracting legislation. However, the obligation to give credit in that case remains doubtful. Generally the dividend as such is exempted from tax (as it was already taxed under the counteracting legislation) and one might argue that there is no basis for a tax credit. On the other hand, the purpose of the treaty would be frustrated if the crediting of taxes could be avoided by simply anticipating the dividend taxation under counteracting legislation. The general principle set out above would suggest that the credit should be granted, though the details may depend on the technicalities of the counteracting measures and the system for crediting foreign taxes against domestic tax, as well as on the particularities of the case (e.g., time lapsed since the taxation of the 'deemed dividend'). However, taxpayers who have recourse to artificial arrangements are taking risks against which they cannot fully be safeguarded by tax authorities." [para. 39]

18.   It may be relevant to point out that certain countries' laws seek to avoid or mitigate economic double taxation, that is, the simultaneous taxation of the company's profits at the level of the company and of dividends at the level of the shareholder. For a detailed consideration of this matter, it may be instructive to refer to paragraphs 40

to 67 in the Commentaries on Article 10 of the OECD Model Convention.

Branch profits taxes

19.   The inclusion of a branch profits tax provision in a revised United Nations Model Convention was discussed at the 1987 and 1991 meetings of the Group of Experts. The issue was further discussed in the 1997 meeting (Eighth Meeting) of the Group of Experts and it was considered that because only a few countries had branch tax, the paragraph might be better placed in the commentaries and not in the main text. It would be left to the Contracting States, if they so desire, during the course of bilateral negotiations to incorporate the provisions relating to the branch profits tax in their bilateral tax treaties. Developing countries were generally not opposed to the principle of branch profits taxation, even if they did not impose a branch profits tax. One member from a developed country stated that imposition of a branch profits tax would conflict with his country's policy of taxing business profits once.

20.   Some members, while citing the justification of branch profits taxation as a means of achieving rough parity in source country taxation whether business in that country is conducted through a subsidiary corporation or a branch, maintained that the principle should be followed logically throughout the Convention. Thus, in this view, contrary to paragraph 3 of article 7 of the United Nations Model Convention, all expenses of the permanent establishment must be deductible as if the permanent establishment were a distinct and separate enterprise dealing wholly independently with the head office.

21.   Another member from a developed country noted that his country imposed the tax in two separate parts: (i) a tax analogous to a dividend withholding tax was imposed on the "dividend equivalent amount" of a branch that was approximately the amount that would likely have been distributed as dividends if the branch were a subsidiary; and (ii) a second tax, analogous to a withholding tax on interest paid by a subsidiary resident in that country to its foreign parent, was

imposed on the excess of the amount of interest deducted by the branch in computing its taxable income over the amount of interest actually paid by the branch. The principal purpose of that system was to minimize the effect of tax considerations on the foreign investor's decision whether to operate in the country in branch or subsidiary form.

22.   If one or both of the Contracting States impose branch profits taxes, they may include in the Convention a provision such as the following:

> "Notwithstanding any other provision of this Convention, where a company which is a resident of a Contracting State has a permanent establishment in the other Contracting State, the profits taxable under article 7, paragraph 1, may be subject to an additional tax in that other State, in accordance with its laws, but the additional charge shall not exceed ___ per cent of the amount of those profits."

23.   The suggested provision does not recommend a maximum branch profits rate. The most common practice is to use the direct investment dividend rate [(e.g., the tax rate in paragraph 2(a))]. At the 1991 meeting of the Group of Experts there was agreement among the supporters of branch profits taxation that, in view of the principles enunciated in support of the system, the rate of tax on branch profits should be the same as that on dividends from direct investments. However, in several treaties the branch profits tax rate was the rate for portfolio investment dividends (typically a higher rate) and in some treaties the branch tax rate was lower than the direct investment dividend rate. Although a branch profits tax is on business profits, the provision may be included in article 10, rather than in article 7, because the tax is intended to be analogous to a tax on dividends.

24.   The provision allows the branch profits tax to be imposed only on profits taxable under article 7, paragraph 1, on account of the permanent establishment. Many treaties further limit the tax base to such profits "after deducting therefrom income tax and other taxes on in-

come imposed thereon in that other State". Other treaties do not contain this clause because the concept is included under domestic law.

25.   At the Group's 1991 meeting, attention was drawn to the fact that a branch profits tax provision could potentially conflict with a treaty's non-discrimination clause. Since a branch profits tax is usually a second level of tax on profits of foreign corporations that is not imposed on domestic corporations carrying on the same activities, it could be viewed, as a technical matter, as prohibited by article 24 (Non-discrimination). However, countries imposing the tax do so as an analogue to the dividend withholding tax paid on dividends from a subsidiary to its foreign parent, and they therefore consider it appropriate to include in the non-discrimination article an explicit exception allowing imposition of the branch tax. The non-discrimination article in several treaties with branch profits tax provisions contains the following paragraph:

> "Nothing in this article shall be construed as preventing either Contracting State from imposing a tax as described in paragraph ___ [branch profits tax provision] of article 10 (Dividends)."

However, the branch profits tax provision suggested above makes this provision unnecessary because it applies "notwithstanding any other provision of this Convention" and thus takes precedence over other treaty provisions, including article 24 (Non-discrimination).

26.   Some members of the Group of Experts pointed out that there are many artificial devices entered into by persons to take advantage of the provisions of article 10 through, inter alia, creation or assignment of shares or other rights in respect of which dividend is paid. While substance over form rules, abuse of rights principle or any similar doctrine could be used to counter such arrangements. Contracting States which may want to specifically address the issue may include a clause on the following lines in their bilateral tax treaties during negotiations, namely:

> "The provisions of this article shall not apply if it was the main purpose or one of the main purposes of any person con-

cerned with the creation or assignment of the shares or other rights in respect of which the dividend is paid to take advantage of this article by means of that creation or assignment."

Article 11

INTEREST

A.   GENERAL CONSIDERATIONS

1.   Article 11 of the United Nations Model Convention reproduces the provisions of Article 11 of the OECD Model Convention with the exception of paragraphs 2 and 4, in which substantive changes have been made.

2.   Interest, which, like dividends, constitutes income from movable capital may be paid to individual savers who have deposits with banks or hold savings certificates, to individual investors who have purchased bonds, to individual suppliers or trading companies selling on a deferred payment basis, to financial institutions which have granted loans or to institutional investors which hold bonds or debentures. Interest may also be paid on loans between associated enterprises.

3.   At the domestic level, interest is usually deductible in calculating profits. Any tax on interest is paid by the beneficiary unless a special contract provides that it should be paid by the payer of the interest. Contrary to what occurs in the case of dividends, interest is not liable to taxation in the hands of both the beneficiary and the payer. If the latter is obliged to withhold a certain portion of the interest as a tax, the amount withheld represents an advance on the tax to which the beneficiary will be liable on his aggregate income or profits for the fiscal year, and the beneficiary can deduct this amount from the tax due from him and obtain reimbursement of any sum by which the amount withheld exceeds the tax finally payable. This mechanism prevents the beneficiary from being taxed twice on the same interest.

4.   At the international level, when the beneficiary of the interest is a resident of one State and the payer of the interest is a resident of another, the interest is subject to taxation in both countries. This double taxation may considerably reduce the net amount of interest received by the beneficiary or, if the payer has agreed to bear the cost of the tax deductible at the source, increase the financial burden on the payer.

5.   The Commentary on the OECD Model Convention notes that although this double taxation could be eliminated by barring the source country or the residence country from taxing the interest,

"A formula reserving the exclusive taxation of interest to one State, whether the State of the beneficiary's residence or the State of source, could not be sure of receiving general approval. Therefore a compromise solution was adopted. It provides that interest may be taxed in the State of residence—but leaves to the State of source the right to impose a tax if its laws so provide, it being implicit in this right that the State of source is free to give up all taxation on interest paid to non-residents. Its exercise of this right will however be limited by a ceiling which its tax cannot exceed . . . The sacrifice that the latter would accept in such conditions will be matched by a relief to be given by the State of residence, in order to take into account the tax levied in the State of source (cf. Article 23 A or 23 B)." [para. 3]

"Certain countries do not allow interest paid to be deducted for the purposes of the payer's tax unless the recipient also resides in the same State or is taxable in that State. Otherwise they forbid the deduction. The question whether the deduction should also be allowed in cases where the interest is paid by a resident of a Contracting State to a resident of the other State is dealt with in paragraph 4 of Article 24." [para. 4]

B.   COMMENTARY ON THE PARAGRAPHS OF ARTICLE 11

Paragraph 1

6.   This paragraph reproduces Article 11, paragraph 1, of the OECD Model Convention, the Commentary on which reads as follows:

> "Paragraph 1 lays down the principle that interest arising in a Contracting State and paid to a resident of the other Contracting State may be taxed in the latter. In doing so, it does not stipulate an exclusive right to tax in favour of the State of residence. The term 'paid' has a very wide meaning, since the concept of payment means the fulfilment of the obligation to put funds at the disposal of the creditor in the manner required by contract or by custom." [para. 5]

> "The Article deals only with interest arising in a Contracting State and paid to a resident of the other Contracting State. It does not, therefore, apply to interest arising in a third State or to interest arising in a Contracting State which is attributable to a permanent establishment which an enterprise of that State has in the other Contracting State . . ." [para. 6]

Paragraph 2

7.   This paragraph reproduces Article 11, paragraph 2, of the OECD Model Convention with one substantive change. The OECD Model Convention provides that the tax in the country of source "shall not exceed 10 per cent of the gross amount of the interest", but the United Nations Model Convention leaves this percentage to be established through bilateral negotiations.

8.   The Group of Experts has amended the main provision of paragraph 2 to bring it in line with that in the OECD Model Convention. Prior to the amendment, it was provided that such interest could also be taxed in the Contracting State in which it arises and according to the laws of that State, but if the recipient is the beneficial owner of the interest the tax was to be charged in the specified manner. This

provision has been changed to provide that if the beneficial owner of the interest is a resident of the other Contracting State, the tax would be charged in the specified manner. The purpose of the amendment is to allow the benefit of this article to a beneficial owner residing in that other Contracting State regardless of the residence of any agent or other intermediary collecting the income on behalf of the beneficial owner, and while continuing to deny this benefit when the beneficial owner was not a resident of the Contracting State, even if the intermediary collecting the income was a resident.

9.   Members from developing countries took the view that the source country should have the exclusive, or at least the primary, right to tax interest. According to that view, it is incumbent on the residence country to prevent double taxation of that income through exemption, credit or other relief measures. These members reason that interest should be taxed where it was earned, that is, where the capital was put to use. Some members from developed countries felt that the home country of the investor should have the exclusive right to tax interest, since in their view that would promote the mobility of capital and give the right to tax to the country that is best equipped to consider the characteristics of the taxpayer. They also pointed out that an exemption of foreign interest from the tax of the investor's home country might not be in the best interests of the developing countries because it could induce investors to place their capital in the developing country with the lowest tax rate.

10.   The members from developing countries agreed to the solution of taxation by both the country of residence and the source country embodied in Article 11, paragraphs 1 and 2, of the OECD Model Convention but found the ceiling of 10 per cent of the gross amount of the interest mentioned in paragraph 2 thereof unacceptable. Since the Group was unable to reach a consensus on an alternative ceiling, the matter was left to bilateral negotiations.

11.   The decision not to recommend a maximum withholding rate can be justified under current treaty practice. The withholding rates for interest adopted in developed/developing country tax treaties range more widely than those for dividends—between complete ex-

emption and 25 per cent. However, some developing countries have reduced the interest withholding rate to attract foreign investment; several of them have adopted rates at or below the OECD rate of 10 per cent.

12.   A precise level of withholding tax for a source country should take into account several factors, including the following: the fact that the capital originated in the residence country; the possibility that a high source rate might cause lenders to pass the cost of the tax on to the borrowers, which would mean that the source country would increase its revenue at the expense of its own residents rather than the foreign lenders; the possibility that a tax rate higher than the foreign tax credit limit in the residence country might deter investment; the fact that a lowering of the withholding rate has revenue and foreign exchange consequences for the source country; and the main direction of interest flows (e.g., from developing to developed countries).

13.   In negotiations on bilateral treaties with a general positive rate for interest withholding, a lower ceiling or even exemption has sometimes been agreed upon for interest in one or more of the following categories:

 (*a*)   Interest paid to Governments or government agencies;

 (*b*)   Interest guaranteed by Governments or government agencies;

 (*c*)   Interest paid to central banks;

 (*d*)   Interest paid to banks or other financial institutions;

 (*e*)   Interest on long-term loans;

 (*f*)   Interest on loans to financing special equipment or public works; or

 (*g*)   Interest on other government-approved types of investment (e.g., export finance).

With respect to bank loans and loans from financial institutions, a major justification for the reduced rate is the high costs associated with these loans, particularly the lender's cost of funds. The withholding tax, because it is a gross basis tax, has a high effective tax rate. If the effective rate is higher than the general tax rate in the lender's country of residence, the borrower is often required to bear the tax through a gross-up feature in the loan agreement. In that case, the withholding tax amounts to an additional tax on residents of the source State. One way to deal with this is to allow the lender to elect to treat such income as business profits under article 7, but this approach raises computation and administrative issues for banks and tax administrators.

14.   A similar justification exists for reduced rates on interest from credit sales. The supplier in such cases often merely passes on to the customer, without additional charge, the price he has had to pay to a bank or export finance agency to finance the credit. For a person selling equipment on credit, the interest is more an element of the sales price than income from invested capital.

15.   In addition, long-term credits correspond to investments that should be profitable enough to be repaid in instalments over a period. In the latter case, interest must be paid out of earnings at the same time as instalments of credit are repaid out of capital. Consequently, any excessive fiscal burden on such interest must be passed on to the book value of the capital goods purchased on credit, with the result that the fiscal charge levied on the interest might, in the last analysis, diminish the amount of tax payable on the profits made by the user of the capital goods.

16.   At the Group's 1991 meeting, some members argued that interest income received by government agencies should be exempted from source country taxation because exemption would facilitate the financing of development projects, especially in developing countries, by eliminating tax considerations from negotiations over interest rates. Some members from developing countries asserted that the financing of such projects would be enhanced even further if the interest income was also exempt from tax in the lender's country of residence.

17.   The predominant treaty practice is to exempt governmental interest from source country tax, but there is a wide range of practice on

the details. In some instances interest income is exempted if paid by a government or paid to a government; in other instances only interest paid to a government is exempt. Also, the definition of "government" varies to include, e.g., local authorities, agencies, instrumentalities, central banks, and financial institutions owned by the government.

18.   The Group has observed that long-term credits often call for special guarantees because of the difficulty of long-term political, economic and monetary forecasting. Moreover, most developed countries, in order to ensure full employment in their capital goods industries or public works enterprises, have adopted various measures to encourage long-term credits, including credit insurance or interest-rate reductions by government agencies. These measures may take the form of direct loans by government agencies tied to loans by private banks or private credit facilities or interest terms more favourable than those obtainable on the money market. These measures are not likely to persist if the preferences are effectively cancelled out or reduced by excessive taxation in the debtor's country. Thus, not only should interest on loans made by a government be exempted, but an argument exists for exempting interest on long-term loans made by private banks where such loans are guaranteed or refinanced by a government or a government agency.

19.   The Commentary on the OECD Model Convention contains the following passages:

"Under paragraph 2, the limitation of tax in the State of source is not available when an intermediary, such as an agent or nominee, is interposed between the beneficiary and the payer, unless the beneficial owner is a resident of the other Contracting State . . . States which wish to make this more explicit are free to do so during bilateral negotiations." [para. 8]

"The paragraph lays down nothing about the mode of taxation in the State of source. It therefore leaves that State free to apply its own laws and, in particular, to levy the tax either by deduction at source or by individual assessment. Procedural questions are not dealt with in this Article. Each State should be able to apply the procedure provided in its own law . . ." [para. 9]

"It does not specify whether or not the relief in the State of source should be conditional upon the interest being subject to tax in the State of residence. This question can be settled by bilateral negotiations." [para. 10]

"The Article contains no provisions as to how the State of the beneficiary's residence should make allowance for the taxation in the State of source of the interest. This question is dealt with in Articles 23 A and 23 B." [para. 11]

"Attention is drawn generally to the following case: the beneficial owner of interest arising in a Contracting State is a company resident in the other Contracting State; all or part of its capital is held by shareholders resident outside that other State; its practice is not to distribute its profits in the form of dividends; and it enjoys preferential taxation treatment (private investment company, base company). The question may arise whether, in the case of such a company, it is justifiable to allow in the State of source of the interest the limitation of tax which is provided in paragraph 2. It may be appropriate, when bilateral negotiations are being conducted, to agree upon special exceptions to the taxing rule laid down in this article, in order to define the treatment applicable to such companies." [para. 12]

"It should, however, be pointed out that the solution adopted, given the combined effect of the right to tax accorded to the State of source and the allowance to be made for the tax levied there against that due in the State of residence, could, in certain cases, result in maintaining partial double taxation and lead to adverse economic consequences. In fact, when the beneficiary of the interest has himself had to borrow in order to finance the operation which earns him interest, the profit he will realize by way of interest will be much smaller than the nominal amount of interest he receives; if the interest he pays and that which he receives balance, there will be no profit at all. In such a case, the allowance to be made under paragraph 2 of Article 23 A, or paragraph 1 of Article 23 B, raises a difficult and sometimes insoluble problem in view of the fact that the tax levied in the State where the interest arises is calculated on the gross amount thereof, whereas the same interest is reflected in the beneficiary's business results at its net amount only. The result of this is that part, or sometimes even the whole amount, of the tax levied in the State where the interest arises cannot be allowed as a credit in the beneficiary's State of residence and so constitutes an excess charge for the beneficiary, who, to that extent, suffers double taxation. Moreover, the latter, in order to avoid the disadvantage just mentioned, will tend to increase the rate of interest he charges his debtor, whose financial burden would then be increased to a corresponding extent. Thus in certain cases the practice of taxation at the source can constitute an obstacle to international trade." [para. 13]

"The disadvantages just mentioned arise in business, particularly with the sale on credit of equipment, other commercial credit sales, and loans granted by banks. The supplier in such cases very often merely passes on to the customer, without any additional charge, the price he will himself have had to pay to a bank or an export finance agency to finance the credit; similarly, the banker generally finances the loan which he grants with funds lent to his bank and, in particular, funds accepted by him on deposit. In the case especially of the person selling equipment on credit, the interest is more an element of the selling price than income from invested capital." [para. 14]

"If two Contracting States, in order to eliminate all risks of double taxation, should desire to avoid the imposition of a tax in the State of source on interest arising from the above-mentioned categories of debts, their common intention can be expressed by an additional paragraph which would follow paragraph 2 of the Article, and which might be in the following terms:

3.   Notwithstanding the provisions of paragraph 2, any such interest as is mentioned in paragraph 1 shall be

taxable only in the Contracting State of which the recipient is a resident, if such recipient is the beneficial owner of the interest and if such interest is paid:

(*a*)   in connection with the sale on credit of any industrial, commercial or scientific equipment,

(*b*)   in connection with the sale on credit of any merchandise by one enterprise to another enterprise, or

(*c*)   on any loan of whatever kind granted by a bank." [para. 15]

"As regards, more particularly, the types of credit sale referred to in subparagraph (*a*) of the text suggested above, they comprise not only sales of complete units, but also sales of separate components thereof. Furthermore, as regards credit sales of the types referred to in subparagraphs (*a*) and (*b*) of the suggested text, it is immaterial whether the interest is stipulated separately and as additional to the sale price, or is included from the outset in the price payable by instalments." [para. 16]

"Contracting States may add to the categories of interest enumerated . . . above other categories in regard to which the imposition of a tax in the State of source might appear to them to be undesirable. They may also agree that the exclusion of a right to tax in the State of source shall be limited to certain of the categories of interest mentioned." [para. 17]

Paragraph 3

20.   This paragraph reproduces Article 11, paragraph 3, of the OECD Model Convention, the Commentary on which reads as follows:

"Paragraph 3 specifies the meaning to be attached to the term 'interest' for the application of the taxation treatment defined by the article. The term designates, in general, income from debt claims of every kind, whether or not secured by mortgage and whether or not carrying a right to participate in profits. The term 'debt claims of every kind' obviously embraces cash deposits and security in the form of money, as well as government securities, and bonds and debentures, although the three latter are specially mentioned because of their importance and of certain peculiarities that they may present. It is recognized, on the one hand, that mortgage interest comes within the category of income from movable capital ('revenus de capitaux mobiliers'), even though certain countries assimilate it to income from immovable property. On the other hand, debt claims, and bonds and debentures in particular, which carry a right to participate in the debtor's profits are nonetheless regarded as loans if the contract by its general character clearly evidences a loan at interest." [para. 18]

"Interest on participating bonds should not normally be considered as a dividend, and neither should interest on convertible bonds until such time as the bonds are actually converted into shares. However, the interest on such bonds should be considered as a dividend if the loan effectively shares the risks run by the debtor company . . . In situations of presumed thin capitalization, it is sometimes difficult to distinguish between dividends and interest and in order to avoid any possibility of overlap between the categories of income dealt with in Article 10 and Article 11 respectively, it should be noted that the term 'interest' as used in Article 11 does not include items of income which are dealt with in Article 10." [para. 19]

"As regards, more particularly, government securities, and bonds and debentures, the text specifies that premiums or prizes attaching thereto constitute interest. Generally speaking, what constitutes interest yielded by a loan security, and may properly be taxed as such in the State of source, is all that the institution issuing the loan pays over and above the amount paid by the subscriber, that is to say, the interest accruing plus any premium paid at redemption or at issue. It follows that when a bond or debenture has been issued at a premium, the excess of the amount paid by the subscriber over that repaid to him may constitute negative interest which should be deducted from the interest that is taxable. On the other hand, any profit or loss which a holder of such a security realizes by the sale thereof to another person does not enter into the concept of interest. Such profit or loss may, depending on the case, constitute either a business profit or a loss, a capital gain or a loss, or income falling under Article 21." [para. 20]

"Moreover, the definition of interest in the first sentence of paragraph 3 is, in principle, exhaustive. It has seemed preferable not to include a subsidiary reference to domestic laws in the text; this is justified by the following considerations:

(*a*)   the definition covers practically all the kinds of income which are regarded as interest in the various domestic laws;

(*b*)   the formula employed offers greater security from the legal point of view and ensures that conventions would be unaffected by future changes in any country's domestic laws;

(*c*)   in the Model Convention references to domestic laws should as far as possible be avoided.

It nevertheless remains understood that in a bilateral convention two Contracting States may widen the formula employed so as to include in it any income which is taxed as interest under either of their domestic laws but which is not covered by the definition and in these circumstances may find it preferable to make reference to their domestic laws." [para. 21]

"The definition of interest in the first sentence of paragraph 3 does not normally apply to payments made under certain kinds of non-traditional financial instruments where there is no underlying debt (for example, interest rate swaps). However, the definition will apply to the extent that a loan is considered to exist under a 'substance over form' rule, and 'abuse of rights' principle, or any similar doctrine." [para. 21.1]

"The second sentence of paragraph 3 excludes from the definition of interest penalty charges for late payment but

Contracting States are free to omit this sentence and treat charges as interest in their bilateral conventions. Penalty charges, which may be payable under the contract, or by customs or by virtue of a judgement, consist either of payments calculated pro rata temporis or else of fixed sums; in certain cases they may combine both forms of payment. Even if they are determined pro rata temporis they constitute not so much income from capital as a special form of compensation for the loss suffered by the creditor through the debtor's delay in meeting his obligations. Moreover, considerations of legal security and practical convenience make it advisable to place all penalty charges of this kind, in whatever form they be paid, on the same footing for the purposes of their taxation treatment. On the other hand, two Contracting States may exclude from the application of Article 11 any kinds of interest which they intend to be treated as dividends." [para. 22]

"Finally, the question arises whether annuities ought to be assimilated to interest; it is considered that they ought not to be. On the one hand, annuities granted in consideration of past employment are referred to in Article 18 and are subject to the rules governing pensions. On the other hand, although it is true that instalments of purchased annuities include an interest element on the purchase capital as well as return of capital, such instalments thus constituting 'fruits civils' which accrue from day to day, it would be difficult for many countries to make a distinction between the element representing income from capital and the element representing a return of capital in order merely to tax the income element under the same category as income from movable capital. Taxation laws often contain special provisions classifying annuities in the category of salaries, wages and pension, and taxing them accordingly." [para. 23]

Paragraph 4

21.   This paragraph, which provides that paragraphs 1 and 2 do not apply to some interest if the recipient has a permanent establishment or fixed base in the source country, reproduces Article 11, paragraph 4,

of the OECD Model Convention, with one modification. The OECD version only applies if the obligation on which the interest is paid is effectively connected with the permanent establishment or fixed base. Since the United Nations Model Convention, unlike the OECD Model Convention, adopts a limited force of attraction rule in article 7, defining the income that may be taxed as business profits, a conforming change is made in article 11, paragraph 4, of the United Nations Model Convention. This modification makes paragraphs 1 and 2 of article 11 inapplicable if the debt claim is effectively connected with the permanent establishment or fixed base or with business activities in the source country of the same or similar kind as those effected through the permanent establishment.

Paragraph 5

22.   This paragraph reproduces Article 11, paragraph 5, of the OECD Model Convention, which specifies that interest is from sources in the residence country of the payer. The first sentence of paragraph 5 was amended in 1999. However, in the course of discussion, the Group agreed that countries might substitute a rule that would identify the source of interest as the State in which the loan giving rise to the interest was used. Where, in bilateral negotiations, the two parties differed on the appropriate rule, a possible solution would be a rule which, in general, would accept the place of residence of the payer as the source of interest; but where the loan was used in the State having a "place of use" rule, the interest would be deemed to arise in that State. The OECD Commentary on Article 11, paragraph 5, reads as follows:

> "This paragraph lays down the principle that the State of source of the interest is the State of which the payer of the interest is a resident. It provides, however, for an exception to this rule in the case of interest-bearing loans which have an obvious economic link with a permanent establishment owned in the other Contracting State by the payer of the interest. If the loan was contracted for the requirements of that establishment and the interest is borne by the latter, the paragraph determines that the source of the interest is in the Contracting State in

which the permanent establishment is situated, leaving aside the place of residence of the owner of the permanent establishment, even when he resides in a third State." [para. 26]

"In the absence of an economic link between the loan on which the interest arises and the permanent establishment, the State where the latter is situated cannot on that account be regarded as the State where the interest arises; it is not entitled to tax such interest, not even within the limits of a 'taxable quota' proportional to the importance of the permanent establishment. Such a practice would be incompatible with paragraph 5. Moreover, any departure from the rule fixed in the first sentence of paragraph 5 is justified only where the economic link between the loan and the permanent establishment is sufficiently clear-cut. In this connection, a number of possible cases may be distinguished:

(*a*)   The management of the permanent establishment has contracted a loan which it uses for the specific requirements of the permanent establishment; it shows it among its liabilities and pays the interest thereon directly to the creditor.

(*b*)   The head office of the enterprise has contracted a loan the proceeds of which are used solely for the purposes of a permanent establishment situated in another country. The interest is serviced by the head office but is ultimately borne by the permanent establishment.

(*c*)   The loan is contracted by the head office of the enterprise and its proceeds are used for several permanent establishments situated in different countries.

In cases (*a*) and (*b*) the conditions laid down in the second sentence of paragraph 5 are fulfilled, and the State where the permanent establishment is situated is to be regarded as the State where the interest arises. Case (*c*), however, falls outside the provisions of paragraph 5, the text of which precludes the attribution of more than one source to the same loan. Such a solution, moreover, would give rise to considerable administrative complications and make it impossible for lenders to calculate in advance the taxation that interest would attract. It is, however, open to two Contracting States to restrict the application of the final provision in paragraph 5 to case (*a*) or to extend it to case (*c*)." [para. 27]

"Paragraph 5 provides no solution for the case, which it excludes from its provisions, where both the beneficiary and the payer are indeed residents of the Contracting States, but the loan was borrowed for the requirements of a permanent establishment owned by the payer in a third State and the interest is borne by that establishment. As paragraph 5 now stands, therefore, only its first sentence will apply in such a case. The interest will be deemed to arise in the Contracting State of which the payer is a resident and not in the third State in whose territory is situated the permanent establishment for the account of which the loan was effected and by which the interest is payable. Thus the interest will be taxed both in the Contracting State of which the payer is a resident and in the Contracting State of which the beneficiary is a resident. But, although double taxation will be avoided between these two States by the arrangements provided in the article, it will not be avoided between them and the third State if the latter taxes the interest on the loan at the source when it is borne by the permanent establishment in its territory." [para. 28]

"It has not, however, been considered possible to refer to such a case in a bilateral convention and provide for it a solution consisting, for example, in obliging the Contracting State of the payer's residence to relinquish its tax at the source in favour of the third State in which is situated the permanent establishment for the account of which the loan was effected and by which the interest is borne. The risk of double taxation just referred to can only be fully avoided through a bilateral convention containing a similar provision to that in paragraph 5, between the Contracting State of which the payer of the interest is a resident and the third State in which the permanent establishment paying the interest is situated, or through a multilateral convention containing such a provision." [para. 29]

"Moreover, in the case—not settled in paragraph 5—where whichever of the two Contracting States is that of the payer's residence and the third State in which is situated the permanent establishment for the account of which the loan is effected and by which the interest is borne together claim the right to tax the interest at the source, there would be nothing to prevent those two States—together with, where appropriate, the State of the beneficiary's residence—from concerting measures to avoid the double taxation that would result from such claims. The proper remedy, it must be said again, would be the establishment between these different States of bilateral conventions, or a multilateral convention, containing a provision similar to that in paragraph 5. Another solution would be for two Contracting States to word the second sentence of paragraph 5 in the following way:

'Where, however, the person paying the interest, whether he is a resident of a Contracting State or not, has in a State other than that of which he is a resident a permanent establishment or a fixed base in connection with which the indebtedness on which the interest is paid was incurred, and such interest is borne by such permanent establishment or fixed base, then such interest shall be deemed to arise in the State in which the permanent establishment or fixed base is situated.'" [para. 30]

"If two Contracting States agree in bilateral negotiations to reserve to the State where the beneficiary of the income resides the exclusive right to tax such income, then ipso facto there is no value in inserting in the convention which fixes their relations that provision in paragraph 5 which defines the State of source of such income. But it is equally obvious that double taxation would not be fully avoided in such a case if the payer of the interest owned, in a third State which charged its tax at the source on the interest, a permanent establishment for the account of which the loan had been borrowed and which bore the interest payable on it. The case would then be just the same as is contemplated . . . above." [para. 31]

Paragraph 6

23.   This paragraph reproduces Article 11, paragraph 6, of the OECD Model Convention, the Commentary on which reads as follows:

"The purpose of this paragraph is to restrict the operation of the provisions concerning the taxation of interest in cases where, by reason of a special relationship between the payer and the beneficial owner or between both of them and some other person, the amount of the interest paid exceeds the amount which would have been agreed upon by the payer and the beneficial owner had they stipulated at arm's length. It provides that in such a case the provisions of the article apply only to that last-mentioned amount and that the excess part of the interest shall remain taxable according to the laws of the two Contracting States, due regard being had to the other provisions of the Convention." [para. 32]

"It is clear from the text that for this clause to apply the interest held excessive must be due to a special relationship between the payer and the beneficial owner or between either of them and some other person. There may be cited as examples cases where interest is paid to an individual or legal person who directly or indirectly controls the payer, or who is directly or indirectly controlled by him or is subordinate to a group having common interest with him. These examples, moreover, are similar or analogous to the cases contemplated by Article 9." [para. 33]

"On the other hand, the concept of special relationship also covers relationship by blood or marriage and, in general, any community of interests as distinct from the legal relationship giving rise to the payment of the interest." [para. 34]

"With regard to the taxation treatment to be applied to the excess part of the interest, the exact nature of such excess will need to be ascertained according to the circumstances of each case, in order to determine the category of income in which it should be classified for the purposes of applying the provisions of the tax laws of the States concerned and the provisions of the Convention. This paragraph permits only the adjustment of the rate at which interest is charged and not the reclassification of the loan in such a way as to give it the character of a contribution to equity capital. For such an adjustment to be possible under paragraph 6 of Article 11 it would be necessary to substitute other words for the phrase 'having regard to the debt claim for which it is paid'. Nevertheless, this paragraph can affect not only the recipient but also the payer of the excessive interest and if the law of the State of source permits, the excess amount can be disallowed as a deduction, due regard being had to other applicable provisions of the Convention. If two Contracting States should have difficulty in determining the other provisions of the Convention applicable, as cases require, to the excess part of the interest, there would be nothing to prevent them from introducing additional clarifications in the last sentence of paragraph 6, as long as they do not alter its general purport." [para. 35]

"Should the principles and rules of their respective laws oblige the two Contracting States to apply different articles of the Convention for the purpose of taxing the excess, it will be necessary to resort to the mutual agreement procedure provided by the Convention in order to resolve the difficulty." [para. 36]

24. Some members of the Group of Experts pointed out that there are many artificial devices entered into by persons to take advantage of the provisions of article 11 through, inter alia, creation or assignment of debt claims in respect of which interest is charged. While substance over form rules, abuse of rights principle or any similar doctrine could be used to counter such arrangements. Contracting States which may want to specifically address the issue may include a clause on the following lines in their bilateral tax treaties during negotiations, namely:

"The provisions of this article shall not apply if it was the main purpose or one of the main purposes of any person concerned with the creation or assignment of the debt claim in respect of which the interest is paid to take advantage of this article by means of that creation or assignment."

Article 12

ROYALTIES

A. GENERAL CONSIDERATIONS

1.   Article 12 of the United Nations Model Convention reproduces Article 12 of the OECD Model Convention, with the following exceptions: first, substantive differences appear in paragraphs 1 and 3; second, paragraphs 2 and 5 do not appear in the OECD Model Convention with the result that the paragraph numbers in the United Nations Model Convention differ from those in the OECD Model Convention; and third, a drafting adjustment is made in paragraph 4.

2.   When the user of a patent or similar property is resident in one country and pays royalties to the owner thereof who is resident in another country, the amount paid by the user is generally subject to withholding tax in his country, the source country. The source country tax is on the gross payments, with no allowance for any related expenses incurred by the owner. Without recognition of expenses, the owner's after-tax profit may in some cases be only a small percentage of gross royalties. Consequently, the owner may take the withholding tax in the source country into account in fixing the amount of the royalty, so that the user and the source country will pay more for the use of the patent or similar property than they would if the withholding tax levied by the source country were lower and took into account the expenses incurred by the owner. A manufacturing enterprise or an inventor may have spent substantial sums on the development of the property generating the royalties, because the work of research and testing involves considerable capital outlays and does not always yield successful results. The problem of determining the appropriate tax rate to be applied by the source country to gross royalty payments is therefore complex, especially since the user may

make a lump sum payment for the use of the patent or similar property, in addition to regular royalty payments.

3.   The Commentary on Article 12 of the OECD Model Convention includes the following preliminary remarks:

> "In principle, royalties in respect of licences to use patents and similar property and similar payments are income to the recipient from a letting. The letting may be granted in connection with an industrial or commercial enterprise (e.g., the use of literary copyright granted by a publisher) or an independent profession (e.g., use of a patent granted by the inventor) or quite independently of any activity of the grantor (e.g., use of a patent granted by the inventor's heirs)." [para. 1]

> "Certain countries do not allow royalties paid to be deducted for the purposes of the payer's tax unless the recipient also resides in the same State or is taxable in that State. Otherwise they forbid the deduction. The question whether the deduction should also be allowed in cases where the royalties are paid by a resident of a Contracting State to a resident of the other State is dealt with in paragraph 4 of Article 24." [para. 2]

B.   COMMENTARY ON THE PARAGRAPHS OF ARTICLE 12

Paragraphs 1 *and* 2

4.   Paragraph 1 drops the word "only" from the corresponding provision of the OECD Model Convention, which provides that "royalties arising in a Contracting State and beneficially owned by a resident of the other Contracting State shall be taxable only in that other State". Paragraph 2 is an addition flowing logically from the premise underlying paragraph 1, which is that royalties should be taxable in the source country as well as the residence country. A member from a developed country has observed that by providing for taxing rights in respect of royalties to be shared between the State of residence and the State of source, the United Nations Model Convention departs from the principle of exclusive residence State's right to tax provided in the OECD Model Convention. In this context, it

should be noted that several member States of OECD have recorded reservations about the approval of exclusive residence State taxation.

5.   The Group of Experts has amended the provisions of paragraph 2 of article 12 in 1999 to bring it in line with the provisions of paragraph 2 of articles 10 and 11. Prior to the amendment, it was provided that such royalties may also be taxed in the Contracting State in which they arise and according to the laws of that State, but if the recipient is the beneficial owner of the royalties, the tax will be charged in the specified manner. The purpose of this amendment is to allow the benefit of this article to the beneficial owner residing in the treaty country regardless of the residence of any agent or other intermediary collecting the income on behalf of the beneficial owner, while continuing to deny this benefit when the beneficial owner was not a resident of the treaty country, even if the intermediary collecting the income was a resident. In this connection, a reference is made to paragraph 5 of the Commentary on article 10.

6.   During discussion by the Group of Experts, members from developing countries argued that, in order to facilitate the conclusion of tax treaties between those countries and developed countries, the primary right to tax royalties should be given to the country where the income arose, that is, the source country. Patents and processes might be licensed to developing countries after they had been fully exploited elsewhere and, according to these members, after the expenses incurred in connection with their development had already been largely recouped.

7.   Members from developed countries responded that it would be unrealistic to assume that enterprises selected the oldest patents for licensing to developing countries. Normally, an enterprise would license its patents to foreign subsidiaries and therefore select the most up-to-date inventions, in the hope of expanding existing markets or opening up new ones. Patents are not merchandise but instruments for promoting industrial production. Several members from developed countries held as a matter of principle that the country of resi-

dence of the owner of a patent or similar property should have the exclusive or primary right to tax royalties paid thereon.

8.   Since the Group reached no consensus on a particular rate for the withholding tax to be charged on royalties on a gross basis, the rate should be established through bilateral negotiations. The following considerations might be taken into account in negotiations:

First, the country of source should recognize both current expenses allocable to the royalty and expenditure incurred in the development of the property whose use gave rise to the royalty. It should be considered that the costs of developing the property are also allocable to profits derived from other royalties or activities, past or future, associated with these expenditures and that expenditure not directly incurred in the development of that property might nevertheless have contributed significantly to that development;

Second, if an expense ratio is agreed upon in fixing a gross rate in the source country, the country of the recipient, if following a credit method, should also use that expense ratio in applying its credit, whenever feasible. Therefore, that matter should be considered under article 23 A or 23 B.

9.   Other factors might influence the determination of the withholding tax on gross royalties, including the developing countries' need to earn revenue and conserve foreign exchange; the fact that royalty payments flow almost entirely from developing countries to developed countries; the extent of assistance that developed countries should, for a variety of reasons, extend to developing countries; and the special importance of providing such assistance in the context of royalty payments; the desirability of preventing a shift of the tax burden to the licensees in the licensing arrangement; the ability that taxation at source confers on a developing country to make selective judgements by which, through reduced taxation or exemption, it could encourage those licensing arrangements if they were considered desirable for its development; the lessening of the risks of tax evasion resulting from taxation at the source; the fact that the country of the licensor supplies the facilities and activities necessary

for the development of the patent and thus undertakes the risks associated with the patent; the desirability of obtaining and encouraging a flow of technology to developing countries; the desirability of expanding the field of activity of the licensor in the utilization of his research; the benefits that developed countries obtain from world development in general; the relative importance of revenue sacrifice; the relation of the royalty decision to other decisions in the negotiations.

10.   Income from film rentals should not be treated as industrial and commercial profits but should be dealt with in the context of royalties. The tax would thus be levied on a gross basis but expenses would be taken into account in fixing the withholding rate. With regard to expenses, there are factors that could be regarded as peculiarly relevant to film rentals. As a general rule, the expenses of film producers might be much higher and the profits lower than in the case of industrial royalties. On the other hand, because a considerable part of film expenses represents high salaries paid to actors and other participants who were taxed solely by the country of residence, and not by the source country, these expenses might not justify any great reduction of the withholding tax at source. However, it could be said that the amounts involved were nevertheless real costs for the producer and should be taken into account, while at the same time all countries involved should join in efforts to make sure that such income did not escape tax. Further, while the write-off of expenses in the country of residence did not mean that the expenses should not be taken into account at source, at some point old films could present a different expense situation.

11.   Some members of the Group believe that because copyright royalties represent cultural efforts, they should be exempted from taxation by the source country. Other members, however, argue that tax would be levied by the residence country, and the reduction at source would not benefit the author. Other members favour exempting copyright royalties at the source, not necessarily for cultural reasons, but because the country of residence is in a better position to evaluate the expenses and personal circumstances of the creator of

the royalties, including the period over which the books or other copyrighted items had been created; a reduction of the source country tax could be supported in some cases by the fact that the tax was too high to be absorbed by the tax credit of the residence country. However, source countries might not be willing to accept that approach to the problem. Furthermore, if the person dealing with the source country might be the publisher and not the author, arguments supporting the exemption of the author's income because of his personal situation obviously do not apply to the publisher.

Paragraph 3

12.   This paragraph reproduces Article 12, paragraph 2, of the OECD Model Convention, but does not incorporate the 1992 amendment thereto which eliminates equipment rental from this article, and paragraph 3 of article 12 includes payments for tapes and royalties which are not included in the corresponding provision of the OECD Model Convention. The following portions of the OECD Commentary are relevant (the bracketed paragraphs being portions of the Commentary on the 1977 OECD Model Convention that are omitted from or altered in the present OECD Commentary):

> "Paragraph 2 contains a definition of the term 'royalties'. These relate, in general, to rights or property constituting the different forms of literary and artistic property, the elements of intellectual property specified in the text and industrial and commercial property specified in the text and information concerning industrial, commercial or scientific experience. The definition applies to payments for the use of, or the entitlement to use, rights of the kind mentioned, whether or not they have been, or are required to be, registered in a public register. The definition covers both payments made under a licence and compensation which a person would be obliged to pay for fraudulently copying or infringing the right . . . [T]he word 'payment', used in the definition, has a very wide meaning since the concept of payment means the fulfilment of the obligation to put funds at the disposal of the creditor in the manner required by contract or by custom. As a guide, certain explana-

tions are given below in order to define the scope of Article 12 in relation to that of other Articles of the Convention, as regards, in particular, [equipment renting and] the provision of information." [para. 8]

"Rents in respect of cinematograph films are also treated as royalties, whether such films are exhibited in cinemas or on the television. It may, however, be agreed through bilateral negotiations that rents in respect of cinematograph films shall be treated as industrial and commercial profits and, in consequence, subjected to the provisions of Articles 7 and 9." [para. 10]

"In classifying as royalties payments received as consideration for information concerning industrial, commercial or scientific experience, paragraph 2 alludes to the concept of 'know-how'. Various specialist bodies and authors have formulated definitions of know-how which do not differ intrinsically. One such definition, given by the 'Association des Bureaux pour la Protection de la Propriété Industrielle' (ANBPPI), states that 'know-how is all the undivulged technical information, whether capable of being patented or not, that is necessary for the industrial reproduction of a product or process, directly and under the same conditions; inasmuch as it is derived from experience, know-how represents what a manufacturer cannot know from mere examination of the product and mere knowledge of the progress of technique'. In the know-how contract, one of the parties agrees to impart to the other, so that he can use them for his own account, his special knowledge and experience which remain unrevealed to the public. It is recognized that the grantor is not required to play any part himself in the application of the formulae granted to the licensee and that he does not guarantee the result thereof. This type of contract thus differs from contracts for the provision of services, in which one of the parties undertakes to use the customary skills of his calling to execute work himself for the other party. Thus, payments obtained as consideration for after-sales service, for services rendered by a seller to the purchaser under a guarantee, for pure technical assistance, or for an opinion given by an engineer, an advocate or an accountant, do not constitute royalties within the meaning of paragraph 2. Such payments generally fall under Article 7 or Article 14. In business practice, contracts are encountered which cover both know-how and the provision of technical assistance. One example, amongst others, of contracts of this kind is that of franchising, where the franchisor imparts his knowledge and experience to the franchisee and, in addition, provides him with varied technical assistance, which, in certain cases, is backed up with financial assistance and the supply of goods. The appropriate course to take with a mixed contract is, in principle, to break down, on the basis of the information contained in the contract or by means of a reasonable apportionment, the whole amount of the stipulated consideration according to the various parts of what is being provided under the contract, and then to apply to each part of it so determined the taxation treatment proper thereto. If, however, one part of what is being provided constitutes by far the principal purpose of the contract and the other parts stipulated therein are only of an ancillary and largely unimportant character, then it seems possible to apply to the whole amount of the consideration the treatment applicable to the principal part." [para. 11]

"Whether payments received as consideration for computer software may be classified as royalties poses difficult problems but is a matter of considerable importance in view of the rapid development of computer technology in recent years and the extent of transfers of such technology across national borders. Software may be described as a program, or series of programs, containing instructions for a computer required either for the operational processes of the computer itself (operational software) or for the accomplishment of other tasks (application software). It can be transferred through a variety of media, for example in writing, on a magnetic tape or disk, or on a laser disk. It may be standardized with a wide range of applications or be tailor-made for single users. It can be transferred as an integral part of computer hardware or in an independent form available for use on a variety of hardware. The rights in computer software are a form of intellectual property. Research into the practices of OECD Member countries has established that all but one protect software rights either explicitly or implicitly under copyright law. Transfers of rights occur in many different ways ranging from the alienation of the entire rights to the sale of a product which is subject to restrictions on the use to which it is put. The consideration paid can also take numerous forms. These factors may make it difficult to determine where the boundary lies between software payments that are properly to be regarded as royalties and other types of payment." [para. 12]

"Three situations are considered. The first is of payments made where less than the full rights in software are transferred. In a partial transfer of rights the consideration is likely to represent a royalty only in very limited circumstances. One such case is where the transferor is the author of the software (or has acquired from the author his rights of distribution and reproduction) and he has placed part of his rights at the disposal of a third party to enable the latter to develop or exploit the software itself commercially, for example by development and distribution of it . . . [E]ven where a software payment is properly to be regarded as a royalty there are difficulties in applying the copyright provisions of the Article to software royalties since paragraph [3] requires that software should be classified as a literary, artistic or scientific work. None of these categories seems entirely apt but treatment as a scientific work might be the most realistic approach. Countries for which it is not possible to attach software to any of those categories might be justified in adopting in their bilateral treaties an amended version of paragraph 2 which either omits all references to the nature of copyrights or refers specifically to software." [para. 13]

"In other cases, the acquisition of the software will generally be for the personal or business use of the purchaser. The payment will then fall to be dealt with as commercial income in accordance with Articles 7 or 14. It is of no relevance that the software is protected by copyright or that there may be restrictions on the use to which the purchaser can put it." [para. 14]

"The second situation is where the payments are made as consideration for the alienation of rights attached to the software. It is clear that where consideration is paid for the transfer of the full ownership, the payment cannot represent a royalty and the provisions of the Article are not applicable. Difficulties can arise where there are extensive but partial alienation of rights involving:

—exclusive right of use during a specific period or in a limited geographical area;

—additional consideration related to usage;

—consideration in the form of a substantial lump sum payment." [para. 15]

"Each case will depend on its particular facts but in general such payments are likely to be commercial income within Article 7 or 14 or a capital gains matter within Article 13 rather than royalties within Article 12. That follows from the fact that where the ownership of rights has been alienated in full or in part, the consideration cannot be for the use of the rights. The essential character of the transaction as an alienation cannot be altered by the form of the consideration, the payment of the consideration in instalments or, in the view of most countries, by the fact that the payments are related to a contingency." [para. 16]

"The third situation is where software payments are made under mixed contracts. Examples of such contracts include sales of computer hardware with built-in software and concessions of the right to use software combined with the provision of services. The methods set out in paragraph 11 above for dealing with similar problems in relation to patent royalties and know-how are equally applicable to computer software.

Where necessary the total amount of the consideration payable under a contract should be broken down on the basis of the information contained in the contract or by means of a reasonable apportionment with the appropriate tax treatment being applied to each apportioned part." [para. 17]

"The suggestions made above regarding mixed contracts could also be applied in regard to certain performances by artists and, in particular, in regard to an orchestral concert given by a conductor or a recital given by a musician. The fee for the musical performance, together with that paid for any simultaneous radio broadcasting thereof, seems to fall to be treated under Article 17. Where, whether under the same contract or under a separate one, the musical performance is recorded and the artist has stipulated that he be paid royalties on the sale or public playing of the records, then so much of the payment received by him as consists of such royalties falls to be treated under Article 12." [para. 18]

"It is further pointed out that variable or fixed payments for the working of mineral deposits, sources or other natural resources are governed by Article 6 and do not, therefore, fall within the present Article. [If two Contracting States should have difficulty from the legal standpoint in applying this distinction in regard to consideration for the use of, or the right to use, equipment, they could add to the text of paragraph 2, after the words 'industrial, commercial or scientific equipment', the words 'not constituting immovable property referred to in Article 6'.]" [para. 19]

13.   Reference is made to the revision of the Commentary on Article 12 concerning software payments that has been approved by the OECD Fiscal Affairs Committee which would replace the Commentary quoted above.

14.   Paragraph 2 of Article 12 of the OECD Model Convention (corresponding to paragraph 3 of article 12 of the United Nations Model Convention) was amended by deleting the words "or the use of, or the right to use, industrial, commercial or scientific equipment"

by the Report entitled "The Revision of the Model Convention" adopted by the Council of the OECD on 23 July 1992. However, a number of OECD member countries have entered reservations on this point.

15.   The Group considered the problems of distinguishing royalties from types of income properly subject to other articles of the Convention. A member from a developed country asserted that the problem was that the "royalties" definition makes an imperfect distinction between revenues that constituted royalties in the strict sense and payments received for brain-work and technical services, such as surveys of any kind (engineering, geological research etc.). The member also mentioned the problem of distinguishing between royalties akin to income from capital and payments received for services. Given the broad definition of "information concerning industrial, commercial or scientific experience", some countries tend to regard the provision of brain-work and technical services as the provision of "information concerning industrial, commercial or scientific experience" and to regard payment for it as royalties.

16.   In order to avoid those difficulties, this member proposed that the definition of royalties be restricted by excluding payments received for "information concerning industrial, commercial or scientific experience". The member also suggested that a protocol should be annexed to the treaty making it clear that such payments should be deemed to be profits of an enterprise to which article 7 would apply and that payments received for studies or surveys of a scientific or technical nature, such as geological surveys, or for consultant or supervisory services, should also be deemed to be business profits subject to article 7. The effect of these provisions would be that the source country could not tax such payments unless the enterprise had a permanent establishment in that country and that taxes should only be imposed on the net income element of such payments attributable to that permanent establishment.

17.   Some members from developing countries interpreted the phrase "information concerning industrial, commercial or scientific experience" to mean specialized knowledge, having intrinsic prop-

erty value relating to industrial, commercial, or managerial processes, conveyed in the form of instructions, advice, teaching or formulas, plans or models, permitting the use or application of experience gathered on a particular subject. They also pointed out that the definition of the term royalties could be broadened through bilateral negotiations to include gains derived from the alienation of any such right or property that were contingent on the productivity, use or disposition thereof. The Group agreed that literary copyrights could be interpreted to include copyrights relating to international news.

Paragraph 4

18.   This paragraph reproduces with modifications Article 12, paragraph 3, of the OECD Model Convention, which states that paragraph 1 does not apply to royalties beneficially owned by a person having a permanent establishment or permanent base in the source country if the right or property from which the royalties derive is effectively connected with the permanent establishment or fixed base. The Group decided to modify paragraph 3 of the OECD Model Convention by introducing a limited force of attraction principle. In addition to royalties excluded from the application of paragraph 1 by paragraph 3 of the OECD Article, paragraph 4 of the United Nations Model Convention excludes royalties which are received in connection with business activities described in subparagraph (*c*) of paragraph 1 of article 7 (business activities of the same or similar kind as those of a permanent establishment in the source country), even if the business activities are not carried on through a permanent establishment or a fixed base. The United Nations Model Convention also modifies the paragraph to refer to paragraph 2 as well as paragraph 1.

Paragraph 5

19.   This paragraph, which provides that royalties are considered income from sources in the residence country of the payer of the royalties, is an innovation of the United Nations Model Convention, not found in Article 12 of the OECD Model Convention.

20.   As in the case of interest, some members suggested that some countries may wish to substitute a rule that would identify the source of a royalty as the State in which the property or right giving rise to the royalty (the patent etc.) is used. Where, in bilateral negotiations, the two parties differ on the appropriate rule, a possible solution would be a rule which, in general, would accept the payer's place of residence as the source of royalty; but where the right or property for which the royalty was paid was used in the State having a place of use rule, the royalty would be deemed to arise in that State.

Paragraph 6

21.   This paragraph reproduces Article 12, paragraph 4, of the OECD Model Convention, the Commentary on which reads as follows:

> "The purpose of this paragraph is to restrict the operation of the provisions concerning the taxation of royalties in cases where, by reason of a special relationship between the payer and the beneficial owner or between both of them and some other person, the amount of the royalties paid exceeds the amount which would have been agreed upon by the payer and the beneficial owner had they stipulated at arm's length. It provides that in such a case the provisions of the Article apply only to that last-mentioned amount and that the excess part of the royalty shall remain taxable according to the laws of the two Contracting States, due regard being had to the other provision of the Convention." [para. 22]

> "It is clear from the text that for this clause to apply the payment held excessive must be due to a special relationship between the payer and the beneficial owner or between both of them and some other person. There may be cited as examples cases where royalties are paid to an individual or legal person who directly or indirectly controls the payer, or who is directly or indirectly controlled by him or is subordinate to a group having common interest with him. These examples, moreover,

are similar or analogous to the cases contemplated by Article 9." [para. 23]

"On the other hand, the concept of special relationship also covers relationship by blood or marriage and, in general, any community of interests as distinct from the legal relationship giving rise to the payment of the royalty." [para. 24]

"With regard to the taxation treatment to be applied to the excess part of the royalty, the exact nature of such excess will need to be ascertained according to the circumstances of each case, in order to determine the category of income in which it should be classified for the purpose of applying the provisions of the tax laws of the States concerned and the provisions of the Convention. If two Contracting States should have difficulty in determining the other provisions of the Convention applicable, as cases required, to the excess part of the royalties there would be nothing to prevent them from introducing additional clarifications in the last sentence of paragraph 4, as long as they do not alter its general purport." [para. 25]

"Should the principles and rules of their respective laws oblige the two Contracting States to apply different Articles of the Convention for the purpose of taxing the excess, it will be necessary to resort to the mutual agreement procedure provided by the Convention in order to resolve the difficulty." [para. 26]

22.   Some members of the Group of Experts pointed out that there are very artificial devices entered into by persons to take advantage of the provisions of article 12 through, inter alia, creation or assignment of agreements for the use, right or information with respect to intangible assets for which royalties are charged. While substance over form rules, abuse of rights principles or any similar doctrine could be used to counter such arrangements, Contracting States which may want to specifically address the issue may include a clause on the following lines in their bilateral tax treaties:

"The provisions of this article shall not apply if it was the main purpose, or one of the main purposes, of any persons con-

cerned with the creation or the assignment of the rights in respect of which the royalties are paid to take advantage of this
article by means of that creation or assignment."

Article 13

CAPITAL GAINS

A. GENERAL CONSIDERATIONS

1.   Article 13 of the United Nations Model Convention consists of
the first three paragraphs of Article 13 of the OECD Model Convention, followed by two new paragraphs (paragraphs 4 and 5) and by
the text of Article 13, paragraph 4, of the OECD Model Convention
renumbered as paragraph 6 and adjusted to take into account the insertion of the two new paragraphs.

2.   The text of this article resulted from a compromise which the
Group felt would be most acceptable to both developed and developing countries. Some members from developed countries advocated
the use of Article 13 of the OECD Model Convention, which (1) allows the source country to tax capital gains from the alienation of immovable property and from movable property that is a part of a
permanent establishment or pertains to a fixed base for performing
independent personal services, (2) permits gains from the alienation
of ships and aircraft to be taxed only in the State of effective management of the relevant enterprises, and (3) reserves to the residence
country the right to tax gains on other forms of alienable property.
Most members from developing countries advocated the right of the
source country to levy a tax in situations in which the OECD reserves
that right to the country of residence.

3.   Concerning the taxation of capital gains in both developed and
developing countries, the following remarks from the preliminary remarks in the Commentary on Article 13 of the OECD Model Convention are pertinent:

"A comparison of the tax laws of the OECD Member countries shows that the taxation of capital gains varies considerably from country to country:

—in some countries capital gains are not deemed to be taxable income;

—in other countries capital gains accrued to an enterprise are taxed, but capital gains made by an individual outside the course of his trade or business are not taxed;

—even where capital gains made by an individual outside the course of his trade or business are taxed, such taxation often applies only in specified cases, e.g., profits from the sale of immovable property or speculative gains (where an asset was bought to be resold)." [para. 1]

"Moreover, the taxes on capital gains vary from country to country. In some OECD Member countries, capital gains are taxed as ordinary income and therefore added to the income from other sources. This applies especially to the capital gains made by the alienation of assets of an enterprise. In a number of OECD Member countries, however, capital gains are subject to special taxes, such as taxes on profits from the alienation of immovable property, or general capital gains taxes, or taxes on capital appreciation (increment taxes). Such taxes are levied on each capital gain or on the sum of the capital gains accrued during a year, mostly at special rates which do not take into account the other income (or losses) of the taxpayer. It does not seem necessary to describe all those taxes." [para. 2]

"The Article does not deal with the above-mentioned questions. It is left to the domestic law of each Contracting State to decide whether capital gains should be taxed and, if they are taxable, how they are to be taxed. The Article can in no way be construed as giving a State the right to tax capital gains if such right is not provided for in its domestic law. The Article does not specify to what kind of tax it applies. It is understood that the Article must apply to all kinds of taxes levied by a Contracting State on capital gains. The wording of Article 2 is large enough to achieve this aim and to include also special taxes on capital gains." [para. 3]

4.   The OECD Commentary on Article 13 contains the following general remarks:

"It is normal to give the right to tax capital gains on a property of a given kind to the State which under the Convention is entitled to tax both the property and the income derived therefrom. The right to tax a gain from the alienation of a business asset must be given to the same State without regard to the question whether such gain is a capital gain or a business profit. Accordingly, no distinction between capital gains and commercial profits is made nor is it necessary to have special provisions as to whether the article on capital gains or Article 7 on the taxation of business profits should apply. It is however left to the domestic law of the taxing State to decide whether a tax on capital gains or on ordinary income must be levied. The Convention does not prejudge this question." [para. 4]

"The Article does not give a detailed definition of capital gains. This is not necessary for the reasons mentioned above. The words 'alienation of property' are used to cover in particular capital gains resulting from the sale or exchange of property and also from a partial alienation, the expropriation, the transfer to a company in exchange for stock, the sale of a right, the gift and even the passing of property on death." [para. 5]

"Most States taxing capital gains do so when an alienation of capital assets takes place. Some of them, however, tax only so-called realized capital gains. Under certain circumstances, though there is an alienation no realized capital gain is recognized for tax purposes (e.g., when the alienation proceeds are used for acquiring new assets). Whether or not there is a realization has to be determined according to the applicable domestic tax law. No particular problems arise when the State which has the right to tax does not exercise it at the time the alienation takes place." [para. 6]

"As a rule, appreciation in value not associated with the alienation of a capital asset is not taxed, since, as long as the owner still holds the asset in question, the capital gain exists only on paper. There are, however, tax laws under which capital appreciation and revaluation of business assets are taxed even if there is no alienation." [para. 7]

"Special circumstances may lead to the taxation of the capital appreciation of an asset that has not been alienated. This may be the case if the value of a capital asset has increased in such a manner that the owner proceeds to the revaluation of this asset in his books. Such revaluation of assets in the books may also occur in the case of a depreciation of the national currency. A number of States levy special taxes on such book profits, amounts put into reserve, an increase in the paid-up capital and other revaluations resulting from the adjustment of the book value to the intrinsic value of a capital asset. These taxes on capital appreciation (increment taxes) are covered by the Convention according to Article 2." [para. 8]

"Where capital appreciation and revaluation of business assets are taxed, the same principle should, as a rule, apply as in the case of the alienation of such assets. It has not been found necessary to mention such cases expressly in the Article or to lay down special rules. The provisions of the Article as well as those of Articles 6, 7 and 21, seem to be sufficient. As a rule, the right to tax is conferred by the above-mentioned provisions on the State of which the alienator is a resident, except that in the cases of immovable property or of movable property forming part of the business property of a permanent establishment or pertaining to a fixed base, the prior right to tax belongs to the State where such property is situated. Special attention must be drawn, however, to the cases dealt with in paragraphs 13 to 17 below." [para. 9]

"In some States the transfer of an asset from a permanent establishment situated in the territory of such State to a permanent establishment or the head office of the same enterprise situated in another State is assimilated to an alienation of property. The Article does not prevent these States from taxing profits or gains deemed to arise in connection with such a transfer, provided, however, that such taxation is in accordance with Article 7." [para. 10]

"The Article does not distinguish as to the origin of the capital gain. Therefore all capital gains, those accruing over a long term, parallel to a steady improvement in economic conditions, as well as those accruing in a very short period (speculative gains), are covered. Also capital gains which are due to depreciation of the national currency are covered. It is, of course, left to each State to decide whether or not such gains should be taxed." [para. 11]

"The Article does not specify how to compute a capital gain, this being left to the domestic law applicable. As a rule, capital gains are calculated by deducting the cost from the selling price. To arrive at cost all expenses incidental to the purchase and all expenditure for improvements are added to the purchase price. In some cases the cost after deduction of the depreciation allowances already given is taken into account. Some tax laws prescribe another base instead of cost, e.g., the value previously reported by the alienator of the asset for capital tax purposes." [para. 12]

"Special problems may arise when the basis for the taxation of capital gains is not uniform in the two Contracting States. The capital gain from the alienation of an asset computed in one State according to the rules mentioned in paragraph 12 above, may not necessarily coincide with the capital gain computed in the other State under the accounting rules used there. This may occur when one State has the right to tax capital gains because it is the State of situs while the other State has the right to tax because the enterprise is a resident of that other State." [para. 13]

"The following example may illustrate this problem: an enterprise of State A bought immovable property situated in State B. The enterprise may have entered depreciation allowances in the books kept in State A. If such immovable property is sold at a price which is above cost, a capital gain may be realized and, in addition, the depreciation allowances granted earlier may be recovered. State B in which the immovable property is situated and where no books are kept does not have to take into account, when taxing the income from the immovable property, the depreciation allowances booked in State A. Neither can State B substitute the value of the immovable property shown in the books kept in State A for the cost at the time of the alienation. State B cannot, therefore, tax the depreciation allowances realized in addition to the capital gain as mentioned in paragraph 12 above." [para. 14]

"On the other hand, State A, of which the alienator is a resident, cannot be obliged in all cases to exempt such book profits fully from its taxes under paragraph 1 of the Article and Article 23 A (there will be hardly any problems for States applying the tax credit method). To the extent that such book profits are due to the realization of the depreciation allowances previously claimed in State A and which had reduced the income or profits taxable in such State A, that State cannot be prevented from taxing such book profits . . ." [para. 15]

"Further problems may arise in connection with profits due to changes of the rate of exchange between the currencies of State A and State B. After the devaluation of the currency of State A, enterprises of such State A may, or may have to, increase the book value of the assets situated outside the territory of State A. Apart from any devaluation of the currency of a State, the usual fluctuations of the rate of exchange may give rise to so-called currency gains or losses. Take for example an enterprise of State A having bought and sold immovable property situated in State B. If the cost and the selling price, both expressed in the currency of State B, are equal, there will be no capital gain in State B. When the value of the currency of State B has risen between the purchase and the sale of the asset in relation to the currency of State A, in the currency of that State a profit will accrue to such enterprise. If the value of the currency of State B has fallen in the meantime, the alienator will sustain a loss which will not be recognized in State B. Such currency gains or losses may also arise in connection with claims and debts contracted in a foreign currency. If the balance sheet of a permanent establishment situated in State B of an enterprise of State A shows claims and debts expressed in the currency of State B, the books of the permanent establishment do not show any gain or loss when repayments are made. Changes of the rate of exchange may be reflected, however, in the accounts of the head office. If the value of the currency of State B has risen (fallen) between the time the claim has originated and its repayment, the enterprise, as a whole will realize a gain (sustain a loss). This is true also with respect to debts if between the time they have originated and their repayment, the currency of State B has fallen (risen) in value." [para. 16]

"The provisions of the article do not settle all questions regarding the taxation of such currency gains. Such gains are in most cases not connected with an alienation of the asset; they may often not even be determined in the State on which the right to tax capital gains is conferred by the Article. Accordingly, the question, as a rule, is not whether the State in which a permanent establishment is situated has a right to tax, but whether the State of which the taxpayer is a resident must, if applying the exemption method, refrain from taxing such currency gains which, in many cases, cannot be shown but in the books kept in the head office. The answer to that latter question depends not only on the Article but also on Article 7 and on Article 23 A. If in a given case differing opinions of two States should result in an actual double taxation, the case should be settled under the mutual agreement procedure provided for by Article 25." [para. 17]

"Moreover, the question arises which Article should apply when there is paid for property sold an annuity during the lifetime of the alienator and not a fixed price. Are such annuity payments, as far as they exceed costs, to be dealt with as a gain from the alienation of the property or as 'income not dealt with' according to Article 21? Both opinions may be supported by arguments of equivalent weight, and it seems difficult to give one rule on the matter. In addition such problems are rare in practice, so it therefore seems unnecessary to establish a rule for insertion in the Convention. It may be left to Contracting States, who may be involved in such a question, to adopt a solution in the mutual agreement procedure provided for by Article 25." [para. 18]

"The Article is not intended to apply to prizes in a lottery or to premiums and prizes attaching to bonds or debentures." [para. 19]

"The Article deals first with the gains which may be taxed in the State where the alienated property is situated. For all other capital gains, paragraph [6] gives the right to tax to the State of which the alienator is a resident." [para. 20]

"As capital gains are not taxed by all States, it may be considered reasonable to avoid only actual double taxation of capital gains. Therefore, Contracting States are free to supplement their bilateral convention in such a way that a State has to forgo its right to tax conferred on it by the domestic laws only if the other State on which the right to tax is conferred by the Convention makes use thereof. In such a case, paragraph [6] of the Article should be supplemented accordingly. Besides, a modification of Article 23 A as suggested in . . . the Commentary on Article 23 A is needed." [para. 21]

B.   COMMENTARY ON THE PARAGRAPHS OF ARTICLE 13

Paragraph 1

5.   This paragraph reproduces Article 13, paragraph 1, of the OECD Model Convention, the Commentary on which is as follows:

"Paragraph 1 states that gains from the alienation of immovable property may be taxed in the State in which it is situated. This rule corresponds to the provisions of Article 6 and of paragraph 1 of Article 22. It applies also to immovable property forming part of the assets of an enterprise or used for performing independent personal services. For the definition of immovable property paragraph 1 refers to Article 6. Paragraph 1 of Article 13 deals only with gains which a resident of a Contracting State derives from the alienation of immovable property situated in the other Contracting State. It does not, therefore, apply to gains derived from the alienation of immovable property situated in the Contracting State of which the alienator is a resident in the meaning of Article 4 or situated in a third State; the provisions of paragraph 1 of Article 21 shall apply to such gains." [para. 22]

"Certain tax laws assimilate the alienation of all or part of the shares in a company, the exclusive or main aim of which is to hold immovable property, to the alienation of such immovable property. In itself paragraph 1 does not allow that practice: a special provision in the bilateral convention can alone provide for such an assimilation. Contracting States are of course free either to include in their bilateral conventions such special provision; or to confirm expressly that the alienation of shares cannot be assimilated to the alienation of the immovable property". [para. 23]

Paragraph 2

6. This paragraph reproduces Article 13, paragraph 2, of the OECD Model Convention, the Commentary on which reads as follows:

"Paragraph 2 deals with movable property forming part of the business property of a permanent establishment of an enterprise or pertaining to a fixed base used for performing independent personal services. The term 'movable property' means all property other than immovable property which is dealt with in paragraph 1. It includes also incorporeal property, such as goodwill, licences etc. Gains from the alienation of such assets may be taxed in the State in which the permanent establishment or fixed base is situated, which corresponds to the rules for business profits and for income from independent personal services (Articles 7 and 14)." [para. 24]

"The paragraph makes clear that its rules apply when movable property of a permanent establishment or fixed base is alienated as well as when the permanent establishment as such (alone or with the whole enterprise) or the fixed base as such is alienated. If the whole enterprise is alienated, then the rule applies to such gains which are deemed to result from the alienation of movable property forming part of the business property of the permanent establishment. The rules of Article 7 should then apply mutatis mutandis without express reference thereto. For the transfer of an asset from a permanent establishment in one State to a permanent establishment (or the head office) in another State, cf. paragraph 10 above." [para. 25]

"On the other hand, paragraph 2 may not always be applicable to capital gains from the alienation of a participation in an enterprise. The provision applies only to property which was owned by the alienator, either wholly or jointly with another person. Under the laws of some countries, capital assets of a partnership are considered to be owned by the partners. Under some other laws, however, partnerships and other associations are treated as body corporate for tax purposes, distinct from their partners (members), which means that participation in such entities are dealt with in the same way as shares in a company. Capital gains from the alienation of such participation like capital gains from the alienation of shares, are therefore taxable only in the State of residence of the alienator. Contracting States may agree bilaterally on special rules governing the taxation of capital gains from the alienation of a participation in a partnership." [para. 26]

"Certain States consider that all capital gains arising from sources in their territory should be subject to their taxes according to their domestic laws, if the alienator has a permanent establishment within their territory. Paragraph 2 is not based on such a conception which is sometimes referred to as 'the force of attraction of the permanent establishment'. The paragraph merely provides that gains from the alienation of movable property forming part of the business property of a permanent establishment or of movable property pertaining to a fixed base used for performing independent personal services may be taxed in the State where the permanent establishment or the fixed base is situated. The gains from the alienation of all other movable property are taxable only in the State of residence of the alienator as provided in paragraph 4 [paragraph 6 of the United Nations text]. The foregoing explanations accord with those in the Commentary on Article 7." [para. 27]

Paragraph 3

7.   This paragraph reproduces Article 13, paragraph 3, of the OECD Model Convention, the Commentary on which is as follows:

"An exception from the rule of paragraph 2 is provided for ships and aircraft operated in international traffic and for boats engaged in inland waterways transport and movable property pertaining to the operation of such ships, aircraft and boats. Gains from the alienation of such assets are taxable only in the State in which the place of effective management of the enterprise operating such ships, aircraft and boats is situated. This rule corresponds to the provisions of Article 8 and of paragraph 3 of Article 22. It is understood that paragraph 3 of Article 8 is applicable if the place of effective management of such enterprise is aboard a ship or a boat. Contracting States which would prefer to confer the exclusive taxing right on the State of residence or to use a combination of the residence criterion and the place of effective management criterion are free, in bilateral conventions, to substitute to paragraph 3 a provision corresponding to those proposed in . . . the Commentary on Article 8." [para. 28]

Paragraph 4

8.   This paragraph, which allows a Contracting State to tax a gain on an alienation of shares of a company or on an alienation of interests in other entities the property of which consists principally of immovable property situated in that State and is not found in the OECD Model Convention, is designed to prevent the avoidance of taxes on the gains from the sale of immovable property. Since it is often relatively easy to avoid taxes on such gains through the incorporation of such property, it is necessary to tax the sale of shares in such a company. This is especially so where ownership of the shares carries the right to occupy the property. In order to achieve its objective, paragraph 4 would have to apply regardless of whether the company is a resident of the Contracting State in which the immovable property is situated or a resident of another State. In 1999, the Group of Experts decided to amend paragraph 4 to expand its scope to include interests in partnerships, trusts and estates which own immovable property. It also decided to exclude from its scope such entities whose property consists directly or indirectly principally of immovable property used by them in their business activities. However, this exclusion will not apply to an immovable property management company, partnership, trust or estate. In order to fulfil its purpose, paragraph 4 must apply whether the company, partnership, trust or estate owns the immovable property directly or indirectly, such as, through one or more interposed entities. Contracting States may agree in bilateral negotiations on paragraph 4 also applying to gains from the alienation of other corporate interests or rights forming part of a substantial participation in a company. For the purpose of this paragraph, the term "principally" in relation to the ownership of an immovable property means the value of such immovable property exceeding 50 per cent of the aggregate value of all assets owned by such company, partnership, trust or estate.

Paragraph 5

9.   The Group of Experts had examined the question of laying down a concessional rate of tax (compared to normal domestic rate)

on gains arising on alienation of shares, other than the shares referred to in paragraph 4, that is, not being shares of principally immovable property owning companies. Since the gains arising on alienation of shares being taxed in a concessional manner is likely to encourage investment in shares, promote foreign direct investment and portfolio investment, and thereby give impetus to the industrialization of the country, the Contracting States may consider discussing this matter during bilateral negotiations and make necessary provision in the bilateral tax treaties.

10.   During the discussion of this paragraph, several members of the Group argued that a Contracting State should be able to tax gain on a sale of shares of a company resident in that State, whether the sale occurs within or outside the State, but it was recognized that for administrative reasons the right to tax should be limited to sale of substantial participation. The determination of what is a substantial participation was left to bilateral negotiations, in the course of which an agreed percentage can be determined.

11.   Some countries might consider that the Contracting State in which a company is resident should be allowed to tax the alienation of its shares only if a substantial portion of the company's assets are situated in that State, and in bilateral negotiations might urge such a limitation. Other countries might prefer that paragraph 5 be omitted entirely.

Paragraph 6

12.   This paragraph reproduces Article 13, paragraph 4, of the OECD Model Convention with a drafting adjustment replacing the words "in paragraphs 1, 2 and 3" with "in paragraphs 1, 2, 3, 4 and 5". The Commentary on Article 13, paragraph 4, of the OECD Model Convention is therefore relevant, mutatis mutandis, to paragraph 6. This Commentary reads as follows:

> "As regards gains from the alienation of any property other than that referred to in paragraphs 1, 2 and 3, paragraph 4 provides that they are taxable only in the State of which the

alienator is a resident. This corresponds to the rules laid down in Article 22." [para. 29]

"The Article does not contain special rules for gains from the alienation of shares in a company or of securities, bonds, debentures and the like. Such gains are, therefore, taxable only in the State of which the alienator is a resident." [para. 30]

"If shares are sold by a shareholder to the issuing company in connection with the liquidation of such company or the reduction of its paid-up capital, the difference between the selling price and the par value of the shares may be treated in the State of which the company is a resident as a distribution of accumulated profits and not as a capital gain. The Article does not prevent the State of residence of the company from taxing such distributions at the rates provided for in Article 10: such taxation is permitted because such difference is covered by the definition of the term 'dividends' contained in paragraph 3 of Article 10 and interpreted in paragraph 28 of the Commentary relating thereto. The same interpretation may apply if bonds or debentures are redeemed by the debtor at a price which is higher than the par value or the value at which the bonds or debentures have been issued; in such a case, the difference may represent interest and, therefore, be subjected to a limited tax in the State of source of the interest in accordance with Article 11." [para. 31]

13.   However, as indicated in paragraph 2 above, most members from developing counries suggested the following alternative to Article 13, paragraph 4, of the OECD Model Convention:

"4.   Gains from the alienation of any property other than those gains mentioned in paragraphs 1, 2 and 3 may be taxed in the Contracting State in which they arise according to the law of that State."

This alternative is equivalent to saying that either or both States may tax according to their own laws and that the State of residence will eliminate double taxation under article 23. Countries choosing this alternative may wish through bilateral negotiations to clarify which particular source rules will apply to establish where a gain shall be considered to arise.

Article 14

INDEPENDENT PERSONAL SERVICES

1.   Article 14 of the United Nations Model Convention reproduces in subparagraph 1(*a*) and paragraph 2 the essential provisions of Article 14 of the OECD Model Convention. Paragraph 1, subparagraph (*b*), allows the country of source to tax in one situation in addition to the one contained in Article 14, paragraph 1, of the OECD Model Convention. More completely, while the OECD Model Convention allows the source country to tax income from independent personal services only if the income is attributable to a fixed base of the taxpayer, the United Nations Model Convention also allows taxation at source if the taxpayer is present in that country for more than 183 days in any twelve-month period commencing or ending in the fiscal year concerned.

2.   In the discussion of article 14, some members from developing countries expressed the view that taxation by the source country should not be restricted by the criteria of existence of a fixed base and length of stay and that the source of income should be the only criterion. Some members from developed countries, on the other hand, felt that the exportation of skills, like the exportation of tangible goods, should not give rise to taxation in the country of destination unless the person concerned has a fixed base in that country comparable to a permanent establishment. They therefore supported the fixed base criterion, although they also accepted that taxation in the source country is justified by continued presence in that country of the person rendering the service. Some members from developing countries also expressed support for the fixed base criterion. Other members from developing countries expressed preference for the criterion based on length of stay.

3.   In developing the 1980 Model, several members from developing countries had proposed a third criterion, namely, that of the amount of remuneration. Under that criterion, remuneration for independent personal services could be taxed by the source country if it exceeded a specified amount, regardless of the existence of a fixed base or the length of stay in that country.

4.   As a compromise, the 1980 Model included three alternative criteria found in subparagraphs (a)-(c) of paragraph 1, the satisfaction of any one of which would give the source country the right to tax the income derived from the performance of personal activities by an individual who is a resident of the other State. However, in 1999, the Group of Experts decided to omit the third criterion, namely, the amount of remuneration, specified in subparagraph (c), retaining subparagraphs (a) and (b).

5.   Subparagraph (a), which reproduces the sole criterion in the OECD Model Convention, provides that the income may be taxed if the individual has a fixed base regularly available to him for performing his activities. Though the presence of a fixed base gives the right to tax, the amount of income that is subject to tax is limited to that which is attributable to the fixed base.

6.   Subparagraph (b) as amended in 1999, extends the source country's right to tax by providing that the source country may tax if the individual is present in the country for a period or periods aggregating at least 183 days in any twelve-month period commencing or ending in the fiscal year concerned, even if there is no fixed base. Only income derived from activities exercised in that country, however, may be taxed. Prior to the amendment, the requirement of minimum stay in the Contracting State was a "period or periods amounting to or exceeding in the aggregate 183 days in the fiscal year concerned". A member from a developed country, however, expressed a preference for retaining the previous wording for technical reasons. By virtue of the amendment, the provisions of article 14, paragraph 1, subparagraph (b), have been brought on a par with those of article 15, paragraph 2, subparagraph (a), relating to the minimum period of stay in the other Contracting State.

7.   Prior to its deletion, subparagraph (c) provided a further criterion for source country tax when neither of the two conditions specified in subparagraphs (a) and (b) is met. It was provided that if the remuneration for the services performed in the source country exceeds a certain amount (to be determined in bilateral negotiations), the source country may tax, but only if the remuneration is received from a resident of the source country or from a permanent establishment or fixed base of a resident of any other country which is situated in that country.

8.   It was observed that any monetary ceiling limit fixed in this behalf becomes meaningless over a period of time due to inflation and would only have the effect of limiting the amount of potentially valuable services that the country will be able to import. Moreover, the provision to this effect appeared only in 6 per cent of the existing bilateral tax treaties finalized between 1980 and 1997. It was, accordingly, decided to delete subparagraph (c) of paragraph 1 of article 14.

9.   The Group discussed the relationship between article 14 and subparagraph 3(b) of article 5. It was generally agreed that remuneration paid directly to an individual for his performance of activity in an independent capacity was subject to the provisions of article 14. Payments to an enterprise in respect of the furnishing by that enterprise of the activities of employees or other personnel are subject to articles 5 and 7. The remuneration paid by the enterprise to the individual who performed the activities is subject either to article 14 (if he is an independent contractor engaged by the enterprise to perform the activities) or article 15 (if he is an employee of the enterprise). If the parties believe that further clarification of the relationship between article 14 and articles 5 and 7 is needed, they may make such clarification in the course of negotiations.

10.   Since article 14 of the United Nations Model Convention contains all the essential provisions of Article 14 of the OECD Model Convention, the Commentary on that Article is relevant. That Commentary reads as follows:

"The Article is concerned with what are commonly known as professional services and with other activities of an independent character. This excludes industrial and commercial activities and also professional services performed in employment, e.g., a physician serving as a medical officer in a factory. It should, however, be observed that the article does not concern independent activities of artistes and sportsmen, these being covered by Article 17." [para. 1]

"The meaning of the term 'professional services' is illustrated by some examples of typical liberal professions. The enumeration has an explanatory character only and is not exhaustive. Difficulties of interpretation which might arise in special cases may be solved by mutual agreement between the competent authorities of the Contracting States concerned." [para. 2]

"The provisions of the Article are similar to those for business profits and rest in fact on the same principles as those of Article 7. The provisions of Article 7 and the Commentary thereon could therefore be used as guidance for interpreting and applying Article 14. Thus the principles laid down in Article 7 for instance as regards allocation of profits between head office and permanent establishment could be applied also in apportioning income between the State of residence of a person performing independent personal services and the State where such services are performed from a fixed base. Equally, expenses incurred for the purposes of a fixed base, including executive and general expenses, should be allowed as deductions in determining the income attributable to a fixed base in the same way as such expenses incurred for the purposes of a permanent establishment. Also in other respects Article 7 and the Commentary thereon could be of assistance for the interpretation of Article 14, e.g., in determining whether computer software payments should be classified as commercial income within article 7 or 14 or as royalties within Article 12." [para. 3]

"Even if Articles 7 and 14 are based on the same principles, it was thought that the concept of permanent establishment should be reserved for commercial and industrial activities. The term 'fixed base' has therefore been used. It has not been thought appropriate to try to define it, but it would cover, for instance, a physician's consulting room or the office of an architect or a lawyer. A person performing independent personal services would probably not as a rule have premises of this kind in any other State than of his residence. But if there is in another State a centre of activity of a fixed or a permanent character, then that State should be entitled to tax the person's activities." [para. 4]

Article 15

DEPENDENT PERSONAL SERVICES

1.   Article 15 of the United Nations Model Convention reproduces Article 15 of the OECD Model Convention, the Commentary on which reads as follows:

"Paragraph 1 establishes the general rule as to the taxation of income from employment (other than pensions), namely, that such income is taxable in the State where the employment is actually exercised. Employment is exercised in the place where the employee is physically present when performing the activities for which the employment income is paid. One consequence of this would be that a resident of a Contracting State who derived remuneration, in respect of an employment, from sources in the other State could not be taxed in that other State in respect of that remuneration merely because the results of this work were exploited in that other State." [para. 1]

"The general rule is subject to exception only in the case of pensions (Article 18) and of remuneration and pensions in respect of government service (Article 19). Non-employment remuneration of members of boards of directors of companies is the subject of Article 16." [para. 2]

"Member countries have generally understood the term 'salaries, wages and other similar remuneration' to include

216

benefits in kind received in respect of an employment (e.g., the use of a residence or automobile, health or life insurance coverage and club memberships)." [para. 2.1]

"Paragraph 2 contains, however, a general exception to the rule in paragraph 1. This exception covers all individuals rendering dependent personal services (sales representatives, construction workers, engineers etc.), to the extent that their remuneration does not fall under the provisions of other Articles, such as those applying to government services or artistes and sportsmen." [para. 3]

"The three conditions prescribed in this paragraph must be satisfied for the remuneration to qualify for the exemption. The first condition is that the exemption is limited to the 183-day period. It is further stipulated that this time period may not be exceeded 'in any twelve-month period commencing or ending in the fiscal year concerned'. This contrasts with the 1963 Draft Convention and the 1977 Model Convention which provided that the 183-day period[15] should not be exceeded 'in the fiscal year concerned', a formulation that created difficulties in cases where the fiscal years of the Contracting States did not coincide and which opened up opportunities in the sense that operations were sometimes organized in such a way that, for example, workers stayed in the State concerned for the last 5½ months of one year and the first 5½ months of the following year. The present wording of subparagraph 2(*a*) does away with such opportunities for tax avoidance." [para. 4]

"Although various formulas have been used by Member countries to calculate the 183-day period, there is only one way which is consistent with the wording of this paragraph: the 'days of physical presence' method. The application of this method is straightforward as the individual is either present in a country or he is not. The presence could also relatively easily

---

[15]The same change was made in 1999 in the United Nations Model Convention.

be documented by the taxpayer when evidence is required by the tax authorities. Under this method the following days are included in the calculation: part of a day, day of arrival, day of departure and all other days spent inside the State of activity such as Saturdays and Sundays, national holidays, holidays before, during and after the activity, short breaks (training, strikes, lockout, delays in supplies), days of sickness (unless they prevent the individual from leaving and he would have otherwise qualified for the exemption) and death or sickness in the family. However, days spent in the State of activity in transit in the course of a trip between two points outside the State of activity should be excluded from the computation. It follows from these principles that any entire day spent outside the State of activity, whether for holidays, business trips, or any other reason, should not be taken into account. A day during any part of which, however brief, the taxpayer is present in a State counts as a day of presence in that State for purposes of computing the 183-day period." [para. 5]

"The second condition is that the employer paying the remuneration must not be a resident of the State in which the employment is exercised. Some Member countries may, however, consider that it is appropriate to extend the exception of paragraph 2 to cases where the employer is not a resident of the State of residence of the employee, as there might then be administrative difficulties in determining the employment income of the employee or in enforcing withholding obligations on the employer. Contracting States that share this view are free to adopt bilaterally the following alternative wording of subparagraph 2(b):

'(b)   the remuneration is paid by, or on behalf of, an employer who is a resident of the first-mentioned State, and'." [para. 7]

"Under the third condition, if the employer has in the State in which the employment is exercised a permanent establishment (or a fixed base if he performs professional services or other activities of an independent character), the exemption is given only on condition that the remuneration is not borne by a permanent establishment or a fixed base which he has in that State." [para. 7.1]

"Paragraph 2 has given rise to numerous cases of abuse through adoption of the practice known as 'international hiring-out of labour'. In this system, a local employer wishing to employ foreign labour for one or more periods of less than 183 days recruits through an intermediary established abroad who purports to be the employer and hires the labour out to the employer. The worker thus fulfils prima facie the three conditions laid down by paragraph 2 and may claim exemption from taxation in the country where he is temporarily working. To prevent such abuse, in situations of this type, the 'employer' should be interpreted in the context of paragraph 2. In this respect, it should be noted that the term 'employer' is not defined in the Convention but it is understood that the employer is the person having rights on the work produced and bearing the relative responsibility and risks. In cases of international hiring-out of labour, these functions are to a large extent exercised by the user. In this context, substance should prevail over form, i.e., each case should be examined to see whether the functions of employer were exercised mainly by the intermediary or by the user. It is therefore up to the Contracting States to agree on situations in which the intermediary does not fulfil the conditions required for him to be considered as the employer within the meaning of paragraph 2. In settling this question, the competent authorities may refer not only to the above-mentioned indications but to a number of circumstances enabling them to establish that the real employer is the user of the labour (and not the foreign intermediary):

—the hirer does not bear the responsibility or risk for the results produced by the employee's work;

—the authority to instruct the worker lies with the user;

—the work is performed at a place which is under the control and responsibility of the user;

—the remuneration to the hirer is calculated on the basis of the time utilized, or there is in other ways a connection between this remuneration and wages received by the employee;

—tools and materials are essentially put at the employee's disposal by the user;

—the number and qualifications of the employees are not solely determined by the hirer." [para. 8]

"Paragraph 3 applies to the remuneration of crews of ships or aircraft operated in international traffic, or of boats engaged in inland waterways transport, a rule which follows up to a certain extent the rule applied to the income from shipping, inland waterways transport and air transport—that is, to tax them in the Contracting State in which the place of effective management of the enterprise concerned is situated. In the Commentary on Article 8, it is indicated that Contracting States may agree to confer the right to tax such income on the State of the enterprise operating the ships, boats or aircraft. The reasons for introducing that possibility in the case of income from shipping, inland waterways and air transport operations are valid also in respect of remuneration of the crew. Accordingly Contracting States are left free to agree on a provision which gives the right to tax such remuneration to the State of the enterprise. Such a provision, as well as that of paragraph 3 of Article 15, assumes that the domestic laws of the State on which the right to tax is conferred allows it to tax the remuneration of a person in the service of the enterprise concerned, irrespective of his residence. It is understood that paragraph 3 of Article 8 is applicable if the place of effective management of a shipping enterprise or of an inland waterways transport enterprise is aboard a ship or boat. According to the domestic laws of some Member countries, tax is levied on remuneration received by non-resident members of the crew in respect of employment aboard ships only if the ship has the nationality of such a State. For that reason conventions concluded between these States provide that the right to tax such remuneration is given to the State of the nationality of the ship. On the other hand many States cannot make use of such a taxation right and the provision could in such cases lead to non-taxation. However, States having that taxation principle in their domestic laws may agree bilaterally to confer the right to tax remuneration in respect of employment aboard ships on the State of the nationality of the ship." [para. 9]

"It should be noted that no special rule regarding the taxation of income of frontier workers is included as it would be more suitable for the problems created by local conditions to be solved directly between the States concerned." [para. 10]

"No special provision has been made regarding remuneration derived by visiting professors or students employed with a view to their acquiring practical experience. Many conventions contain rules of some kind or other concerning such cases, the main purpose of which is to facilitate cultural relations by providing for a limited tax exemption. Sometimes, tax exemption is already provided under domestic taxation laws. The absence of specific rules should not be interpreted as constituting an obstacle to the inclusion of such rules in bilateral conventions whenever this is felt desirable." [para. 11]

2.   Although articles 14, 15, 19 and 23 may generally be adequate to prevent double taxation of visiting teachers, some countries may wish to include a visiting teachers article in their treaties. Reference is made to paragraphs 11 to 13 of the Commentary on article 20 for a comprehensive treatment of this subject.

Article 16

DIRECTORS' FEES AND REMUNERATION OF TOP-LEVEL MANAGERIAL OFFICIALS

1.   Article 16, paragraph 1, of the United Nations Model Convention reproduces Article 16 of the OECD Model Convention.

2.   Since article 16, paragraph 1, of the United Nations Model Convention reproduces the whole of Article 16 of the OECD Model Convention, the Commentary on the latter Article, which reads as follows, is relevant:

> "This Article relates to remuneration received by a resident of a Contracting State, whether an individual or a legal person, in the capacity of a member of a board of directors of a company which is a resident of the other Contracting State. Since it might sometimes be difficult to ascertain where the services are performed, the provision treats the services as performed in the State of residence of the company." [para. 1]

> "Member countries have generally understood the term 'fees and other similar payments' to include benefits in kind received by a person in that person's capacity as a member of the board of directors of a company (e.g., the use of a residence or automobile, health or life insurance coverage and club memberships)." [para. 1.1]

> "A member of the board of directors of a company often also has other functions with the company, e.g., as ordinary employee, adviser, consultant etc. It is clear that the Article does not apply to remuneration paid to such a person on account of such other functions." [para. 2] [This position does not apply under the United Nations Model Convention.]

> "In some countries organs of companies exist which are similar in function to the board of directors. Contracting States are free to include in bilateral conventions such organs of companies under a provision corresponding to Article 16." [para. 3]

3.   Article 16 of the United Nations Model Convention also includes a second paragraph not in the OECD Model Convention, dealing with remuneration received by top-level managerial officials.

4.   The Group of Experts decided that where a top-level managerial position of a company resident in a Contracting State is occupied by a resident of the other Contracting State, the remuneration paid to that official should be subject to the same principle as directors' fees.

The term "top-level managerial position" refers to a limited group of positions that involve primary responsibility for the general direction of the affairs of the company, apart from the activities of the directors. The term covers a person acting as both a director and a top-level manager.

Article 17

ARTISTES AND SPORTSPERSONS

1.   Article 17 of the United Nations Model Convention reproduces Article 17 of the OECD Model Convention with one modification. Instead of the word "sportsman" used in the OECD Model Convention (in place of "athlete" earlier used in both the United Nations and OECD Model Conventions), it has been decided to use the gender-neutral word "sportsperson", which unlike the term "entertainer" was not followed in paragraph 1 by illustrative examples but is nevertheless likewise to be construed in a broad manner consistent with the spirit and purpose of the article.

2.   The Commentary on Article 17 of the OECD Model Convention is as follows:

> "Paragraph 1 provides that artistes and sportsmen who are residents of a Contracting State may be taxed in the other Contracting State in which their personal activities as such are performed, whether these are of an independent or of a dependent nature. This provision is an exception to the rules in Article 14 and to that in paragraph 2 of Article 15, respectively." [para. 1]

> "This provision makes it possible to avoid the practical difficulties which often arise in taxing artistes and sportsmen performing abroad. Moreover, too strict provisions might in certain cases impede cultural exchanges. In order to overcome this disadvantage, the States concerned may, by common agreement, limit the application of paragraph 1 to independent activities. To achieve this it would be sufficient to amend the text of the Article so that an exception is made only to the provisions of Article 14. In such a case, artistes and sportsmen

performing for a salary or wages would automatically come within Article 15 and thus be entitled to the exemptions provided for in paragraph 2 of that Article." [para. 2]

"Paragraph 1 refers to artistes and sportsmen. It is not possible to give a precise definition of 'artiste', but paragraph 1 includes examples of persons who would be regarded as such. These examples should not be considered as exhaustive. On the one hand, the term 'artiste' clearly includes the stage performer, film actor, actor (including for instance a former sportsman) in a television commercial. The Article may also apply to income received from activities which involve a political, social, religious or charitable nature, if an entertainment character is present. On the other hand, it does not extend to a visiting conference speaker or to administrative or support staff (e.g., cameramen for a film, producers, film directors, choreographers, technical staff, road crew for a pop group etc.). In between there is a grey area where it is necessary to review the overall balance of the activities of the person concerned." [para. 3]

"An individual may both direct a show and act in it, or may direct and produce a television programme or film and take a role in it. In such cases it is necessary to look at what the individual actually does in the State where the performance takes place. If his activities in that State are predominantly of a performing nature, the Article will apply to all the resulting income he derives in that State. If, however, the performing element is a negligible part of what he does in that State, the whole of the income will fall outside the Article. In other cases an apportionment should be necessary." [para. 4]

"Whilst no precise definition is given of the term 'sportsmen', it is not restricted to participants in traditional athletic events (e.g., runners, jumpers, swimmers). It also covers, for example, golfers, jockeys, footballers, cricketers and tennis players, as well as racing drivers." [para. 5]

"The Article also applies to income from other activities which are usually regarded as of an entertainment character, such as those deriving from billiards and snooker, chess and bridge tournaments." [para. 6]

"Income received by impresarios etc. for arranging the appearance of an artiste or sportsman is outside the scope of the Article, but any income they receive on behalf of the artiste or sportsman is of course covered by it." [para. 7]

"Paragraph 1 applies to income derived directly and indirectly by an individual artiste or sportsman. In some cases the income will not be paid directly to the individual or his impresario or agent. For instance, a member of an orchestra may be paid a salary rather than receive payment for each separate performance: a Contracting State where a performance takes place is entitled, under paragraph 1, to tax the proportion of the musician's salary which corresponds to such a performance. Similarly, where an artiste or sportsman is employed by, e.g., a one-person company, the State where the performance takes place may tax an appropriate proportion of any remuneration paid to the individual. In addition, where its domestic laws 'look through' such entities and treat the income as accruing directly to the individual, paragraph 1 enables that State to tax income derived from appearances in its territory and accruing in the entity for the individual's benefit, even if the income is not actually paid as remuneration to the individual." [para. 8]

"Besides fees for their actual appearances, artistes and sportsmen often receive income in the form of royalties or of sponsorship or advertising fees. In general, other Articles would apply whenever there was no direct link between the income and a public exhibition by the performer in the country concerned. Royalties for intellectual property rights will normally be covered by Article 12 rather than Article 17 (cf. paragraph 18 of the Commentary on Article 12), but in general, advertising and sponsorship fees will fall outside the scope of Article 12. Article 17 will apply to advertising or sponsorship income etc. which is related directly or indirectly to performances or appearances in a given State. Similar income which could not be attributed to such performances or appearances would fall under the standard rules of Article 14 or Article 15, as appropriate. Payments received in the event of the cancellation of a performance are also outside the scope of Article 17, and fall under Articles 7, 14 or 15, as the case may be." [para. 9]

"The Article says nothing about how the income in question is to be computed. It is for a Contracting State's domestic law to determine the extent of any deductions for expenses. Domestic laws differ in this area, and some provide for taxation at source, at a low rate based on the gross amount paid to artistes and sportsmen. Such rules may also apply to income paid to groups or incorporated teams, troupes etc." [para. 10]

"Paragraph 1 of the Article deals with income derived by individual artistes and sportsmen from their personal activities. Paragraph 2 deals with situations where income from their activities accrues to other persons. If the income of an entertainer or sportsman accrues to another person, and the State of source does not have the statutory right to look through the person receiving the income to tax it as income of the performer, paragraph 2 provides that the portion of the income which cannot be taxed in the hands of the performer may be taxed in the hands of the person receiving the remuneration. If the person receiving the income is an enterprise, tax may be applied by the source country even if the income is not attributable to a permanent establishment there. If the person receiving the income is an individual, the income may be taxed even in the absence of a fixed base. But it will not always be so. There are three main situations of this kind.

(a)   The first is the management company which receives income for the appearance of, e.g., a group of sportsmen (which is not itself constituted as a legal entity).

(b)   The second is the team, troupe, orchestra etc. which is constituted as a legal entity. Income for performances may be paid to the entity. Individual members of the team, orchestra etc. will be liable to tax under paragraph 1, in the State in which a performance is given, on any remuneration (or income accruing for their benefit) as a counterpart to the performance; however, if the members are paid a fixed periodic remuneration and it would be difficult to allocate a portion of that income to a particular performance, Member countries may decide, unilaterally or bilaterally, not to tax it. The profit element accruing from a performance to the legal entity would be liable to tax under paragraph 2.

(c) The third situation involves certain tax avoidance devices in cases where remuneration for the performance of an artiste or sportsman is not paid to the artiste or sportsman himself but to another person, e.g., a so-called artiste company, in such a way that the income is taxed in the State where the activity is performed neither as personal service income to the artiste or sportsman nor as profits of the enterprise, in the absence of a permanent establishment. Some countries 'look through' such arrangements under their domestic law and deem the income to be derived by the artiste or sportsman; where this is so, paragraph 1 enables them to tax income resulting from activities in their territory. Other countries cannot do this. Where a performance takes place in such a country, paragraph 2 permits it to impose a tax on the profits diverted from the income of the artiste or sportsman to the enterprise. It may be, however, that the domestic laws of some States do not enable them to apply such a provision. Such States are free to agree to other solutions or to leave paragraph 2 out of their bilateral conventions." [para. 11]

"Where, in the cases dealt with in paragraphs 1 and 2, the exemption method for relieving double taxation is used by the State of residence of the person receiving the income, that State would be precluded from taxing such income even if the State where the activities were performed could not make use of its right to tax. It is therefore understood that the credit method should be used in such cases. The same result could be achieved by stipulating a subsidiary right to tax for the State of residence of the person receiving the income, if the State where the activities are performed cannot make use of the right conferred on it by paragraphs 1 and 2. Contracting States are free to choose any of these methods in order to ensure that the income does not escape taxation." [para. 12]

"Article 17 will ordinarily apply when the artiste or sportsman is employed by a Government and derives income from that Government . . . Certain conventions contain provisions excluding artistes and sportsmen employed in organizations which are subsidized out of public funds from the application of Article 17." [para. 13]

"Some countries may consider it appropriate to exclude from the scope of the Article events supported from public funds. Such countries are free to include a provision to achieve this but the exemptions should be based on clearly definable and objective criteria to ensure that they are given only where intended. Such a provision might read as follows:

'The provisions of paragraphs 1 and 2 shall not apply to income derived from activities performed in a Contracting State by artistes or sportsmen if the visit to that State is wholly or mainly supported by public funds of one or both of the Contracting States or political subdivisions or local authorities thereof. In such a case, the income is taxable only in the Contracting State in which the artiste or the sportsman is a resident.' " [para. 14]

3. Some members of the Group indicated that the examples given in the Commentary on Article 17, paragraph 2, of the OECD Model Convention should not be understood as limiting the field of application of taxation to the incomes mentioned in that Commentary. In fact, the wording of the Commentary would allow taxation of the enterprise in the other Contracting State, with the same limitations as those imposed for artistes or sportspersons resident in a Contracting State and carrying out activities in the other State.

4. On the other hand, members expressed the view that some countries might wish paragraph 2 to have a narrower scope.

Article 18

PENSIONS AND SOCIAL SECURITY PAYMENTS

A.   GENERAL CONSIDERATIONS

1.   Two alternative versions are given for article 18 of the United Nations Model Convention, article 18 A and article 18 B. Article 18 A, like Article 18 of the OECD Model Convention, assigns to the country of residence the exclusive right to tax pensions and other similar remuneration, but it departs from the OECD Article by granting to the source country the exclusive right to tax when the payments involved are made within the framework of a public scheme which is part of the social security system of that State or a political subdivision or a local authority thereof. Article 18 B provides for a sharing between the country of residence and the country of source of the right to tax pensions and other similar remuneration when the payments involved are not made within the framework of a public scheme which is part of the social security system of a State or a political subdivision or a local authority thereof. In the latter case, the right to tax belongs only to the source country.

2.   Some members of the Group pointed out that some countries wanted to be able to negotiate the question whether the country of residence should have the right to tax residents on social security payments.

B.   COMMENTARY ON THE TWO ALTERNATIVE VERSIONS OF ARTICLE 18

Commentary on the paragraphs of article 18 A

Paragraph 1

3.   Since article 18 A reproduces in its first paragraph the text of Article 18 of the OECD Model Convention, the Commentary on the latter Article is relevant. However, since the United Nations Model Convention provides a separate rule in paragraph 2, dealing with so-

cial security benefits, the discussion in the OECD Commentary of social security benefits is moved in this Commentary to the discussion of paragraph 2. The OECD Commentary observes:

> "According to this Article, pensions paid in respect of private employment are taxable only in the State of residence of the recipient. The provision also covers widows' and orphans' pensions and other similar payments such as annuities paid in respect of past employment. It also applies to pensions in respect of services rendered to a State or a political subdivision or local authority thereof which are not covered by the provisions of paragraph 2 of Article 19." [para. 1]

> "The treatment under the taxation laws of the . . . countries of amounts paid to an employee on the cessation of his employment is highly diversified. Some States regard such a payment as a pension, private or Government as the case may be, paid as a lump sum. In such a case it would be natural to consider the income as falling under Article 18 or 19. In the tax laws of other States such a payment is looked upon as the final remuneration for the work performed. Then it should of course be treated under Article 15 or 19, as the case may be. Others again consider such a payment as a bonus which is not taxable under their income tax laws but perhaps subjected to a gift tax or a similar tax. It has not been possible to reach a common solution on the tax treatment of payments of this kind under the Model Convention. If the question of taxing such payments should arise between Contracting States, the matter therefore has to be solved by recourse to the provisions of Article 25." [para. 3]

Paragraph 2

4.   This paragraph assigns to the country of source the exclusive right to tax pensions paid out and other payments made within the framework of a public scheme which is part of the social security system of that State or a political subdivision or a local authority thereof. As can be seen from paragraph 2 of the OECD Commentary quoted

below, no consensus emerged within the OECD Committee on Fiscal Affairs on the inclusion in the text of Article 18 of such an exclusive right. The assignment to the source country of the exclusive right to tax pensions paid out and other payments made under a public scheme which is part of the social security system is predicated on the rationale that the payments involved are wholly or largely financed out of the tax revenues of the source country. This is the case when there are no contributions by the prospective beneficiaries of the payments or when the contractual savings contributed under the social security scheme have to be supplemented by the tax revenues of the source country. Such may not always be the case however when the social security system functions on the basis of the capitalization principle rather than that of the distribution principle. The OECD Commentary observes:

"Some States consider pensions paid out under a public pension scheme which is part of their social security system similar to Government pensions. Such States argue on that basis that the State of source, i.e., the State from which the pension is paid, should have a right to tax such pensions. Many conventions concluded by these States contain provisions to that effect, sometimes including also other payments made under the social security legislation of the State of source. Such payments are for instance sickness benefits, unemployment benefits and benefits on account of industrial injury. Contracting States having that view may agree bilaterally on an additional paragraph to the Article giving the State of source a right to tax payments made under its social security legislation. A paragraph of that kind could be drafted along the following lines:

'Notwithstanding the provisions of paragraph 1, pensions and other payments made under the social security legislation of a Contracting State may be taxed in that State.'

Where the State of which the recipient of such payments is a resident applies the exemption method the payments will be taxable only in the State of source, while States using the credit method may tax the payments and give credit for the tax levied in the State of source. Some States using the credit method as the general method in their conventions may, however, consider that the State of source should have an exclusive right to tax such payments. Such States should then substitute the words 'shall be taxable only' for the words 'may be taxed' in the above draft provision." [para. 2]

5.   The Group of Experts had suggested that the provisions of paragraph 2 of article 18 (alternative A) and paragraph 3 of article 18 (alternative B) may require amendment to deal with the consequences of privatization of social security systems.

6.   As of 1999, there does not appear to be any treaty text which clearly addresses the issue of privatization of social security systems. It is true that in some treaty texts, the right to tax the social security payments is attributed to the State of residence, rather than the State of source, though this does not address the issue raised above.

7.   Privatized social security systems can be found in a number of countries in Latin America and East Europe. The issues concerning double taxation consequent upon the introduction of privatized social security systems have not been noticed so far. This issue is still under examination and the results of enquiry in this behalf will be brought to the notice of the Group of Experts in due course.

Commentary on the paragraphs of article 18 B

8.   During the discussion, several members of the Group of Experts from developing countries expressed the view that pensions should not be taxed exclusively in the beneficiary's country of residence. They pointed out that, since pensions were in substance a form of deferred compensation for services performed in the source country, they should be taxed at source as normal employment income would be. They further observed that pension flows between some developed and developing countries were not reciprocal and in some cases represented a relatively substantial net outflow for the developing country. Several members said they favoured exclusive tax-

ation of pensions at source but would be willing to grant an exemption from source taxation for amounts equivalent to the personal exemptions allowable in the source country. Other members were generally of the view that pensions should be taxed only in the beneficiary's country of residence. They suggested that, since the amounts involved were generally not substantial, countries would not suffer measurably if they agreed to taxation in the country of residence. Those members also made the point that the country of residence is probably in a better position than the source country to tailor its taxation of pensions to the taxpayer's ability to pay.

9.   A question was raised about how pension payments would be taxed in the case of employees who had performed services consecutively in several different countries—a fairly common practice among employees of transnational corporations. If such employees were taxed in each jurisdiction in which they had previously worked to earn the pension, then each pension payment might be taxed in several jurisdictions. It was also observed that it would be very difficult for the head office of a company to allocate each pension among the various countries in which the pensioner had worked during his years of employment. It was generally agreed, therefore, that taxation of pension at source should be construed to mean taxation at the place in which the pension payments originated, not the place in which the services had been performed.

Paragraph 1

10.   This paragraph, although it recognizes the right of the country of residence to tax pensions and other similar remuneration, leaves open the possibility that the country of source may also be given the right to tax in certain conditions which are defined in paragraph 2.

Paragraph 2

11.   As indicated above, the country of source may be allowed to tax but only if the payments involved are made by a resident of that country or a permanent establishment situated therein.

Paragraph 3

12.   Since paragraph 3 of article 18 B is identical to paragraph 2 of article 18 A, the Commentary on the latter paragraph (see above) is fully applicable to the former.

13.   The OECD Model Convention in the Commentary on Article 18 at paragraphs 4 to 37 has dealt with the question of tax treatment of contributions to foreign pension schemes. Some members of the Group of Experts pointed out that incorporation of these paragraphs in the United Nations Model Convention dealing with this subject would send a strong positive signal to potential inward investors. Allowing recognition of cross-border pension contributions will also stimulate movement of personnel to foreign countries. It is, therefore, considered important to reproduce paragraphs 4 to 37 of the OECD Commentary as under:

"The tax treatment of contributions to
foreign pension schemes

A.   *General comments*

It is characteristic of multinational enterprises that their staff are expected to be willing to work outside their home country from time to time. The terms of service under which staff are sent to work in other countries are of keen interest and importance to both the employer and the employee. One consideration is the pension arrangements that are made for the employee in question." [para. 4]

"Employees sent abroad to work will often wish to continue contributing to a pension scheme in their home country during their absence abroad. This is because switching schemes can lead to a loss of rights and benefits, and because many practical difficulties can arise from having pension arrangements in a number of countries." [para. 5]

"The tax treatment accorded to pension contributions of employees who are assigned to work outside their home country varies both from country to country and depending on the circumstances of the individual case. Before taking up an overseas assignment, employees commonly qualify for tax relief on pension contributions paid in the home country. When assigned abroad, employees in some cases continue to qualify for relief. Where an individual, for example, remains resident and fully taxable in the home country, pension contributions made to a pension scheme established in the home country will generally continue to qualify for relief there. But frequently, contributions paid in the home country by an individual assigned to work abroad do not qualify for relief under the domestic laws of either the home country or the host country. Where this is the case it can become expensive, if not prohibitive, to maintain membership of a pension scheme in the home country during a foreign assignment. Paragraph 11 below suggests a provision which Member countries can, if they wish, include in bilateral treaties to provide reliefs for the pension contributions of employees assigned to work outside their home country." [para. 6]

"However, some Member countries may not consider that the solution to the problem lies in a treaty provision, preferring, for example, the pension scheme to be amended to secure deductibility of contributions in the host State. Other countries may be opposed to including the provision in treaties where domestic legislation allows deductions only for contributions paid to residents. In such cases it may be appropriate to include the suggested provision in a bilateral treaty." [para. 7]

"The suggested provision does not address itself to contributions made to social security schemes (general State pension schemes dependent upon contribution records, whether or not contributors are employees) as the right or obligation to join a social security scheme is primarily a matter of social legislation rather than tax law. Many Member countries have entered into bilateral social security totalization agreements which may help to avoid the problem with respect to contributions to social security schemes. The provision also does not contain provisions relating either to the deductibility by the employer of employer pension contributions in respect of employees working abroad or to the treatment of income accrued within the plan. All of these issues can be dealt with in bilateral negotiations." [para. 8]

"The provision is confined to the tax treatment of contribution to pension schemes by or on behalf of individuals who exercise employments within the meaning of Article 15 away from their home State. It does not deal with contributions by individuals who render independent personal services within the meaning of Article 14. However, Member countries may wish, in bilateral negotiations, to agree on a provision covering individuals rendering services within both Article 14 and Article 15." [para. 9]

"B.   *Aim of the provision*

The aim of the provision is to ensure that, as far as possible, an employee is not discouraged from taking up an overseas assignment by the tax treatment of contributions made to a home country pension scheme by an employee working abroad. The provision seeks, first, to determine the general equivalence of pension plans in the two countries and then to establish limits to the deductibility of employee contributions based on the limits in the laws of both countries." [para. 10]

"C.   *Suggested provision*

The following is the suggested text of the provision that could be included in bilateral conventions to deal with the problem identified above:

(*a*)   Contributions borne by an individual who renders dependent personal services in a Contracting State to a pension scheme established in and recognized for tax purposes in the other Contracting State shall be deducted, in the first-mentioned State, in determining the individual's taxable income, and treated in that State, in the same way and subject to the same conditions and limitations as contributions made to a pension scheme that is recognized for tax purposes in that first-mentioned State, provided that:

(i)   the individual was not a resident of that State, and was contributing to the pension scheme, immediately before he began to exercise employment in that State; and

(ii)   the pension scheme is accepted by the competent authority of that State as generally corresponding to a pension scheme recognized as such for tax purposes by that State.

(b)   For the purposes of subparagraph (a):

(i)   the term 'a pension scheme' means an arrangement in which the individual participates in order to secure retirement benefits payable in respect of the dependent personal services referred to in subparagraph (a); and

(ii)   a pension scheme is recognized for tax purposes in a State if the contributions to the scheme would qualify for tax relief in that State." [para. 11]

"Subparagraph (a) of the suggested provision lays down the characteristics of both the employee and the contributions to which the provision applies. It also provides the principle that contributions borne by an individual rendering dependent personal services within the meaning of Article 15 in one Contracting State (the host State) to a defined pension scheme in the other Contracting State (the home State) are to be relieved from tax in the host State, subject to the same conditions and limitations as relief for contributions to domestic pension schemes of the host State." [para. 12]

"Relief for contributions to the home country pension scheme under the conditions outlined can be given by either the home country, being the country where the pension scheme is situated or by the host country, where the economic activities giving rise to the contributions are carried out." [para. 13]

"A solution in which relief would be given by the home country might not be effective, since the employee might have no or little taxable income in that country. Practical considerations therefore suggest that it would be preferable for relief to be given by the host country and this is the solution adopted in the suggested provision." [para. 14]

"In looking at the characteristics of the employee, sub-paragraph (*a*) makes it clear that, in order to get the relief from taxation in the host State, the employee must not have been resident in the host State immediately prior to working there." [para. 15]

"Subparagraph (*a*) does not, however, limit the application of the provision to secondees who become resident in their host State. In many cases employees working abroad who remain resident in their home State will continue to qualify for relief there, but this will not be so in all cases. The suggested provision therefore applies to non-residents working in the host State as well as to secondees to the host State who attain residence status there. In some Member countries the domestic legislation may restrict deductibility to contributions borne by residents, and these Member countries may wish to restrict the suggested provision to cater for this. Also, States with a special regime for non-residents (e.g., taxation at special low rate) may, in bilateral negotiations, wish to agree on a provision restricted to residents." [para. 16]

"In the case where individuals temporarily cease to be resident in the host country in order to join a pension scheme in a country with more relaxed rules, individual States may want a provision which would prevent the possibility of abuse. One form such a provision could take would be a nationality test which could exclude from the suggested provision individuals who are nationals of the host State." [para. 17]

"As it is not unusual for employees to be seconded to a number of different countries in succession, the suggested provision is not limited to employees who are residents of the home State immediately prior to exercising employment in the host State. The provision covers an employee coming to the host State from a third country as it is only limited to employees who were not resident in the host country before taking up employment there. However, Article 1 restricts the scope of the Convention to residents of one or both Contracting States. An employee who is neither a resident of the host State nor of the home State where the pension scheme is established is therefore outside the scope of the Convention between the two States." [para. 18]

"The suggested provision places no limits on the length of time for which an employee can work in a host State. It could be argued that, if an employee works in the host State for long enough, it in effect becomes his home country and the provision should no longer apply. Indeed, some host countries already restrict relief for contributions to foreign employee/ employer pension schemes to cases where the seconded employees are present on a temporary basis." [para. 19]

"In addition, the inclusion of a time limit may be helpful in preventing the possibility of abuse outlined in paragraph 17 above. In bilateral negotiations, individual countries may find it appropriate to include a limit on the length of time for which an employee may exercise an employment in the host State after which reliefs granted by the suggested provision would no longer apply." [para. 20]

"In looking at the characteristics of the contributions, sub-paragraph (a) provides a number of tests. It makes clear that the provision applies only to contributions borne by an individual to a pension scheme established in and recognized for tax purposes in the home State. The phrase 'recognized for tax purposes' is further defined in subdivision (b)(ii) of the suggested provision." [para. 21]

"The second test applied to the characteristics of the contributions is that the contributions should be made to a home State scheme recognized by the competent authority of the host State as generally corresponding to a scheme recognized as such for tax purposes by the host State. This operates on the premise that only contributions to recognized schemes qualify for relief in Member countries. This limitation does not, of course necessarily secure equivalent tax treatment of contributions paid where an employee was working abroad and of contributions while working in the home country. If the host State's rules for recognizing pension schemes were narrower than those of the home State, the employee could find that contributions to his home country pension scheme were less favourably treated when he was working in the host country than when working in the home country." [para. 22]

"However, it would not be in accordance with the stated aim of securing, as far as possible, equivalent tax treatment of employee contributions to give relief for contributions which do not—at least broadly—correspond to domestically recognized schemes. To do so would mean that the amount of relief in the host State would become dependent on legislation in the home State. In addition, it could be hard to defend treating employees working side by side differently depending on whether their pension scheme was at home or abroad (and if abroad, whether it was one country rather than another). By limiting the suggested provision to schemes which generally correspond to those in the host country such difficulties are avoided." [para. 23]

"The suggested provision makes it clear that it is for the competent authority of the host State to determine whether the scheme in the home State generally corresponds to recognized schemes in the host State. Individual States may wish, in bilateral negotiations, to establish what interpretation the competent authority places on the term 'generally corresponding'; for example how widely it is interpreted and what tests are imposed." [para. 24]

"The contributions covered by the provision are limited to payments to schemes to which the employee was contributing before he began to exercise his employment in the host State. This means that contributions to new pension schemes which an employee joins while in the host State are excluded from the suggested provision." [para. 25]

"It is, however, recognized that special rules may be needed to cover cases where new pension schemes are substituted for previous ones. For instance, in some Member countries the common practice may be that, if a company employer is taken over by another company, the existing company pension scheme for its employees may be ended and a new scheme opened by the new employer. In bilateral negotiations, therefore, individual States may wish to supplement the provision to cover such substitution schemes." [para. 26]

"Subparagraph (*a*) also sets out the relief to be given by the host State if the characteristics of the employee and the contributions fall within the terms of the provision. In brief, the relief is to be given in a way which corresponds to the manner in which relief would be given if the contributions were to a scheme established in the host State." [para. 27]

"This measure of relief does not, of course, necessarily secure equivalent tax treatment given to contributions paid when an employee is working abroad and contributions paid when he is working in the home country. Similar considerations apply here to those discussed in paragraphs 22 and 23 above. The measure does, however, ensure equivalent treatment of the contributions of colleagues. The following example is considered. The home country allows relief for pension contributions subject to a limit of 18 per cent of income. The host country allows relief subject to a limit of 20 per cent. The suggested provision in paragraph 11 would require the host country to allow relief up to its domestic limit of 20 per cent. Countries wishing to adopt the limit in the home country would need to amend the wording of the provision appropriately." [para. 28]

"The amount and method of giving the relief would depend upon the domestic tax treatment of pension contributions by the host State. This would settle such questions as whether such contributions qualify for relief in full, or only in part, and whether relief should be given as a deduction in computing taxable income (and if so, which income, e.g., only employment income or all income) or as a tax credit." [para. 29]

"Being assigned to work abroad may not only mean that an employee's contributions to a pension scheme in his home country cease to qualify for tax relief. It may also mean that contributions to the pension scheme by the employer are regarded as employee's income for tax purposes. In some Member countries employees are taxed on employer's contributions to domestic scheme whilst working in the home country whereas in others these contributions remain exempt. The provision, therefore, is silent on the treatment of such contributions, although Member countries may wish to extend the suggested provision in bilateral treaties, to ensure that the employer's contributions in the context of employees' tax liability are accorded the same treatment that such contributions to domestic schemes would receive." [para. 30]

"Subdivision (b)(i) defines a pension scheme for the purposes of subparagraph (a). It makes it clear that, for these purposes, a pension scheme is an arrangement in which the individual who makes the payments participates in order to secure retirement benefits. These benefits must be payable in respect of the exercise of the employment in the host State. All the above conditions must apply to the pension scheme before it can qualify for relief under the suggested provision." [para. 31]

"Subdivision (b)(i) refers to the participation of the individual in the pension scheme in order to secure retirement benefits. This definition is intended to ensure that the proportion of contributions made to secure benefits other than periodic pension payments on retirement, e.g., a lump sum on retirement, will also qualify for relief under the provision." [para. 32]

"The initial definition of a pension scheme is 'an arrangement'. This is a widely drawn term, the use of which is intended to encompass the various forms that pension schemes may take in individual member countries." [para. 33]

"Although subdivision (b)(i) sets out that participation in this scheme has to be by the individual who exercises the employment referred to in subparagraph (a) there is no reference to the identity of the recipient of the retirement benefits secured by participation in the scheme. This is to ensure that any proportion of contributions intended to generate a widow or dependant's pension may be eligible for relief under the suggested provision." [para. 34]

"The definition of a pension scheme makes no distinction between pensions paid from State-run occupational pension schemes and similar privately run schemes. Both are covered by the scope of the provision. Any pensions, such as pensions from general State pension schemes dependent on contribution records whether or not contributors are employees, are excluded from the provision as the individual will not contribute to such schemes in order to receive benefits payable in respect of dependant personal services rendered." [para. 35]

"Subdivision (b)(ii) further defines the phrase 'recognized for tax purposes'. As the aim of the provision is, so far as possible, to ensure that the contributions are neither more nor less favourably treated for tax purposes than they would be if the employee was resident in his home State, it is right to limit the provision to contributions which would have qualified for relief if the employee had remained in the home State. The provision seeks to achieve this aim by limiting its scope to contributions made to a scheme only if contributions to this scheme would qualify for tax relief in that State." [para. 36]

"This method of attempting to achieve parity of treatment assumes that in all Member countries only contributions to recognized pension schemes qualify for relief. The tax treatment of contributions to pension schemes under Member countries' tax systems may differ from this assumption. It is recognized that, in bilateral negotiations, individual countries may wish to further define the qualifying pension schemes in terms that match the respective domestic laws of the treaty partners." [para. 37]

Article 19

GOVERNMENT SERVICE

1.   In 1999, three changes were made in article 19. Firstly, the title of article 19 was changed from "Remuneration and pensions in respect of government service" to "Government service". Secondly, in paragraphs 1 and 3, the word "remuneration" was replaced by the expression "salaries, wages and other similar remuneration". Thirdly, paragraph 3 was amended to refer to article 17. As a result, article 19 of the United Nations Model Convention reproduces Article 19 of the OECD Model Convention. The Group observed that, while the provisions of the article were generally acceptable to its members, some developing countries might in bilateral negotiations desire to place a monetary ceiling on the amount subject to subparagraph 2(*b*), which precludes a Contracting State from taxing pension payments that it makes to a resident or a national of the other State. The Group also felt that some developing countries might prefer that payments dealt with in article 19 should be taxed only by the beneficiary's country of residence.

2.   Since article 19 of the United Nations Model Convention incorporates all the provisions of Article 19 of the OECD Model Convention, the following Commentary on the OECD Article is relevant:

"This Article applies to salaries, wages and other similar remuneration in respect of government service. Similar provisions in old bilateral conventions were framed in order to conform with the rules of international courtesy and mutual respect between sovereign States. They were therefore rather limited in scope. However, the importance and scope of Article 19 has increased on account of the fact that, consequent on the growth of the public sector in many countries, governmental activities abroad have been considerably extended. According to the original version of paragraph 1 of Article 19 in the 1963 Draft Convention, the paying State had a right to tax payments made for services rendered to that State or political subdivision or local authority thereof. The expression 'may be taxed' was used and this did not connote an exclusive right of taxation." [para. 1]

"... subparagraphs (*a*) of paragraphs 1 and 2 are both based on the principle that the paying State shall have an exclusive right to tax the payments. Countries using the credit method as the general method for relieving double taxation in their conventions are thus, as an exception to that method, obliged to exempt from tax such payments to their residents as are dealt with under paragraphs 1 and 2. If both the Contracting States apply the exemption method for relieving double taxation, they can continue to use the expression 'may be taxed' instead of 'shall be taxable only'. In relation to such countries the effect will of course will be the same irrespective of which of these expressions they use. It is understood that the expression 'shall be taxable only' shall not prevent a Contracting State from taking into account the income exempted under subparagraph (*a*) of paragraphs 1 and 2 in determining the rate of tax to be imposed on income derived by its residents from other sources. The principle of giving the exclusive taxing right to the paying State is contained in so many of the existing conventions between OECD Member countries that it can be said to be already internationally accepted. It is also in conformity with the conception of international courtesy which is at the basis of the Article and with the provisions of the Vienna Conventions on Diplomatic and Consular Relations. It should, however, be observed that the Article is not intended to restrict the operation of any rules originating from international law in the case of diplomatic missions and consular posts (cf. Article 27) but deals with cases not covered by such rules." [para. 2]

"In 1994, a further amendment was made to paragraph 1 by replacing the term 'remuneration' by the words 'salaries, wages, and other similar remuneration'. This amendment was intended to clarify the scope of the Article, which only applies to State employees and to persons deriving pensions from past employment by a State, and not to persons rendering independent services to a State or deriving pensions related to such services." [para. 2.1]

"Member countries have generally understood the term 'salaries, wages and other similar remuneration . . . paid' to include benefits in kind received in respect of services rendered to a State or political subdivision or local authority thereof (e.g., the use of a residence or automobile, health or life insurance coverage and club memberships)." [para. 2.2]

"The provisions of the Article apply to payments made not only by a State but also by its political subdivisions and local authorities (constituent states, regions, provinces, '*départements*', cantons, districts, '*arrondissements*', '*Kreise*', municipalities, or groups of municipalities etc.)." [para. 3]

"An exception from the principle of giving exclusive taxing power to the paying State is contained in subparagraph (*b*) of paragraph 1. It is to be seen against the background that, according to the Vienna Conventions mentioned above, the receiving State is allowed to tax remuneration paid to certain categories of personnel of foreign diplomatic missions and consular posts, who are permanent residents or nationals of that State. Given that pensions paid to retired government officials ought to be treated for tax purposes in the same way as salaries or wages paid to such employees during their active time, an exception like the one in subparagraph (*b*) of paragraph 1 is incorporated also in subparagraph (*b*) of paragraph 2 regarding pensions. Since the condition laid down in subdivision (*b*)(ii) of paragraph 1 cannot be valid in relation to a pensioner, the only prerequisite for the receiving State's power to tax the pension is that the pensioner must be one of its own residents and nationals. It should be noted that the expression 'out of funds created by' in subparagraph (*a*) of paragraph 2 covers the situation where the pension is not paid directly by the State, a political subdivision or a local authority but out of separate funds created by them." [para. 4]

"According to Article 19 of the 1963 Draft Convention, the services rendered to the State, political subdivision or local authority had to be rendered 'in the discharge of functions of a governmental nature'. That expression was deleted in the 1977 Model Convention. Some OECD Member countries, however, thought that the exclusion would lead to a widening of the scope of the Article. Contracting States who are of that view and who feel that such a widening is not desirable may continue to use, and preferably specify, the expression 'in the discharge of functions of a governmental nature' in their bilateral conventions." [para. 5]

"Paragraphs 1 and 2 do not apply if the services are performed in connection with business carried on by the State, or one of its political subdivisions or local authorities, paying the salaries, wages or other similar remuneration, or the pensions. In such cases the ordinary rules apply: Article 15 for wages and salaries, Article 16 for directors' fees and other similar payments, Article 17 for artistes and sportsmen and Article 18 for pensions. Contracting States, wishing for specific reasons to dispense with paragraph 3 in their bilateral conventions, are free to do so, thus bringing in under paragraphs 1 and 2 also services rendered in connection with business. In view of the specific functions carried out by certain public bodies, e.g., State Railways, the Post Office, State-owned theatres etc., Contracting States wanting to keep paragraph 3 may agree in bilateral negotiations to include under the provisions of paragraphs 1 and 2 remuneration paid by such bodies, even if they could be said to be performing business activities." [para. 6]

3.   It was the intention of the Group that all pensions paid in respect of services rendered to a Contracting State, political subdivision or local authority thereof should be subject to article 19, even if they were paid under the social security system of one of the States. In most cases the treatment would be the same whether such payments were subject to article 18 or article 19. The treatment differs, however, in those cases described in subparagraph 2(b) of article 19—where the recipient is both a resident and a national of the other State. Under article 19, government service pensions received by such individuals are taxable only in the country of residence. If they

were to be subject to tax under article 18, they would be taxable only in the country of source. The purpose of this paragraph is to indicate that a public service pension paid by one country, even if it is paid under its social security system, to a resident of the other country who is a national of that other country is taxable only in the latter country.

4.   It was proposed that the question of tax treatment of a Government meeting the expenses of artistes resident of one Contracting State performing their activities in another Contracting State might be dealt with in the Commentaries. However, it was considered that the Contracting States, if they so desire, may discuss the matter during bilateral negotiations. A reference is made to the Commentaries on article 17 in this connection.

Article 20

STUDENTS

1.   Article 20 of the United Nations Model Convention, as presently worded, reproduces substantially Article 20 of the OECD Model Convention. In 1999, paragraph 2, containing new provisions dealing with grants and scholarships and remuneration from employment not covered by paragraph 1, was omitted.

2.   Since article 20 of the United Nations Model Convention reproduces Article 20 of the OECD Model Convention, the following Commentary on the latter Article is relevant:

> "The rule established in this Article concerns certain payments received by students or business apprentices for the purpose of their maintenance, education or training. All such payments received from sources outside the State in which the student or business apprentice concerned is staying shall be exempted from tax in that State." [para. 1]

> "The word 'immediately' [makes] clear that the Article does not cover a person who has once been a resident of a Con-

tracting State but has subsequently moved his residence to a third State before visiting the other Contracting State." [para. 2]

3.   The question whether paragraph 2 of article 20 should be deleted from the United Nations Model Convention had engaged the attention of the Group of Experts for some time. In this connection, it is relevant to reproduce paragraphs 25 to 29 of the Report of the Ad Hoc Group of Experts on International Cooperation in Tax Matters on the Work of its Seventh Meeting held in December 1995 (ST/ESA/250):

> "At its July 1995 meeting, the Steering Committee recommended that the group consider deleting from the Model Convention article 20, paragraph 2, which provided that if a visiting student had income not exempted by paragraph 1 from taxation in the visited country, the student should, in the taxation of non-exempted income, be entitled to the same exemptions, reliefs, and reductions as were allowed to residents of that country." [para. 25]

> "A participant argued that the provision should be retained because it allowed visiting students to be taxed in the same way as resident students. Another participant responded that such parity was sometimes elusive because the resident student was taxable on all income, whereas a visiting student was taxable only on income from sources in the visited country." [para. 26]

> "A proponent of deleting the provision noted that article 24, paragraph 4 (second sentence), stated that a country is not required to allow non-residents any personal allowances or other reliefs 'on account of civil status or family responsibilities' which might be allowed to residents; article 20, paragraph 2, it was argued, contradicted the provision of article 24." [para. 27]

> "A participant noted that, as an alternative to article 14, paragraph 1(c), a treaty might provide for exemption in the host State, for the normal duration of studies, of remuneration not exceeding a certain annual amount, but only to the extent

that the remuneration was also not exempted in the other State." [para. 28] [Paragraph 1(*c*) of article 14 was deleted in 1999.]

"After discussion, it was concluded that a majority of the Group, but not a consensus, favoured deletion of article 20, paragraph 2." [para. 29]

4.   The matter was considered again at the ninth meeting of the Group of Experts, in May 1999, and the Group agreed to delete paragraph 2 of article 20. Article 20 thus conforms to Article 20 of the OECD Model Convention, with the addition of the word "trainee".

5.   Paragraph 2 in the 1980 version of the United Nations Model Convention read as follows:

"(2)   in respect of grants, scholarships and remuneration from employment not covered by paragraph 1, a student or business apprentice described in paragraph 1 shall, in addition, be entitled during such education or training to the same exemptions, reliefs or reductions in respect of taxes available to residents of the State which he is visiting."

6.   Although, as worded, paragraph 2 covers grants and scholarships that have their source in the country visited as well as income from an employment in the country visited, the Commentaries to the 1980 Model made it clear that the paragraph was mainly concerned with income from employment. The wording was intended to put visiting students etc. on exactly the same basis as students who were residents for tax purposes of the State where they were studying, but not to treat visiting students more favourably than tax-resident students.

7.   Experience with the application of paragraph 2 in practice has shown that, as presently worded, it can give rise to difficult problems of administration. For example, if the visiting student is subject to tax in the State visited only on income from sources in that country, and not on his worldwide income, should the visitor be entitled to the full allowances which a resident who is taxed on his worldwide income is allowed? Similarly, should a married student, whose spouse does not come to the country with the student, be entitled to the married

person's allowance? These issues cannot be settled from a strict reading of the text of paragraph 2 as it stands.

8.   A particular question that is begged by the inclusion of paragraph 2 is the tax residence status of a visiting student or business apprentice under the normal rules of residence in article 4. A student who is following a full-time course of studies may become a tax resident of the host State: in which case, he will become liable to tax there in respect of his worldwide income, and be entitled to all the personal reliefs, without the need of any special provision in article 20.

9.   Moreover, as the commentaries to the 1980 version went on to show, there are a number of further ways in which the countries may wish to consider expanding article 20 in the course of negotiations in order to cover particular problems which may arise in special bilateral situations. Examples are given, without suggesting any particular form of words to give effect to their intentions. The 1980 Commentaries said:

> ". . . some countries in bilateral negotiations might wish to expand the article by adding a paragraph permitting a further exemption (beyond that generally applicable as a personal exemption or similar allowance under the internal law of the Contracting State) of employment income under certain conditions. Some countries may, for example, wish to extend the exemption to remuneration received for services performed in the country where the student or business apprentice is present, but to limit the exemption to a specified amount of remuneration. In fixing the amount, countries may take into account the fact that students or business apprentices may incur additional costs because they are away from their home country. It may also be appropriate, in cases where the exemption is extended, to place a time limit on such exemption in the cases of business apprentices, and also perhaps in the cases of students, a longer period presumably being allowed in the latter situation."

10.   In the light of the practical difficulties of applying paragraph 2, and the fact that there are a number of other issues affecting students and business apprentices that may need to be addressed in bilateral negotiations, the Group of Experts decided that, rather than attempt a comprehensive rewording, it was preferable to omit paragraph 2 from the Model Convention. Countries wishing to broaden the scope of article 20 to cover sources of income arising in the country visited should aim to draft a suitable provision as tightly as possible to meet their specific circumstances.

Article for teachers

11.   During the course of discussions in the Seventh Meeting of the Ad Hoc Group of Experts, several participants argued for the addition to the Model Convention of an article dealing with visiting teachers. Currently, under the Model Convention visiting teachers were subject to article 14, if the teaching services were performed in an independent capacity; article 15, if the services were dependent; or article 19, if the remuneration was paid by a Contracting State. Many treaties have an additional article or paragraph dealing specifically with teachers and, sometimes, researchers, which typically exempted them from taxation in the source country if their stay did not exceed a prescribed length. It was noted that articles 14 and 15 commonly did not exempt a visiting teacher's compensation from taxation at source because they generally allowed source taxation of service performers who were present in the host country for more than 183 days, and many teaching assignments exceeded that period of time.

12.   There was considerable controversy among participants about the need to provide an independent article in the United Nations Model Convention dealing exclusively with visiting teachers. But substantially, all participants agreed that an article on teachers, if included in the Model Convention, should not have the effect of exempting a teacher from tax both in the home country and the country visited. One member suggested a compromise on the issue: that the Model Convention should not be amended to include a provision on

visiting teachers but that an addition should be made in the Commentary, noting that many treaties contained such articles and providing advice for bilateral negotiations on the subject. There was general consensus for this suggestion.

13.   Accordingly, the Group appointed a drafting committee to formulate language for inclusion in the Commentary on the Model Convention. After being discussed and amended, the following inclusion was adopted by the Group in 1999:

> "No special Model Convention provision has been made regarding remuneration derived by visiting professors and other teachers. In the absence of a special provision, articles 14, 15, 19 or 23 of the Model Convention, depending on the circumstances, would apply. Many bilateral conventions, however, contain rules of some kind or other concerning such persons, the main purpose of which is to facilitate cultural relations and the exchange of knowledge by providing for a limited tax exemption in the host country for visiting teachers. Sometimes, tax exemption is already provided under domestic taxation laws, which many consider to be the preferred way of solving double taxation problems of visiting teachers.
>
> Notwithstanding the applicability of articles 14, 15, 19 and 23 to prevent double taxation, some countries may wish to include an article on teachers. The variety of domestic tax rules in different countries, on the one hand, or the absence of such rules, on the other, constitute an impediment to a specific provision on teachers in the Model Convention. If, however, in bilateral negotiations, the Contracting States choose to include a provision relating to visiting teachers, the following issues should be considered in preparing such a provision:
>
> (*a*)   The purpose of a tax treaty generally is to avoid double taxation, and double exemption of teachers is not desirable;
>
> (*b*)   It is advisable to limit benefits for visits of a maximum duration (normally two years), and the time limit should be subject to expansion in individual cases by mu-

tual agreement between competent authorities of the Contracting States. It should be determined whether income from the visits exceeding the time limit should be taxable as of the beginning of the visit or merely from the date beyond the expiration of the time limit;

(*c*) Whether the benefits should be limited to teaching services performed at certain institutions 'recognized' by the Contracting States in which the services are performed;

(*d*) Whether, in the case of visiting professors and other teachers who also do research, to limit benefits remuneration for research performed in the public (vs. private) interest;

(*e*) Whether an individual may be entitled to the benefits of the article more than once."

Article 21

OTHER INCOME

1. Article 21 of the United Nations Model Convention reproduces Article 21 of the OECD Model Convention in its entirety and also has an additional paragraph (paragraph 3) containing a general provision relating to items of income of a resident of a Contracting State not dealt with in the preceding articles and arising in the other Contracting State.

2. The article covers not only income of a class not expressly dealt with in the preceding articles, but also income from sources not expressly referred to therein. The article covers income arising in third States as well as income from a Contracting State.

Paragraph 1

3.   This paragraph reproduces Article 21, paragraph 1, of the OECD Model Convention. Part of the Commentary on the latter paragraph, quoted below, is relevant:

"Under this paragraph the exclusive right to tax is given to the State of residence. In cases of conflict between two residences, Article 4 will also allocate the taxation right in respect of third-State income." [para. 2]

"[W]hen income arises in a third State and the recipient of this income is considered as a resident by both Contracting States under their domestic law, the application of Article 4 will result in the recipient being treated as a resident of one Contracting State only and being liable to comprehensive taxation ('full tax liability') in that State only. In this case, the other Contracting State may not impose tax on the income arising from the third State, even if the recipient is not taxed by the State of which he is considered a resident under Article 4. In order to avoid non-taxation, Contracting States may agree to limit the scope of the Article to income which is taxed in the Contracting State of which the recipient is a resident and may modify the provisions of the paragraph accordingly . . ." [para. 3]

A reference is also invited to paragraph 5 of the Commentary below.

Paragraph 2

4.   This paragraph reproduces Article 21, paragraph 2, of the OECD Model Convention. The Commentary on the latter paragraph, quoted below, is therefore relevant:

"This paragraph provides for an exception from the provisions of paragraph 1 where the income is associated with the activity of a permanent establishment or fixed base which a resident of a Contracting State has in the other Contracting State. The paragraph includes income from third States. In such a case, a right to tax is given to the Contracting State in which the permanent establishment or the fixed base is situated. Paragraph 2 does not apply to immovable property for which, according to paragraph 4 of Article 6, the State of situs has a primary right to tax . . . Therefore, immovable property situated in a Contracting State and forming part of the business property of a permanent establishment of an enterprise of that State situated in the other Contracting State shall be taxable only in the first-mentioned State in which the property is situated and of which the recipient of the income is a resident. This is in consistency with the rules laid down in Articles 13 and 22 in respect of immovable property since paragraph 2 of those Articles applies only to movable property of a permanent establishment." [para. 4]

"The paragraph also covers the case where the beneficiary and the payer of the income are both residents of the same Contracting State, and the income is attributed to a permanent establishment or a fixed base, which the beneficiary of the income has in the other Contracting State. In such a case a right to tax is given to the Contracting State in which the permanent establishment or the fixed base is situated. Where double taxation occurs, the State of residence should give relief under the provisions of Article 23 A or 23 B. However, a problem may arise as regards the taxation of dividends and interest in the State of residence as the State of source: the combination of Articles 7 and 23 A prevents that State from levying tax on that income, whereas if it were paid to a resident of the other State, the first State, being the State of source of the dividends or interest, could tax such dividends or interest at the rates provided for in paragraph 2 of Articles 10 and 11. Contracting States which find this position unacceptable may include in their conventions a provision according to which the State of residence would be entitled, as State of source of the dividends or interest, to levy a tax on such income at the rates provided for in paragraph 2 of Articles 10 and 11. The State where the permanent establishment is situated would give a credit for such tax on the lines of the provisions of paragraph 2 of Article 23 A or of paragraph 1 of Article 23 B; of course, this credit should not be given in cases where the State in which the permanent establishment is situated does not tax the dividends or interest attributed to the permanent establishment, in accordance with its domestic laws." [para. 5]

"Some States which apply the exemption method (Article 23 A) may have reason to suspect that the treatment accorded in paragraph 2 may provide an inducement to an enterprise of a Contracting State to attach assets such as shares, bonds or patents, to a permanent establishment situated in the other Contracting State in order to obtain more favourable tax treatment there. To counteract such arrangements which they consider would represent abuse, some States might take the view that the transaction is artificial and, for this reason, would regard the assets as not effectively connected with the permanent establishment. Some other States may strengthen their position by adding in paragraph 2 a condition providing that the paragraph shall not apply to cases where the arrangements were primarily made for the purpose of taking advantage of this provision." [para. 6]

Paragraph 3

5.   This paragraph constitutes an addition to Article 21 of the OECD Model Convention. It is intended to permit the country in which the income arises to tax such income if its law so provides while the provisions of paragraph 1 would permit taxation in the country of residence. The concurrent application of the provisions of the two paragraphs may result in double taxation. In such a situation, the provisions of article 23 A or 23 B as appropriate would be applicable, as in other cases of double taxation. In some cases paragraphs 2 and 3 may overlap; they would then produce the same result.

6.   During the Ninth Meeting of the Group of Experts held in 1999, there was extensive discussion regarding inclusion of a new paragraph dealing with new financial instruments. Three options were identified. First, the Contracting States could adopt article 21 of

the United Nations Model Convention with the three paragraphs. Second, the Contracting States could adopt paragraph 3 of article 21 but add a reduced rate of tax in respect of income referred to in paragraph 3. Third, the Contracting States could adopt the United Nations Model Convention with the OECD version with paragraphs 1 and 2 only. These alternatives were considered useful in dealing with this subject. It was noted that the application of new financial products is relevant for options 2 and 3.

Optional additional paragraph

7.   The following Commentary to Article 21 in the OECD Model Convention is relevant:

> "Some countries have encountered difficulties in dealing with income arising from certain non-traditional financial instruments when the parties to the instrument have a special relationship. These countries may wish to add the following paragraph to Article 21:

>> '[4].   Where, by reason of a special relationship between the person referred to in paragraph 1 and some other person, or between both of them and some third person, the amount of the income referred to in paragraph 1 exceeds the amount (if any) which would have been agreed upon between them in the absence of such a relationship, the provisions of this Article shall apply only to the last-mentioned amount. In such a case, the excess part of the income shall remain taxable according to the laws of each Contracting State, due regard being had to the other applicable provisions of this Convention.' " [para. 7]

> "This paragraph restricts the operation of the provisions concerning the taxation of income not dealt with in other Articles in the same way that paragraph 6 of Article 11 restricts the operation of the provisions concerning the taxation of interest . . ." [para. 8]

> "Although the restriction could apply to any income otherwise subject to Article 21, it is not envisaged that in practice it

is likely to be applied to payments such as alimony payments or social security payments but rather that it is likely to be most relevant where certain non-traditional financial instruments are entered into in circumstances and on terms such that they would not have been entered into in the absence of a special relationship . . ." [para. 9]

"The restriction of Article 21 differs from the restriction of Article 11 in two important respects. First, the paragraph permits, where the necessary circumstances exist, all of the payments under a non-traditional financial instrument to be regarded as excessive. Second, income that is removed from the operation of the interest Article might still be subject to some other Article of the Convention . . . Income to which Article 21 would otherwise apply is by definition not subject to any other Article. Therefore, if the Article 21 restriction removes a portion of income from the operation of that Article, then Articles 6 through 20 of the Convention are not applicable to that income at all, and each Contracting State may tax it under its domestic law." [para. 10]

"Other provisions of the Convention, however, will continue to be applicable to such income, such as Article 23 (Relief from Double Taxation), Article 25 (Mutual Agreement Procedure), and Article 26 (Exchange of Information)." [para. 11]

"The Committee on Fiscal Affairs is actively studying the taxation of non-traditional financial instruments. Further changes to the Model or Commentaries may be necessary. The inclusion of proposed paragraph [4] carries no implication about the treatment of innovative financial transactions between independent persons or under other provisions of the Convention." [para. 12]

8.   Some members of the Group of Experts pointed out that there are very artificial devices entered into by persons to take advantage of the provisions of article 21—especially if paragraph 3 is omitted or provides for only a reduced rate of tax in the source State—through, inter alia, creation or assignment of rights with re-

spect to which income from, e.g., financial instruments arises. While substance over form rules, abuse of rights principles or any similar doctrine could be used to counter such arrangements, Contracting States which may want to address the issue specifically may include a clause on the following lines in their bilateral tax treaties:

> "The provisions of this article shall not apply if it was the main purpose or one of the main purposes of any person concerned with the creation or assignment of the rights in respect of which the income is paid to take advantage of this article by means of that creation or assignment."

Commentary on chapter IV

TAXATION OF CAPITAL

Article 22

CAPITAL

1.   In the United Nations Model Convention, article 22 deals with taxes on capital, to the exclusion of taxes on estates and inheritances and on gifts and of transfer duties.

2.   The question whether paragraphs 1 to 4 should continue to be placed within brackets has been examined by the Group of Experts. There is a general agreement that brackets are not required for the first three paragraphs but it was decided to retain them so far as paragraph 4 was concerned. There was a strong argument that the situs State would have the right to tax where the property was situated in that country; that would bring it into line with the treatment of the United Nations Model Convention of other income referred to in article 21. In 1999, it has been decided, to retain the brackets so far as paragraph 4 is concerned.

3.   Should the negotiating parties decide to include an article on the taxation of capital, they will have to determine whether to use the wording of paragraph 4 as shown or wording that leaves taxation to the State in which the capital is located. If the wording of paragraph 4 of the OECD Model Convention is used, the whole Commentary on Article 22, reproduced below, will be relevant.

"This Article deals only with taxes on capital, to the exclusion of taxes on estates and inheritances and on gifts and of transfer duties. Taxes on capital to which the article applies are those referred to in Article 2." [para. 1]

"Taxes on capital generally constitute complementary taxation of income from capital. Consequently, taxes on a given element of capital can be levied, in principle, only by the State which is entitled to tax the income from this element of capital. However, it is not possible to refer purely and simply to the rules relating to the taxation of such class of income, for not all items of income are subject to taxation exclusively in one State." [para. 2]

"The Article, therefore, enumerates first property which may be taxed in the State in which they are situated. To this category belong immovable property, referred to in Article 6, which a resident of a Contracting State owns and which is situated in the other Contracting State (paragraph 1), and movable property forming part of the business property of a permanent establishment which an enterprise of a Contracting State has in the other Contracting State, or pertaining to a fixed base which a resident of a Contracting State has in the other Contracting State for the performance of independent personal services (paragraph 2)." [para. 3]

"Ships and aircraft operated in international traffic and boats engaged in inland waterways transport and movable property pertaining to the operation of such ships, boats or aircraft shall be taxable only in the State in which the place of effective management of the enterprise is situated (paragraph 3). This rule corresponds to the provisions of Article 8 and of paragraph 3 of Article 13. It is understood that paragraph 3 of Article 8 is applicable if the place of effective management of a shipping enterprise or of an inland waterways transport enterprise is aboard a ship or boat. Contracting States which would prefer to confer the exclusive taxing right on the State of residence or to use a combination of the residence criterion and the place of effective management criterion are free in bilateral conventions to substitute for paragraph 3 a provision corresponding to those proposed in paragraphs 2 and 3 of the Commentary on Article 8. Immovable property pertaining to the operation of ships, boats or aircraft may be taxed in the State in which they are situated, in accordance with the rule laid down in paragraph 1." [para. 4]

"As regards elements of capital other than those listed in paragraphs 1 to 3, the article provides that they are taxable only in the Contracting State of which the person to whom they belong is a resident (paragraph 4)." [para. 5]

"If, when the provisions of paragraph 4 are applied to elements of movable property under usufruct, double taxation subsists because of the disparity between domestic laws, the States concerned may resort to the mutual agreement procedure or settle the question by means of bilateral negotiations." [para. 6]

"The Article does not provide any rule about the deductions of debts. The laws of OECD Member countries are too different to allow a common solution for such a deduction. The problem of the deduction of debts which could arise when the taxpayer and the creditor are not residents of the same State is dealt with in paragraph 4 of Article 24." [para. 7]

Commentary on chapter V

METHODS FOR THE ELIMINATION
OF DOUBLE TAXATION

Article 23

METHODS FOR THE ELIMINATION
OF DOUBLE TAXATION

A. GENERAL CONSIDERATIONS

1.   The United Nations Model Convention takes the same approach as the OECD Model Convention concerning methods for the elimination of double taxation and therefore reproduces the two alternative versions of Article 23 embodied in that Convention, namely article 23 A on the exemption method and article 23 B on the credit method.

2.   The method by which a country gives relief from double taxation depends primarily on its general tax policy and the structure of its tax system. Owing to the differences which exist in the various tax systems, bilateral tax treaties provide the most flexible instrument for reconciling conflicting tax systems and for avoiding or mitigating double taxation.

3.   Members of the Group from developing countries felt that, as regards relief measures to be applied by developed countries, the methods of tax exemption and tax credit could be used as appropriate. The exemption method was considered eminently suitable where exclusive tax jurisdiction over certain income was allotted to the country of source under a treaty; it might take the form of an exemption with progression. One of the principal defects of the foreign tax credit method, in the eyes of the developing countries, is that the benefit of low taxes in developing countries or of special tax concessions granted by them may in large part inure to the benefit of the treasury of the capital-exporting country rather than to the foreign investor for

whom the benefits were designed. Thus, revenue is shifted from the developing country to the capital-exporting country.

4.   The effectiveness of the tax incentive measures introduced by most developing countries thus depends on the interrelationship between the tax systems of the developing countries and those of the capital-exporting countries from which the investment originates. It is of primary importance to developing countries to ensure that the tax incentive measures shall not be made ineffective by taxation in the capital-exporting countries using the foreign tax credit system. This undesirable result is to some extent avoided in bilateral treaties through a "tax-sparing" credit, by which a developed country grants a credit not only for the tax paid but for the tax spared by incentive legislation in the developing country. It is also avoided by the exemption method. The members of the Group from developing countries considered it necessary to underline their understanding that either the exemption method or the tax-sparing clause is, for these countries, a basic and fundamental aim in the negotiation of tax treaties. On the other hand, some members noted that studies have shown that tax factors may not themselves be decisive in the process of investment decisions and, therefore, in their view, tax sparing may not be an appropriate policy.

5.   Many members from both developed and developing countries agreed with the view that tax-sparing credits should be included in treaties between developed and developing countries, where the developed country used the credit method. However, a member from a developed country expressed the view that for a variety of reasons tax-sparing credits are not an appropriate tool for economic development, an objective that can better be served by other measures.

6.   While the exemption method of providing relief for double taxation eliminates the undesirable effects of the residence country's taxes on the source country's tax incentive scheme, many developed countries are unprepared to include this system in their treaties. Where the investor's home country applies the principle of foreign tax credit, the most effective method of preserving the effect of the tax incentives and concessions extended by developing countries is a

tax-sparing credit. Three alternatives might be considered to cope with the problem.

7.   First, a tax incentive granting country's internal legislation might include provisions allowing the incentive only if the taxpayer can show to the satisfaction of the tax administration that, upon remittance of its profits abroad, the laws of the country to which the profits are remitted will not, directly or indirectly, tax the income covered by the incentive or will give credit for tax forgone by the incentive. Such a provision would foreclose the possibility of the benefits of a tax incentive flowing from the developing country's fisc to the taxpayer and thence to the fisc of the developed country.

8.   Second, a tax convention might include a provision barring each Contracting State from taxing the profits of an enterprise resident in that State from activities in the other State benefiting from tax incentives granted by the latter until the profits are repatriated or otherwise directly or indirectly remitted to the first Contracting State. Thus, those profits would have to be reinvested in the developing country in order to remain untaxed. Some accounting rules would have to be developed to reflect this provision, and a schedule or timetable for repatriation could be agreed upon by the Contracting States.

9.   Third, the first Contracting State might be allowed to tax such profits, but be required, pursuant to a revenue-sharing agreement, to turn over to the Contracting State where the income was produced the amounts of tax revenue that can reasonably be attributed to the tax incentive granted by the country of source. This proposal has the attraction of preserving the incentive value of the developing country's fiscal sacrifice and of being relatively easy to administer. The existing rules in many developed countries for apportioning the source and nature of foreign income earned by its taxpayers may provide most of the information required to determine the tax revenues that can be attributed to a tax incentive.

10.   On the other hand, some members contended that, theoretically, it could be argued that the effectiveness of the tax incentive measures introduced by many developing countries thus depends, in

part, on the interrelationship between the tax systems of the developing countries and those of the capital-exporting countries which use the foreign tax credit system, that their tax incentives are "matched" by means of a "tax-sparing" credit, granted by the developed country. By a "tax-sparing" credit is meant a credit granted in respect of tax not only actually paid, but actually forgone under its incentive legislation.

11.   In some 20 years which have elapsed since the original publication of the United Nations Model Convention, there have been various studies undertaken of the economic justification for adopting fiscal incentives with the objective of stimulating investment. According to these members, these studies have demonstrated that tax factors may not themselves be decisive in the process of investment decisions made by the enterprises and therefore, in their view, tax sparing may not be an appropriate policy. Other factors play a greater role in forming the so-called "investment climate" of any given country, for example, political and economic stability, a judicial system perceived as impartial, the availability of a skilled workforce, and labour laws and social security costs that do not serve as unintended obstacles to the development of enterprise. It has been argued that fiscal incentives undermine the tax base and can lead to the damaging effects of tax incentive competition which then takes place between neighbouring States, as they try to outdo each other's incentives and lend themselves to fiscal manipulation. Moreover, where "matching" credit provisions have been included in tax treaties, there have been examples of the artificial structuring of business transactions in order to take advantage of them, leading both to erosion of the tax base and to an unintended economic distortion in the process of investment decision-making.

12.   That said, the reality is that, as a policy matter, countries remain free to adopt those investment incentives that seem to them to be useful or unavoidable, given the pressure resulting from the existence of preferential tax regimes, such as tax-free zones in the other jurisdictions, although, as a matter of observation, there is a tendency in more recent years for these to be more narrowly targeted than for-

merly. For example, they may be restricted to specific areas of economic activity, or to specific geographical regions; and, instead of being open-ended, they tend to be relatively tightly time-limited. Where developing countries choose to adopt such fiscal incentives, some experts from developing countries consider that they should continue to have, as a treaty negotiating aim, the inclusion of a "matching" or "tax-sparing" provision in treaties with capital-exporting countries which have a foreign tax credit system. Studies of recent tax treaties concluded between developed and developing countries show that tax-sparing provisions are still features, although these provisions, in their turn, now show a tendency to be more strictly time-limited than previously. Sometimes, there is a "break" or "sunset" clause, providing for the provision to be terminated after, say, five years, unless the treaty partner States agree to an extension. Where such clauses are included, it is the view of some experts from developing countries that the capital-importing country should provide, both in its domestic tax laws and in its treaties, some protection against a future decision by the treaty partner to refuse to extend the life of the tax-sparing provision. This might, for instance, take the form of a so-called "soak-up tax", which consists of a tax or levy designed to reduce the benefit granted by means of the domestic tax incentive legislation, by the amount which would otherwise be transferred to the treasury of the treaty partner, in the absence of a tax-sparing provision. Some countries do not, however, allow a foreign tax credit for soak-up taxes.

13.   The flow of international investment can also be hampered if a country's system of eliminating double taxation, although following article 23 in form, does not lead to the elimination of double taxation in practice. For example, a system's mechanical features may lead to unusable foreign tax credits. Not only is this inconsistent with the spirit of article 23, but it also might impede foreign investment.

14.   The Commentary on Articles 23 A and 23 B of the OECD Model Convention, which is fully relevant in the case of the United Nations Model Convention, contains the following preliminary remarks.

"A.   *The scope of the Articles*

These Articles deal with the so-called juridical double taxation where the same income or capital is taxable in the hands of the same person by more than one State." [para. 1]

"This case has to be distinguished especially from the so-called economic double taxation, i.e., where two different persons are taxable in respect of the same income or capital. If two States wish to solve problems of economic double taxation, they must do so in bilateral negotiations." [para. 2]

"International juridical double taxation may arise in three cases:

(*a*)   where each Contracting State subjects the same person to tax on his worldwide income or capital (concurrent full liability to tax); [Please see paragraph 4 below]

(*b*)   where a person is a resident of a Contracting State (R)[16] and derives income from, or owns capital in, the other Contracting State (S or E) and both States impose tax on that income or capital; [Please see paragraph 5 below]

(*c*)   where each Contracting State subjects the same person, not being a resident of either Contracting State, to tax on income derived from, or capital owned in, a Contracting State: this may result, for instance, in the case where a non-resident person has a permanent establishment or fixed base in one Contracting State (E) through which he derives income from, or owns capital in, the other Contracting State (S) (concurrent limited tax liability)." [para. 3] [Please see paragraph 11 below]

"The conflict in case (*a*) is reduced to that of case (*b*) by virtue of Article 4. This is because that Article defines the term 'resident of a Contracting State' by reference to the liability to tax of a person under domestic law by reason of his domicile,

---

[16]Throughout the Commentary on Articles 23 A and 23 B, the letter "R" stands for the State of residence within the meaning of the Convention, "S" for the State of source or situs, and "E" for the State where a permanent establishment or a fixed base is situated.

residence, place of management or any other criterion of a similar nature (paragraph 1 of Article 4) and by listing special criteria for the case of double residence to determine which of the two States is the State of residence (R) within the meaning of the Convention (paragraphs 2 and 3 of Article 4)" [para. 4] .

"The conflict in case (b) may be solved by allocation of the right to tax between the Contracting States. Such allocation may be made by renunciation of the right to tax either by the State of source or situs (S) or of the situation of the permanent establishment or the fixed base (E), or by the State of residence (R), or by a sharing of the right to tax between the two States. The provisions of the Chapters III and IV of the Convention, combined with the provisions of Article 23 A or 23 B, govern such allocation." [para. 5]

"For some items of income or capital, an exclusive right to tax is given to one of the Contracting States, and the relevant article states that the income or capital in question 'shall be taxable only' in a Contracting State.[17] The words 'shall be taxable only' in a Contracting State preclude the other Contracting State from taxing, thus double taxation is avoided. The State to which the exclusive right to tax is given is normally the State of which the taxpayer is a resident within the meaning of Article 4, that is, State R, but in four Articles[18] the exclusive right may be given to the other Contracting State (S) of which the taxpayer is not a resident within the meaning of Article 4." [para. 6]

"For other items of income or capital, the attribution of the right to tax is not exclusive, and the relevant Article then states that the income or capital in question 'may be taxed' in the

---

[17]Cf. first sentence of paragraph 1 of Article 7, paragraphs 1 and 2 of Article 8, . . . paragraphs 3 and [6] of Article 13, first sentence of paragraph 1 of Article 14, first sentence of paragraph 1 and paragraph 2 of Article 15, Article 18 [except paragraphs 1 and 2 of alternative B], paragraphs 1 and 2 of Article 19, paragraph 1 of Article 21 and paragraphs 3 and 4 of Article 22.

[18]Cf. paragraphs 1 and 2 of Article 8, paragraph 3 of Article 13, subparagraph (a) of paragraphs 1 and 2 of Article 19 and paragraph 3 of Article 22.

Contracting State (S or E) of which the taxpayer is not a resident within the meaning of Article 4. In such case the State of residence (R) must give relief so to avoid the double taxation. Paragraphs 1 and 2 of Article 23 A and paragraph 1 of Article 23 B are designed to give the necessary relief." [para. 7]

"Articles 23 A and 23 B apply to the situation in which a resident of State R derives income from, or owns capital in, the other Contracting State E or S (not being the State of residence within the meaning of the Convention) and that such income or capital, in accordance with the Convention, may be taxed in such other State E or S. The Articles, therefore, apply only to the State of residence and do not prescribe how the other Contracting State E or S has to proceed." [para. 8]

"Where a resident of the Contracting State R derives income from the same State R through a permanent establishment or a fixed base which he has in the other Contracting State E, State E may tax such income (except income from immovable property situated in State R) if it is attributable to the said permanent establishment or fixed base (paragraph 2 of Article 21). In this instance too, State R must give relief under Article 23 A or Article 23 B for income attributable to the permanent establishment or fixed base situated in State E, notwithstanding the fact that the income in question originally arises in State R... However, where the Contracting States agree to give to State R which applies the exemption method a limited right to tax as the State of source of dividends or interest within the limits fixed in paragraph 2 of the Articles 10 or 11 ... then the two States should also agree upon a credit to be given by State E for the tax levied by State R, along the lines of paragraph 2 of Article 23 A or of paragraph 1 of Article 23 B." [para. 9]

"Where a resident of State R derives income from a third State through a permanent establishment or a fixed base which he has in State E, such State E may tax such income (except income from immovable property situated in the third State) if it is attributable to such permanent establishment or fixed base (paragraph 2 of Article 21). State R must give relief under Article 23 A or Article 23 B in respect of income attributable to the permanent establishment or fixed base in State E. There is no provision in the Convention for relief to be given by Contracting State E for taxes levied in the third State where the income arises: however, under paragraph 4 of Article 24 any relief provided for in the domestic laws of State E (double taxation conventions excluded) for residents of State E is also to be granted to a permanent establishment in State E of an enterprise of State R . . ." [para. 10]

"The conflict in case (*c*) of paragraph 3 above is outside the scope of the Convention as, under Article 1, it applies only to persons who are residents of one or both of the States. It can, however, be settled by applying the mutual agreement procedure . . ." [para. 11]

"B.   *Description of methods for elimination of double taxation*

In the existing conventions, two leading principles are followed for the elimination of double taxation by the State of which the taxpayer is a resident. For purposes of simplicity, only income tax is referred to in what follows; but the principles apply equally to capital tax." [para. 12]

"1.   *The principle of exemption*

Under the principle of exemption, the State of residence R does not tax the income which according to the Convention may be taxed in State E or S (nor, of course, also income which shall be taxable only in State E or S . . .)." [para. 13]

"The principle of exemption may be applied by two main methods:

(*a*)   the income which may be taxed in State E or S is not taken into account at all by State R for the purposes of its tax; State R is not entitled to take the income so exempted into consideration when determining the tax to be imposed on the rest of the income; this method is called 'full exemption';

(*b*)   the income which may be taxed in State E or S is not taxed by State R, but State R retains the right to take that income into consideration when determining the tax to be imposed on the rest of the income; this method is called 'exemption with progression'." [para. 14]

"2.   *The principle of credit*

Under the principle of credit, the State of residence R calculates its tax on the basis of the taxpayer's total income including the income from the other State E or S which, according to the Convention, may be taxed in that other State (but not including income which shall be taxable only in State S . . .). It then allows a deduction from its own tax for the tax paid in the other State." [para. 15]

"The principle of credit may be applied by two main methods:

(*a*)   State R allows the deduction of the total amount of tax paid in the other State on income which may be taxed in that State; this method is called 'full credit';

(*b*)   The deduction given by State R for the tax paid in the other State is restricted to that part of its own tax which is appropriate to the income which may be taxed in the other State; this method is called 'ordinary credit'." [para. 16]

"Fundamentally, the difference between the methods is that the exemption methods look at income, while the credit methods look at tax." [para. 17]

"C.   *Operation and effects of the methods*

An example in figures will facilitate the explanation of the effects of the various methods. Suppose the total income to be 100,000, of which 80,000 is derived from one State (State of residence R) and 20,000 from the other State (State of source S). Assume that in State R the rate of tax on an income of 100,000 is 35 per cent and on an income of 80,000 is 30 per cent. Assume further that in State S the rate of tax is either 20 per cent—case (i) or 40 per cent—case (ii), so that the tax payable therein on 20,000 is 4,000 in case (i) or 8,000 in case (ii), respectively." [para. 18]

"If the taxpayer's total income of 100,000 arises in State R, his tax would be 35,000. If he had an income of the same amount, but derived in the manner set out above, and if no relief is provided for in the domestic laws of State R and no conventions exist between State R and State S, then the total amount of tax would be, in case (i): 35,000 plus 4,000 = 39,000, and in case (ii): 35,000 plus 8,000 = 43,000." [para. 19]

"1. *Exemption methods*

Under the exemption methods, State R limits its taxation to that part of the total income which, in accordance with the various articles of the Convention, it has a right to tax, i.e., 80,000.

(*a*) *Full exemption*

State R imposes tax on 80,000 at the rate of tax applicable to 80,000, i.e., at 30 per cent.

	Case (i)	Case (ii)
Tax in State R, 30 per cent of 80,000 . . .	24,000	24,000
Plus tax in State S	4,000	8,000
Total taxes	28,000	32,000
Relief has been given by State R in the amount of	11,000	11,000

(*b*) *Exemption with progression*

State R imposes tax on 80,000 at the rate of tax applicable to total income wherever it arises (100,000), i.e., at 35 per cent.

	Case (i)	Case (ii)
Tax in State R, 35 per cent of 80,000. . .	28,000	28,000
Plus tax in State S	4,000	8,000
Total taxes	32,000	36,000
Relief has been given by State R in the amount of	7,000	7,000"

[para. 20]

"In both cases, the level of tax in State S does not affect the amount of tax given up by State R. If the tax on the income from State S is lower in State S than the relief to be given by State R—cases (a)(i), (a)(ii), and (b)(i)—then the taxpayer will fare better than if his total income were derived solely from State R. In the converse case—case (b)(ii)—the taxpayer will be worse off." [para. 21]

"The example shows also that the relief given where State R applies the full exemption method may be higher than the tax levied in State S, even if the rates of tax in State S are higher than those in State R. This is due to the fact that under the full exemption method, not only the tax of State R on the income from State S is surrendered (35 per cent of 20,000 = 7,000 as under the exemption with progression) but also the tax on remaining income (80,000) is reduced by an amount corresponding to the differences in rates at the two income levels in State R (35 less 30 = 5 per cent applied to 80,000 = 4,000)." [para. 22]

"2.   *Credit methods*

Under the credit methods, State R retains its right to tax the total income of the taxpayer, but against the tax so imposed, it allows a deduction.

(*a*)   *Full credit*

State R computes tax on total income of 100,000 at the rate of 35 per cent and allows the deduction of the tax due in State S on the income from S.

	Case (i)	Case (ii)
Tax in State R, 35 per cent of 100,000 . .	35,000	35,000
Less tax in State S	- 4,000	- 8,000
Tax due	31,000	27,000
Total taxes	35,000	35,000
Relief has been given by State R in the amount of	4,000	8,000

(b)   Ordinary credit

State R computes tax on total income of 100,000 at the rate of 35 per cent and allows the deduction of the tax due in State S on the income from S, but in no case it allows more than the portion of tax in State R attributable to the income from S (maximum deduction). The maximum deduction would be 35 per cent of 20,000 = 7,000.

	Case (i)	Case (ii)
Tax in State R, 35 per cent of 100,000 . .	35,000	35,000
Less tax in State S	- 4,000	
Less maximum deduction.		- 7,000
Tax due	31,000	28,000
Total taxes	35,000	36,000
Relief has been given by State R in the amount of	4,000	7,000"

[para. 23]

"A characteristic of the credit methods compared with the exemption methods is that State R is never obliged to allow a deduction of more than the tax due in State S." [para. 24]

"Where the tax due in State S is lower than the tax of State R appropriate to the income from State S (maximum deduction), the taxpayer will always have to pay the same amount of taxes as he would have had to pay if he were taxed only in State R, i.e., as if his total income were derived solely from State R." [para. 25]

"The same result is achieved, where the tax due in State S is the higher, while State R applies the full credit, at least as long as the total tax due to State R is as high as or higher than the amount of the tax due in State S." [para. 26]

"Where the tax due in State S is higher and where the credit is limited (ordinary credit), the taxpayer will not get a deduction for the whole of the tax paid in State S. In such event the result would be less favourable to the taxpayer than if his whole income arose in State R, and in these circumstances the ordinary credit method would have the same effect as the method of exemption with progression." [para. 27]

"D.   *The methods proposed in the Articles*

In the conventions concluded between OECD Member countries both leading principles have been followed. Some States have a preference for the first one, some for the other. Theoretically, a single principle could be held to be more desirable, but, on account of the preferences referred to, each State has been left free to make its own choice." [para. 28]

"On the other hand, it has been found important to limit the number of methods based on each leading principle to be employed. In view of this limitation, the Articles have been drafted so that Member countries are left free to choose between two methods:

—the exemption method with progression (Article 23 A), and

—the ordinary credit method (Article 23 B)." [para. 29]

"If two Contracting States both adopt the same method, it will be sufficient to insert the relevant Article in the convention. On the other hand, if the two Contracting States adopt different methods, both Articles may be amalgamated in one, and the name of the State must be inserted in each appropriate part of the Article, according to the method adopted by that State." [para. 30]

"Contracting States may use a combination of the two methods. Such combination is indeed necessary for a Contracting State R which generally adopts the exemption method in the case of income which under Articles 10 and 11 may be subjected to a limited tax in the other Contracting State S. For such case, Article 23 A provides in paragraph 2 a credit for the limited tax levied in the other Contracting State S. Moreover, States which in general adopt the exemption method may wish to exclude specific items of income from exemption and to apply to such items the credit method. In such case, paragraph 2 of Article 23 A could be amended to include these items of income." [para. 31]

"The two Articles are drafted in a general way and do not give detailed rules on how the exemption or credit is to be computed, this being left to the domestic laws and practice applicable. Contracting States which find it necessary to settle any problem in the convention itself are left free to do so in bilateral negotiations". [para. 32]

B. COMMENTARY ON THE PARAGRAPHS OF ARTICLE 23 A

14. Since article 23 A of the United Nations Model Convention reproduces Article 23 A of the OECD Model Convention, the Commentary on that Article is fully relevant:

"Paragraph 1

A. *The obligation of the State of residence to give exemption*

In the Article it is laid down that the State of residence R shall exempt from tax income and capital, which in accordance with the Convention 'may be taxed' in the other State E or S." [para. 33]

"The State of residence must accordingly give exemption whether or not the right to tax is in effect exercised by the other State. This method is regarded as the most practical one since it relieves the State of residence from undertaking investigations of the actual taxation position in the other State." [para. 34]

"Occasionally, negotiating States may find it reasonable in certain circumstances to make an exception to the absolute obligation on the State of residence to give exemption. Such may be the case, in order to avoid non-taxation, where under the domestic laws of the State of source no tax on specific items of income or capital is provided, or tax is not effectively collected owing to special circumstances such as the set-off of losses, a mistake, or the statutory time limit having expired. To avoid non-taxation of specific items of income, Contracting States may agree to amend the relevant Article itself . . . One might also make an exception to the general rule, in order to achieve a certain reciprocity, where one of the States adopts the exemption method and the other the credit method. Finally, another exception to the general rule may be made where a State wishes to apply to specific items of income the credit method rather than exemption . . . ." [para. 35]

"As already mentioned . . . , the exemption method does not apply to such items of income which according to the Convention may be taxed in the State of residence but may also be subject to a limited tax in the other Contracting State. For such items of income, paragraph 2 of Article 23 A provides for the credit method . . . ." [para. 36]

15.   In the United Nations Model Convention, the right to tax in the country of source extends in many cases to income which under the OECD Model Convention is taxable only in the country of residence. As a consequence, many countries adopting the exemption method in their bilateral conventions may wish to restrict the application of paragraph 1 of article 23 A, e.g., by limiting the exemption from tax to income effectively taxed in the country of source or by applying to some items of income the tax credit provided for in paragraph 2 of article 23 A rather than the tax exemption. Also, because article 23 A, paragraph 1, of the United Nations Model Convention has a much broader scope than the corresponding provision of the OECD Model Convention, a State which generally chooses the exemption method may elect the credit method for specific items of income not mentioned in paragraph 2 of article 23 A.

16.   The OECD Commentary continues as follows:

"B.   *Alternative formulation of the Article*

An effect of the exemption method as it is drafted in the Article is that the taxable income or capital in the State of residence is reduced by the amount exempted in that State. If in a particular State the amount of income as determined for income tax purposes is used as a measure for other purposes, e.g., social benefits, the application of the exemption method in the form proposed may have the effect that such benefits may be given to persons who ought not to receive them. To avoid such consequences the Article may be altered so that the income in question is included in the taxable income in the State of residence. The State of residence must, in such cases, give up that part of the total tax appropriate to the income concerned. This procedure would give the same result as the Article in the form proposed. States can be left free to make such modifications in the drafting of the Article. If a State wants to draft the Article as indicated above, paragraph 1 may be drafted as follows:

'Where a resident of a Contracting State derives income or owns capital which, in accordance with the provisions of this Convention, shall be taxable only or may be taxed in the other Contracting State, the first mentioned State shall, subject to the provisions of paragraph 2, allow as a deduction from the income tax or capital tax that part of the income tax or capital tax, respectively, which is applicable, as the case may be, to the income derived from or the capital owned in that other State.'

If the Article is so drafted, paragraph 3 would not be necessary and could be omitted." [para. 37]

"C.   *Miscellaneous problems*

Article 23 A contains the principle that the State of residence has to give exemption, but does not give detailed rules on how the exemption has to be implemented. This is consistent with the general pattern of the Convention. Articles 6 to

22 too lay down rules attributing the right to tax in respect of the various types of income or capital without dealing, as a rule, with the determination of taxable income or capital, deductions, rate of taxes etc. (cf., however, paragraph 3 of Article 7 and Article 24). Experience has shown that many problems may arise. This is especially true with respect to Article 23 A. Some of them are dealt with in the following paragraphs. In the absence of a specific provision in the Convention, the domestic laws of each Contracting State are applicable. Some conventions contain an express reference to the domestic laws but of course this would not help where the exemption method is not used in the domestic laws. In such cases, Contracting States which face this problem should establish rules for the application of Article 23 A, if necessary, after having consulted with the competent authority of the other Contracting State (paragraph 3 of Article 25)." [para. 38]

"1. *Amount to be exempted*

The amount of income to be exempted from tax by the State of residence is the amount which, but for the Convention, would be subjected to domestic income tax according to the domestic laws governing such tax. It may, therefore, differ from the amount of income subjected to tax by the State of source according to its domestic laws." [para. 39]

"Normally, the basis for the calculation of income tax is the total net income, i.e., gross income less allowable deductions. Therefore, it is the gross income derived from the State of source less any allowable deductions (specified or proportional) connected with such income which is to be exempted." [para. 40]

"Problems arise from the fact that most countries provide in their respective taxation laws for additional deductions from total income or specific items of income to arrive at the income subject to tax. A numerical example may illustrate the problem:

(a)	Domestic income (gross less allowable expenses) . . .	100
(b)	Income from the other State (gross less allowable expenses)	100
(c)	Total income	200
(d)	Deductions for other expenses provided for under the laws of the State of residence which are not connected with any of the income under (a) or (b), such as insurance premiums, contributions to welfare institutions	- 20
(e)	'Net' income	180
(f)	Personal and family allowances	- 30
(g)	Income subject to tax	150

The question is, what amount should be exempted from tax, e.g.:

—100 (line (b)), leaving a taxable amount of 50;

—90 (half of line (e), according to the ratio between line (b) and line (c)), leaving 60 (line (f) being fully deducted from domestic income);

—75 (half of line (g), according to the ratio between line (b) and line (c)), leaving 75;

—or any other amount." [para. 41]

"A comparison of the laws and practices of the OECD Member countries shows that the amount to be exempted varies considerably from country to country. The solution adopted by a State will depend on the policy followed by that State and its tax structure. It may be the intention of a State that its residents always enjoy the full benefit of their personal and family allowances and other deductions. In other States these tax free amounts are apportioned. In many States personal or family allowances form part of the progressive scale, are granted as a deduction from tax, or are even unknown, the family status being taken into account by separate tax scales." [para. 42]

"In view of the wide variety of fiscal policies and techniques in the different States regarding the determination of tax, especially deductions, allowances and similar benefits, it is preferable not to propose an express and uniform solution in the Convention, but to leave each State free to apply its own legislation and technique. Contracting States which prefer to have special problems solved in their convention are, of course, free to do so in bilateral negotiations. Finally, attention is drawn to the fact that the problem is also of importance for States applying the credit method . . ." [para. 43]

"2. *Treatment of losses*

Several States in applying Article 23 A treat losses incurred in the other State in the same manner as they treat income arising in that State: as State of residence (State R), they do not allow deduction of a loss incurred from immovable property or a permanent establishment situated in the other State (E or S). Provided that this other State allows carry over of such loss, the taxpayer will not be at any disadvantage as he is merely prevented from claiming a double deduction of the same loss namely in State E (or S) and in State R. Other States may, as State of residence R, allow a loss incurred in State E (or S) as a deduction from the income they assess. In such a case State R should be free to restrict the exemption under paragraph 1 of Article 23 A for profits or income which are made subsequently in the other State E (or S) by deducting from such subsequent profits or income the amount of earlier losses which the taxpayer can carry over in State E (or S). As the solution depends primarily on the domestic laws of the Contracting States and as the laws of the OECD Member countries differ from each other substantially, no solution can be proposed in the Article itself, it being left to the Contracting States, if they find it necessary, to clarify the above-mentioned question and other problems connected with losses . . . bilaterally, either in the Article itself or by way of a mutual agreement procedure (paragraph 3 of Article 25)." [para. 44]

"3. *Taxation of the rest of income*

Apart from the application of progressive tax rates which is now dealt with in paragraph 3 of the Article . . . some problems may arise from specific provisions of the tax laws. Thus, e.g., some tax laws provide that taxation starts only if a minimum amount of taxable income is reached or exceeded (tax-exempt threshold). Total income before application of the Convention may clearly exceed such tax-free threshold; but by virtue of the exemption resulting from the application of the Convention which leads to a deduction of the tax-exempt income from total taxable income, the remaining taxable income may be reduced to an amount below this threshold. For the reasons mentioned in paragraph 43 above, no uniform solution can be proposed. It may be noted, however, that the problem will not arise, if the alternative formulation of paragraph 1 of Article 23 A . . . is adopted." [para. 45]

"Certain States have introduced special systems for taxing corporate income . . . In States applying a split-rate corporation tax . . . , the problem may arise whether the income to be exempted has to be deducted from undistributed income (to which the normal rate of tax applies) or from distributed income (to which the reduced rate applies) or whether the income to be exempted has to be attributed partly to distributed and partly to undistributed income. Where, under the laws of a State applying the split-rate corporation tax, a supplementary tax is levied in the hands of a parent company on dividends which it received from a domestic subsidiary company but which it does not redistribute (on the grounds that such supplementary tax is a compensation for the benefit of a lower tax rate granted to the subsidiary on the distributions), the problem arises whether such supplementary tax may be charged where the subsidiary pays its dividends out of income exempt from tax by virtue of the Convention. Finally, a similar problem may arise in connection with taxes ('précompte', Advance Corporation Tax) which are levied on distributed profits of a corporation in order to cover the tax credit attributable to the shareholders . . . The question is whether such special taxes connected with the distribution of profits could be levied in so far as distributions are made out of profits exempt from tax. It is left to Contracting States to settle these questions by bilateral negotiations." [para. 46]

"Paragraph 2

In Articles 10 and 11 the right to tax dividends and interest is divided between the State of residence and the State of source. In these cases, the State of residence is left free not to tax if it wants to do so . . . and to apply the exemption method also to the above-mentioned items of income. However, where the State of residence prefers to make use of its right to tax such items of income, it cannot apply the exemption method to eliminate the double taxation since it would thus give up fully its right to tax the income concerned. For the State of residence, the application of the credit method would normally seem to give a satisfactory solution. Moreover, as already indicated in paragraph 31 above, States which in general apply the exemption method may wish to apply to specific items of income the credit method rather than exemption. Consequently, the paragraph is drafted in accordance with the ordinary credit method. The Commentary on Article 23 B hereafter applies mutatis mutandis to paragraph 2 of Article 23 A." [para. 47]

"In the cases referred to in the previous paragraph, certain maximum percentages are laid down for tax reserved to the State of source. In such cases, the rate of tax in the State of residence will very often be higher than the rate in the State of source. The limitation of the deduction which is laid down in the second sentence of paragraph 2 and which is in accordance with the ordinary credit method is therefore of consequence only in a limited number of cases. If, in such cases, the Contracting States prefer to waive the limitation and to apply the full credit method, they can do so by deleting the second sentence of paragraph 2 . . ." [para. 48]

"Dividends from substantial holdings by a company

The combined effect of paragraphs 1 and 2 of Article 10 and Article 23 (Article 23 A and 23 B as appropriate) is that the State of residence of the shareholder is allowed to tax dividends arising in the other State, but that it must credit against its own tax on such dividends the tax which has been collected by the State where the dividends arise at a rate fixed under paragraph 2 of Article 10. This regime equally applies when the recipient of the dividends is a parent company receiving dividends from a subsidiary; in this case, the tax withheld in the State of the subsidiary—and credited in the State of the parent company—is limited to [5] per cent of the gross amount of the dividends by the application of subparagraph (*a*) of paragraph 2 of Article 10." [para. 49]

"These provisions effectively avoid the juridical double taxation of dividends but they do not prevent recurrent corporate taxation on the profits distributed to the parent company: first at the level of the subsidiary and again at the level of the parent company. Such recurrent taxation creates a very important obstacle to the development of international investment. Many States have recognized this and have inserted in their domestic laws provisions designed to avoid this obstacle. Moreover, provisions to this end are frequently inserted in double taxation conventions." [para. 50]

"The Committee on Fiscal Affairs has considered whether it would be appropriate to modify Article 23 of the Convention in order to settle this question. Although many States favoured the insertion of such a provision in the Model Convention this met with many difficulties, resulting from the diverse opinions of States and the variety of possible solutions. Some States, fearing tax evasion, preferred to maintain their freedom of action and to settle the question only in their domestic laws." [para. 51]

"In the end, it appeared preferable to leave States free to choose their own solution to the problem. For States preferring to solve the problem in their conventions, the solutions would most frequently follow one of the principles below:

(a) Exemption with progression

The State of which the parent company is a resident exempts the dividends it receives from its subsidiary in the other State, but it may nevertheless take these dividends into account in computing the tax due by the parent company on the remaining income (such a provision will frequently be favoured by States applying the exemption method specified in Article 23 A).

(b) Credit for underlying taxes

As regards dividends received from the subsidiary, the State of which the parent company is a resident gives credit as provided for in paragraph 2 of Article 23 A or in paragraph 1 of Article 23 B, as appropriate, not only for the tax on dividends as such, but also for the tax paid by the subsidiary on the profits distributed (such a provision will frequently be favoured by States applying as a general rule the credit method specified in Article 23 B).

(c) Assimilation to a holding in a domestic subsidiary

The dividends that the parent company derives from a foreign subsidiary are treated, in the State of the parent company, in the same way for tax purposes as dividends received from a subsidiary which is a resident of that State." [para. 52]

"When the State of the parent company levies taxes on capital, a similar solution should also be applied to such taxes." [para. 53]

"Moreover, States are free to fix the limits and methods of application of these provisions (definition and minimum duration of holding of the shares, proportion of the dividends deemed to be taken up by administrative or financial expenses) or to make the relief granted under the special regime subject to the condition that the subsidiary is carrying out a genuine economic activity in the State of which it is a resident, or that it derives the major part of its income from that State or that it is subject to a substantial taxation on profits therein." [para. 54]

"Paragraph 3

The 1963 Draft Convention reserved expressly the application of the progressive scale of tax rates by the State of residence (last sentence of paragraph 1 of Article 23 A) and most conventions concluded between OECD Member countries which adopt the exemption method follow this principle. According to paragraph 3 of Article 23 A, the State of residence retains the right to take the amount of exempted income or capital into consideration when determining the tax to be imposed on the rest of the income or capital. The rule applies even where the exempted income (or items of capital) and the taxable income (or items of capital) accrue to those persons (e.g., husband and wife) whose incomes (or items of capital) are taxed jointly according to the domestic laws. This principle of progression applies to income or capital exempted by virtue of paragraph 1 of Article 23 A as well as to income or capital which under any other provision of the Convention 'shall be taxable only' in the other Contracting State . . . This is the reason why, in the 1977 Model Convention, the principle of progression was transferred from paragraph 1 of Article 23 A to a new paragraph 3 of the said Article, and reference is made to exemption 'in accordance with any provision of the Convention'." [para. 55]

"Paragraph 3 of Article 23 A relates only to the State of residence. The form of the Article does not prejudice the application by the State of source of the provisions of its domestic laws concerning the progression." [para. 56]

C.   COMMENTARY ON THE PARAGRAPHS OF ARTICLE 23 B

18.   Since article 23 B of the United Nations Model Convention reproduces Article 23 B of the OECD Model Convention, the Commentary on that Article, quoted below, is fully relevant:

"Paragraph 1

A. *Methods*

Article 23 B, based on the credit principle, follows the ordinary credit method: the State of residence (R) allows, as a deduction from its own tax on the income or capital of its resident, an amount equal to the tax paid in the other State E (or S) on the income derived from, or capital owned in, that other State E (or S), but the deduction is restricted to the appropriate proportion of its own tax." [para. 57]

"The ordinary credit method is intended to apply also for a State which follows the exemption method but has to give credit, under paragraph 2 of Article 23 A, for the tax levied at limited rates in the other State on dividends and interest . . . The possibility of some modification . . . could, of course, also be of relevance in the case of dividends and interest paid to a resident of a State which adopted the ordinary credit method . . ." [para. 58]

"It is to be noted that Article 23 B applies in a State R only to items of income or capital which, in accordance with the Convention, 'may be taxed' in the other State E (or S). Items of income or capital which according to Article 8, to paragraph 3 of Article 13, to subparagraph (*a*) of paragraphs 1 and 2 of Article 19 and to paragraph 3 of Article 22, 'shall be taxable only' in the other State, are from the outset exempt from tax in State R . . . , and the Commentary on Article 23 A applies to such exempted income and capital. As regards progression, reference is made to paragraph 2 of the Article . . ." [para. 59]

"Article 23 B sets out the main rules of the credit method, but does not give detailed rules on the computation and operation of the credit. This is consistent with the general pattern of the Convention. Experience has shown that many problems may arise. Some of them are dealt with in the following paragraphs. In many States, detailed rules on credit for foreign tax already exist in their domestic laws. A number of conventions, therefore, contain a reference to the domestic laws of the Contracting States and further provide that such domestic rules shall not affect the principle laid down in Article 23 B. Where the credit method is not used in the domestic laws of a Contracting State, this State should establish rules for the application of Article 23 B, if necessary after consultation with the competent authority of the other Contracting State (paragraph 3 of Article 25)." [para. 60]

"The amount of foreign tax for which a credit has to be allowed is the tax effectively paid in accordance with the Convention in the other Contracting State. Problems may arise, e.g., where such tax is not calculated on the income of the year for which it is levied but on the income of a preceding year or on the average income of two or more preceding years. Other problems may arise in connection with different methods of determining the income or in connection with changes in the currency rates (devaluation or revaluation). However, such problems could hardly be solved by an express provision in the Convention." [para. 61]

"According to the provisions of the second sentence of paragraph 1 of Article 23 B, the deduction which the State of residence (R) is to allow is restricted to that part of the income tax which is appropriate to the income derived from the State S or E (so-called 'maximum deduction'). Such maximum deduction may be computed either by apportioning the total tax on total income according to the ratio between the income for which credit is to be given and the total income, or by applying the tax rate for total income to the income for which credit is to be given. In fact, in cases where the tax in State E (or S) equals or exceeds the appropriate tax of State R, the credit method will have the same effect as the exemption method with progression. Also under the credit method, similar problems as regards the amount of income, tax rate etc. may arise as are mentioned in the Commentary on Article 23 A . . . For the same reasons mentioned in paragraphs 42 and 43 above, it is preferable also for the credit method, not to propose an express and uniform solution in the Convention, but to leave each State free to apply its own legislation and technique. This is also true for some further problems which are dealt with below." [para. 62]

"The maximum deduction is normally computed as the tax on net income, i.e., on the income from State E (or S) less allowable deductions (specified or proportional) connected with such income . . . For such reason, the maximum deduction in many cases may be lower than the tax effectively paid in State E (or S). This may especially be true in the case where, for instance, a resident of State R deriving interest from State S has borrowed funds from a third person to finance the interest-producing loan. As the interest due on such borrowed money may be offset against the interest derived from State S, the amount of net income subject to tax in State R may be very small, or there may even be no net income at all. This problem could be solved by using the full credit method in State R as mentioned in paragraph 48 above. Another solution would be to exempt such income from tax in State S, as it is proposed in the Commentary in respect of interest on credit sales and on loans granted by banks . . ." [para. 63]

"If a resident of State R derives income of different kinds from State S, and the latter State, according to its tax laws, imposes tax only on one of these items, the maximum deduction which State R is to allow will normally be that part of its tax which is appropriate only to that item of income which is taxed in State S. However, other solutions are possible, especially in view of the following broader problem: the fact that credit has to be given, e.g., for several items of income on which tax at different rates is levied in State S, or for income from several States, with or without conventions, raises the question whether the maximum deduction or the credit has to be calculated separately for each item of income, or for each country, or for all foreign income qualifying for credit under domestic laws and under conventions. Under an 'overall credit' system, all foreign income is aggregated, and the total of foreign taxes is credited against the domestic tax appropriate to the total foreign income." [para. 64]

"Further problems may arise in case of losses. A resident of State R, deriving income from State E (or S), may have a loss in State R, or in State E (or S) or in a third State. For purposes of the tax credit, in general, a loss in a given State will be set off against other income from the same State. Whether a loss suffered outside State R (e.g., in a permanent establishment) may be deducted from other income, whether derived from State R or not, depends on the domestic laws of State R. Here similar problems may arise, as mentioned in the Commentary on Article 23 A (paragraph 44 above). When the total income is derived from abroad, and no income but a loss not exceeding the income from abroad arises in State R, then the total tax charged in State R will be appropriate to the income from State S, and the maximum deduction which State R is to allow will consequently be the tax charged in State R. Other solutions are possible." [para. 65]

"The aforementioned problems depend very much on domestic laws and practice, and the solution must, therefore, be left to each State. In this context, it may be noted that some States are very liberal in applying the credit method. Some States are also considering or have already adopted the possibility of carrying over unused tax credits. Contracting States are, of course, free in bilateral negotiations to amend the Article to deal with any of the aforementioned problems." [para. 66]

"In so-called thin 'capitalizations' situations, the Model Convention allows the State of the borrower company, under certain conditions, to treat an interest payment as a distribution of dividends in accordance with its domestic legislation; the essential condition is that the contributor of the loan should effectively share the risks run by the borrower company. This gives rise to two consequences:

—the taxing at source of such 'interest' at the rate for dividends (paragraph 2 of Article 10);

—the inclusion of such 'interest' in the taxable profits of the lender company." [para. 67]

"If the relevant conditions are met, the State of residence of the lender would be obliged to give relief for any juridical or economic double taxation of the interest as if the payment was in fact a dividend. It should then give credit for tax effectively withheld on this interest in the State of residence of the borrower at the rate applicable to dividends and, in addition, if the lender is the parent company of the borrower company, apply to such 'interest' any additional relief under its parent/subsidiary regime. This obligation may result:

(*a*)   from the actual wording of Article 23 of the Convention, when it grants relief in respect of income defined as dividends in Article 10 or of items of income dealt with in Article 10;

(*b*)   from the context of the Convention, i.e., from a combination of Articles 9, 10, 11, and 23 and, if need be, by way of the mutual agreement procedure

—where the interest has been treated in the country of residence of the borrower company as a dividend under rules which are in accordance with paragraph 1 of Article 9 or paragraph 6 of Article 11 and where the State of residence of the lender agrees that it has been properly so treated and is prepared to apply a corresponding adjustment;

—when the State of residence of the lender applies similar thin capitalization rules and would treat the payment as a dividend in a reciprocal situation, i.e., if the payment were made by a company established in its territory to a resident in the other Contracting State;

—in all other cases where the State of residence of the lender recognizes that it was proper for the State of residence of the borrower to treat the interest as a dividend." [para. 68].

"B.   *Remarks concerning capital tax*

As paragraph 1 is drafted, credit is to be allowed for income tax only against income tax and for capital tax only against capital tax. Consequently, credit for or against capital tax will be given only if there is a capital tax in both Contracting States." [para. 70]

"In bilateral negotiations, two Contracting States may agree that a tax called a capital tax is of a nature closely related to income tax and may, therefore, wish to allow credit for it against income tax and vice versa. There are cases where because one State does not impose a capital tax or because both States impose capital taxes only on domestic assets, no double taxation of capital will arise. In such cases it is, of course, understood that the reference to capital taxation may be deleted. Furthermore, States may find it desirable, regardless of the nature of the taxes under the convention, to allow credit for the total amount of tax in the State of source or situs against the total amount of tax in the State of residence. Where, however, a convention includes both real capital taxes and capital taxes which are in their nature income taxes, the States may wish to allow credit against income tax only for the latter capital taxes. In such cases, States are free to alter the proposed Article so as to achieve the desired effect." [para. 71]

"C.   *The relation in special cases between the taxation in the State of source and the ordinary credit method*

In certain cases a State, especially a developing country, may for particular reasons give concessions to taxpayers, e.g., tax incentive reliefs to encourage industrial output. In a similar way, a State may exempt from tax certain kinds of income, e.g., pensions to war-wounded soldiers." [para. 72]

"When such a State concludes a convention with a State which applies the exemption method, no restriction of the relief given to the taxpayers arises, because that other State must give exemption regardless of the amount of tax, if any, imposed in the State of source (see paragraph 34 above). But when the other State applies the credit method, the concession may be nullified to the extent that such other State will allow a deduction only of the tax paid in the State of source. By reason of the concessions, that other State secures what may be called an uncovenanted gain for its own Exchequer." [para. 73]

"Should the two States agree that the benefit of the concessions given to the taxpayers in the State of source are not to be nullified, a derogation from paragraph 2 of Article 23 A, or from Article 23 B will be necessary." [para. 74]

"Various formulae can be used to this effect as for example:

(*a*)   the State of residence will allow as a deduction the amount of tax which the State of source could have imposed in accordance with its general legislation or such amount as limited by the Convention (e.g., limitations of rates provided for dividends and interest in articles 10 and 11) even if the State of source, as a developing country, has waived all or part of that tax under special provisions for the promotion of its economic development;

(*b*)   as a counterpart for the tax sacrifice which the developing country makes by reducing in a general way its tax at the source, the State of residence agrees to allow a deduction against its own tax of an amount (in part fictitious) fixed at a higher rate;

(*c*)   the State of residence exempts the income which has benefited from tax incentives in the developing country.

Contracting States are free to devise other formulae in the course of bilateral negotiations." [para. 75]

"If a Contracting State agrees to stimulate especially investments in the other State being a developing country, the above provisions will generally be accompanied by guarantees for the investors, that is to say, the convention will limit the rate of tax which can be imposed in the State of source on dividends, interest and royalties." [para. 76]

"Moreover, time restrictions or time limits can be provided for the application of the advantages referred to in formula (*a*), and possibly (*c*), above: the extended credit (or the exemption) may be granted only in respect of incentives applied temporarily in developing countries, or only for investments made or contracts concluded in the future (for instance, from the date of entry into force of the convention) or for a determined period of time." [para. 77]

"Thus, there exist a considerable number of solutions to this problem. In fact, the concrete effects of the provisions concerned can also vary as a result of other factors such as the amount to be included in the taxable income in the State of residence (formulae (*a*) and (*b*) above); it may be the net income derived (after deduction of the tax effectively paid in the State of source), or the net income grossed-up by an amount equal to the tax effectively paid in the State of source, or to the tax which could have been levied in accordance with the convention (rates provided for in Articles 10 and 11) or to the tax which the State of residence agrees to allow as a deduction." [para. 78]

"*Paragraph* 2

This paragraph has been added to enable the State of residence to retain the right to take the amount of income or capital exempted in that State into consideration when determining the tax to be imposed on the rest of the income or capital. The right so retained extends to income or capital which 'shall be taxable only' in the other State. The principle of progression is thus safeguarded for the State of residence, not only in relation to income or capital which 'may be taxed' in the other State, but also for income or capital which 'shall be taxable only' in that other State. The Commentary on paragraph 3 of Article 23 A in relation to the State of source also applies to paragraph 2 of Article 23 B". [para. 79]

Commentary on chapter VI

SPECIAL PROVISIONS

Article 24

NON-DISCRIMINATION

1.   Article 24 of the United Nations Model Convention reproduces Article 24 of the OECD Model Convention. In 1999, the definition of the term "national" which had previously been included in this article was moved to article 3 as was also done in the OECD Model Convention. (Cf. paragraph 9 of the Commentary on article 3 above).

Paragraph 1

2.   Since this paragraph reproduces Article 24, paragraph 1, of the OECD Model Convention, the Commentary on that paragraph is fully relevant:

"This paragraph establishes the principle that for purposes of taxation discrimination on the grounds of nationality is forbidden, and that, subject to reciprocity, the nationals of a Contracting State may not be less favourably treated in the other Contracting State than nationals of the latter State in the same circumstances." [para. 1]

"It is noteworthy that the principle of non-discrimination, under various descriptions and with a more or less wide scope, was applied in international fiscal relations well before the appearance, at the end of the 19th century, of the classic type of double taxation conventions. Thus, in a great many agreements of different kinds (consular or establishment conventions, treaties of friendship or commerce etc.) concluded by States, especially in the 19th century, in order to extend and strengthen the diplomatic protection of their nationals wherever resident, there are clauses under which each of the two

Contracting States undertakes to accord nationals of the other State equality of treatment with their own nationals. The fact that such clauses subsequently found their way into double taxation conventions has in no way affected their original justification and scope. The text of paragraph 1 provides that the application of this paragraph is not restricted by Article 1 to nationals solely who are residents of a Contracting State, but on the contrary, extends to all nationals of each Contracting State, whether or not they be residents of one of them. In other words, all nationals of a Contracting State are entitled to invoke the benefit of this provision as against the other Contracting State. This holds good, in particular, for nationals of the Contracting States who are not residents of either of them but of a third State." [para. 2]

"The expression 'in the same circumstances' refers to taxpayers (individuals, legal persons, partnerships and associations) placed, from the point of view of the application of the ordinary taxation laws and regulations, in substantially similar circumstances both in law and in fact. The expression 'in particular with respect to residence' makes clear that the residence of the taxpayer is one of the factors that are relevant in determining whether taxpayers are placed in similar circumstances. The expression 'in the same circumstances' would be sufficient by itself to establish that a taxpayer who is a resident of a Contracting State and one who is not a resident of that State are not in the same circumstances. In fact, whilst the expression 'in particular with respect to residence' did not appear in the 1963 Draft Convention or in the 1977 Model Convention, the Member countries have consistently held, in applying and interpreting the expression 'in the same circumstances', that the residence of the taxpayer must be taken into account. However, in revising the Model Convention, the Committee on Fiscal Affairs felt that a specific reference to the residence of the taxpayers would be a useful clarification as it would avoid any possible doubt as to the interpretation to be given to the expression 'in the same circumstances' in this respect." [para. 3]

"In applying paragraph 1, therefore, the underlying question is whether two persons who are residents of the same State are being treated differently solely by reason of having a different nationality. Consequently, if a Contracting State, in giving relief from taxation on account of family responsibilities, distinguishes between its own nationals according to whether they reside in its territory or not, that State cannot be obliged to give nationals of the other State who do not reside in its territory the same treatment as it gives its resident nationals but it undertakes to extend to them the same treatment as is available to its nationals who reside in the other State. Similarly, paragraph 1 does not apply where a national of a Contracting State (State R) who is also a resident of State R is taxed less favourably in the other Contracting State (State S) than a national of State S residing in a third State (for instance, as a result of the application of provisions aimed at discouraging the use of tax havens) as the two persons are not in the same circumstances with respect to their residence." [para. 4]

"Likewise, the provisions of paragraph 1 are not to be construed as obliging a State which accords special taxation privileges to its own public bodies or services as such, to extend the same privileges to the public bodies and services of the other State." [para. 5]

"Neither are they to be construed as obliging a State which accords special taxation privileges to private institutions not for profit whose activities are performed for purposes of public benefit, which are specific to that State to extend the same privileges to similar institutions whose activities are not for its benefit." [para. 6]

"To take the first of these two cases, if a State accords immunity from taxation to its own public bodies and services, this is justified because such bodies and services are integral parts of the State and at no time can their circumstances be comparable to those of the public bodies and services of the other State. Nevertheless, this reservation is not intended to apply to State corporations carrying on gainful undertakings. To the extent that these can be regarded as being on the same footing as private industrial and commercial undertakings, the provisions of paragraph 1 will apply to them." [para. 7]

"As for the second case, if a State accords taxation privileges to certain private institutions not for profit, this is clearly justified by the very nature of these institutions' activities and by the benefit which that State and its nationals will derive from those activities." [para. 8]

"Furthermore, paragraph 1 has been deliberately framed in a negative form. By providing that the nationals of a Contracting State may not be subjected in the other Contracting State to any taxation or any requirement connected therewith which is other or more burdensome than the taxation and connected requirements to which nationals of the other Contracting State in the same circumstances are or may be subjected, this paragraph has the same mandatory force as if it enjoined the Contracting States to accord the same treatment to their respective nationals. But since the principal object of this clause is to forbid discrimination in one State against the nationals of the other, there is nothing to prevent the first State from granting to persons of foreign nationality, for special reasons of its own, or in order to comply with a special stipulation in a double taxation convention, such as, notably, the requirement that profits of permanent establishments are to be taxed on the basis of separate accounts, certain concessions or facilities which are not available to its own nationals. As it is worded, paragraph 1 would not prohibit this." [para. 9]

"Subject to the foregoing observation, the words '. . . shall not be subjected . . . to any taxation or any requirement connected therewith which is other or more burdensome . . .' mean that when a tax is imposed on nationals and foreigners in the same circumstances, it must be in the same form as regards both the basis of charge and the method of assessment, its rate must be the same and, finally, the formalities connected with the taxation (returns, payment, prescribed times etc.) must not be more onerous for foreigners than for nationals." [para. 10]

"In view of the legal relationship created between the company and the State under whose law it is constituted, which from certain points of view is closely akin to the relationship of nationality in the case of individuals, it seems justifiable not to deal with legal persons, partnerships and associations in a special provision, but to assimilate them with individuals under paragraph 1. This result is achieved through the definition of the term 'national' in subparagraph (f) of paragraph 1 of Article 3." [para. 11]

Paragraph 2

3. Since this paragraph reproduces Article 24, paragraph 2, of the OECD Model Convention, the Commentary on the latter paragraph, which reads as follows, is fully relevant:

"On 28th September, 1954, a number of States concluded in New York a Convention relating to the status of stateless persons, under article 29 of which stateless persons must be accorded national treatment. The signatories of the Convention include several OECD Member countries." [para. 12]

"It should, however, be recognized that the provisions of paragraph 2 will, in a bilateral convention, enable national treatment to be extended to stateless persons who, because they are in one of the situations enumerated in paragraph 2 of article 1 of the above-mentioned Convention of 28th September, 1954, are not covered by that Convention. This is mainly the case, on the one hand, of persons receiving at the time of signature of that Convention protection or assistance from organs or agencies of the United Nations other than the United Nations High Commissioner for Refugees, and, on the other hand, of persons who are residents of a country and who there enjoy and are subject to the rights and obligations attaching to the possession of that country's nationality." [para. 13]

"The purpose of paragraph 2 is to limit the scope of the clause concerning equality of treatment with nationals of a Contracting State solely to stateless persons who are residents of that or the other Contracting State." [para. 14]

"By thus excluding stateless persons who are residents of neither Contracting State, such a clause prevents their being privileged in one State as compared with nationals of the other State." [para. 15]

"However, if States were to consider it desirable in their bilateral relations, to extend the application of paragraph 2 to all stateless persons, whether residents of a Contracting State or not, so that in all cases they enjoy the most favourable treatment accorded to nationals of the State concerned, in order to do this they would need only to adopt the following text which contains no condition as to residence in a Contracting State:

'Notwithstanding the provisions of Article 1, stateless persons shall not be subjected in a Contracting State to any taxation or any requirement connected therewith which is other or more burdensome than the taxation and connected requirements to which nationals of that State in the same circumstances are or may be subjected.' " [para. 16]

"It is possible that in the future certain States will take exception to the provisions of paragraph 2 as being too liberal in so far as they entitle stateless persons who are residents of one State to claim equality of treatment not only in the other State but also in their State of residence and thus benefit in particular in the latter from the provisions of double taxation conventions concluded by it with third States. If such States wished to avoid this latter consequence, they would have to modify paragraph 3 as follows:

'Stateless persons who are residents of a Contracting State shall not be subjected in the other Contracting State to any taxation or any requirement connected therewith which is other or more burdensome than the taxation and connected requirements to which nationals of that other

State in the same circumstances, in particular with respect to residence, are or may be subjected.' " [para. 17]

"Finally, it should be understood that the definition of the term 'stateless person' to be used for the purposes of such a clause can only be that laid down in paragraph 1 of Article 1 of the Convention of 28th September, 1954, which defines a stateless person as 'a person who is not considered as a national by any State under the operation of its law'." [para. 18]

Paragraph 3

4.   Since this paragraph reproduces Article 24, paragraph 3, of the OECD Model Convention, the Commentary on that paragraph is fully relevant:

"Strictly speaking, the type of discrimination which this paragraph is designed to end is discrimination based not on nationality but on the actual situs of an enterprise. It therefore affects without distinction, and irrespective of their nationality, all residents of a Contracting State who have a permanent establishment in the other Contracting State." [para. 19]

"It appears necessary first to make it clear that the wording of the first sentence of paragraph 3 must be interpreted in the sense that it does not constitute discrimination to tax non-resident persons differently, for practical reasons, from resident persons, as long as this does not result in more burdensome taxation for the former than for the latter. In the negative form in which the provision concerned has been framed, it is the result alone which counts, it being permissible to adapt the mode of taxation to the particular circumstances in which the taxation is levied." [para. 20]

"By the terms of the first sentence of paragraph 3, the taxation of a permanent establishment shall not be less favourably levied in the State concerned than the taxation levied on enterprises of that State carrying on the same activities. The purpose of this provision is to end all discrimination in the treatment of permanent establishments as compared with resident enterprises belonging to the same sector of activities, as regards taxes based on industrial and commercial activities, and especially taxes on business profits." [para. 21]

"However, the second sentence of paragraph 3 specifies the conditions under which the principle of equal treatment set forth in the first sentence should be applied to individuals who are residents of a Contracting State and have a permanent establishment in the other State. It is designed mainly to ensure that such persons do not obtain greater advantages than residents, through entitlement to personal allowances and reliefs for family responsibilities, both in the State of which they are residents, by the application of its domestic laws, and in the other State by virtue of the principle of equal treatment. Consequently, it leaves it open to the State in which the permanent establishment is situated whether or not to give personal allowances and reliefs to the persons concerned in the proportion which the amount of the permanent establishment's profits bears to the world income taxable in the other State." [para. 22]

"As regards the first sentence, experience has shown that it was difficult to define clearly and completely the substance of the principle of equal treatment and this has led to wide differences of opinion with regard to the many implications of this principle. The main reason for difficulty seems to reside in the actual nature of the permanent establishment which is not a separate legal entity but only a part of an enterprise that has its head office in another State. The situation of the permanent establishment is different from that of a domestic enterprise, which constitutes a single entity all of whose activities, with their fiscal implications, can be fully brought within the purview of the State where it has its head office. The implications of the equal treatment clause will be examined below under several aspects of the levying of tax." [para. 23]

"A. *Assessment of tax*

With regard to the basis of assessment of tax, the principle of equal treatment normally has the following implications:

(*a*) Permanent establishments must be accorded the same right as resident enterprises to deduct the trading expenses that are, in general, authorized by the taxation law to be deducted from taxable profits in addition to the right to attribute to the permanent establishment a proportion of the overheads of the head office of the enterprise. Such deductions should be allowed without any restrictions other than those also imposed on resident enterprises.

(*b*) Permanent establishments must be accorded the same facilities with regard to depreciation and reserves. They should be entitled to avail themselves without restriction not only of the depreciation facilities which are customarily available to enterprises (straight line depreciation, declining balance depreciation), but also of the special systems that exist in a number of countries ('wholesale' writing down, accelerated depreciation etc.). As regards reserves, it should be noted that these are sometimes authorized for purposes other than the offsetting—in accordance with commercial accounting principles—of depreciation on assets, expenses or losses which have not yet occurred but which circumstances make likely to occur in the near future. Thus, in certain countries, enterprises are entitled to set aside, out of taxable profit provisions or 'reserves' for investment. When such a right is enjoyed by all enterprises, or by all enterprises in a given sector of activity, it should normally also be enjoyed, under the same conditions, by non-resident enterprises, with respect to their permanent establishments situated in the State concerned, in so far, that is, as the activities to which such provisions or reserves would pertain are taxable in that State.

(*c*) Permanent establishments should also have the option that is available in most countries to resident enterprises of carrying forward or backward a loss brought out at the close of an accounting period within a certain period of time (e.g., 5 years). It is hardly necessary to specify that in the case of permanent establishments it is the loss on their own business activities, as shown in the separate accounts for these activities, which will qualify for such carry-forward.

(*d*) Permanent establishments should further have the same rules applied to resident enterprises, with regard to the taxation of capital gains realized on the alienation of assets, whether during or on the cessation of business." [para. 24]

"Although the general rules mentioned above rarely give rise to any difficulties with regard to the principle of non-discrimination, the same does not always hold good for the tax incentive measures which most countries, faced with such problems as decentralization of industry, development of economically backward regions, or the promotion of new activities necessary for the expansion of the economy, have introduced in order to facilitate the solution of these problems by means of tax exemptions, reductions or other tax advantages given to enterprises for investment which is in line with official objectives." [para. 25]

"As such measures are in furtherance of objectives directly related to the economic activity proper of the State concerned, it is right that the benefit of them should be extended to permanent establishments of enterprises of another State which has a double taxation convention with the first embodying the provisions of Article 24, once they have been accorded the right to engage in industrial or commercial activity in that State, either under its legislation or under an international agreement (treaties of commerce, establishment conventions etc.) concluded between the two States." [para. 26]

"It should, however, be noted that although non-resident enterprises are entitled to claim these tax advantages in the State concerned, they must fulfil the same conditions and requirements as resident enterprises. They may, therefore, be denied such advantages if their permanent establishments are unable or refuse to fulfil the special conditions and requirements attached to the granting of them." [para. 27]

"Finally, it goes without saying that non-resident enterprises are not entitled to tax advantages attaching to activities the exercise of which is strictly reserved, on grounds of national interest, defence, protection of the national economy etc., to domestic enterprises, since non-resident enterprises are not allowed to engage in such activities." [para. 28]

"B. *Special treatment of dividends received in respect of holdings owned by permanent establishments*

In many countries special rules exist for the taxation of dividends distributed between companies (parent company-subsidiary treatment, the 'Schachtelprivileg', the rule 'non bis in idem'). The question arises whether such treatment should by effect of the provisions of paragraph 3 also be enjoyed by permanent establishments in respect of dividends on holdings forming part of their assets." [para. 29]

"On this point opinions differ. Some States consider that such special treatment should be accorded to permanent establishments. They take the view that such treatment was enacted in order to avoid double taxation on profits made by a subsidiary and distributed to a parent company. In principle profits tax should be levied once, in the hands of the subsidiary performing the profit-generating activities. The parent company should be exempted from tax on such profits when received from the subsidiary or should, under the indirect credit method, be given relief for the taxation borne by the subsidiary. In cases where shares are held as direct investment by a permanent establishment the same principle implies that such a permanent establishment receiving dividends from the subsidiary should likewise be granted the special treatment in view of the fact that a profits tax has already been levied in the hands of the subsidiary. On the other hand, it is hardly conceivable on this line of thought to leave it to the State where the head office of the parent company is situated to give relief from double taxation brought about by a second levying of tax in the State of the permanent establishment. The State of the parent company, in which no activities giving rise to the doubly taxed profits have taken place, will normally exempt the profits in question or will levy a profits tax which is not sufficient to bear a double credit (i.e., for the profits tax on the subsidiary as well as for such tax on the permanent establishment). All this assumes that the shares held by the permanent establishment are effectively connected with its activity. Furthermore, an obvious additional condition is that the profits out of which the dividends are distributed should have borne a profits tax." [para. 30]

"Other States, on the contrary, consider that assimilating permanent establishments to their own enterprises does not entail any obligation to accord such special treatment to the former. They justify their position on various grounds. The purpose of such special treatment is to avoid economic double taxation of dividends and it should be for the recipient company's State of residence and not the permanent establishment's State to bear its cost, because it is more interested in the aim in view. Another reason put forward relates to the sharing of tax revenue between States. The loss of tax revenue incurred by a State in applying such special treatment is partly offset by the taxation of the dividends when they are redistributed by the parent company which has enjoyed such treatment (withholding tax on dividends, shareholder's tax). A State which accorded such treatment to permanent establishments would not have the benefit of such a compensation. Another argument made is that when such treatment is made conditional upon redistribution of the dividends its extension to permanent establishments would not be justified, for in such a case the permanent establishment, which is only a part of a company of another State and does not distribute dividends, would be more favourably treated than a resident company. Finally, the States which feel that paragraph 3 does not entail any obligation to extend such treatment to permanent establishments argue that there is a risk that companies of one State might transfer their holdings in companies of another State to their permanent establishments in that other State for the sole purpose of availing themselves of such treatment." [para. 31]

"The fact remains that there can be very valid reasons for a holding being owned and managed by a permanent establishment rather than by the head office of the enterprise, viz.,

—reasons of necessity arising principally from a legal or regulatory obligation on banks and financial institutions and insurance companies to keep deposited in countries where they operate a certain amount of assets, particularly shares, as security for the performance of their obligations;

—or reasons of expediency, where the holdings are in companies which have business relations with the permanent establishment or whose head offices are situated in the same country as the permanent establishment;

—or simple reasons of practical convenience, in line with the present tendency towards decentralization of management functions in large enterprises." [para. 32]

"In view of these divergent attitudes, as well as of the existence of the situations just described, it would be advisable for States, when concluding bilateral conventions, to make clear the interpretation they give to the first sentence of paragraph 3. They can, if they so desire, explain their position, or change it as compared with their previous practice, in a protocol or any other document annexed to the convention." [para. 33]

"A solution could also be provided in such a document to meet the objection mentioned above that the extension of the treatment of holdings in a State (A) to permanent establishments of companies which are residents of another State (B) results in such companies unduly enjoying privileged treatment as compared with other companies which are residents of the same State and whose head offices own holdings in the capital of companies which are residents of State A, in that whereas the dividends on their holdings can be repatriated by the former companies without bearing withholding tax, such tax is levied on dividends distributed to the latter companies at the rate of 5 or 15 per cent as the case may be. Tax neutrality and the equality of tax burdens as between permanent establishments and subsidiary companies, as advocated by the States concerned, could be ensured by adapting, in the bilateral convention between States A and B, the provisions of paragraphs 2 and 4 of Article 10, so as to enable withholding tax to be levied in State A on dividends paid by companies which are residents of that State to permanent establishments of companies which are residents of State B in the same way as if they are received directly, i.e., by the head offices of the latter companies, viz., at the rate of:

—5 per cent in the case of a holding of at least 25 per cent;

—15 per cent in all other cases." [para. 34]

[It is to be noted that paragraph 2 of Article 10 in the United Nations Model Convention differs from the terms quoted above.]

"Should it not be possible, because of the absence of appropriate provisions in the domestic laws of the State concerned, to levy a withholding tax there on dividends paid to permanent establishments, the treatment of inter-company dividends could be extended to permanent establishments, as long as its application is limited in such manner that the tax levied by the State of source of the dividends is the same whether the dividends are received by a permanent establishment of a company which is a resident of the other State or are received directly by such a company." [para. 35]

"C. *Structure and rate of tax*

In countries where enterprises, mainly companies, are charged a tax on their profits which is specific to them, the provisions of paragraph 3 raise, with regard to the rate applicable in the case of permanent establishments, especially difficult and delicate problems, which here too arise from the fact that the permanent establishment is only a part of a legal entity which is not under the jurisdiction of the State where the permanent establishment is situated." [para. 36]

"When the taxation of profits made by companies which are residents of a given State is calculated according to a progressive scale of rates, such a scale should, in principle, be applied to permanent establishments situated in that State. If in applying the progressive scale, the permanent establishment's State takes into account the profits of the whole company to which such a permanent establishment belongs, such a rule would not appear to conflict with the equal treatment rule, since resident companies are in fact treated in the same way . . . States that tax their own companies in this way could therefore define in their bilateral conventions the treatment applicable to permanent establishments." [para. 37]

"When a system of taxation based on a progressive scale of rates includes a rule that a minimum rate is applicable to permanent establishments, it cannot be claimed a priori that such a rule is incompatible with the equal treatment principle. The profits of the whole enterprise to which the permanent establishment belongs should be taken into account in determining the rate applicable according to the progressive scale. The provisions of the first sentence of paragraph 3 are not observed only if the minimum rate is higher." [para. 38]

"However, even if the profits of the whole enterprise to which the permanent establishment belongs is taken into account when applying either a progressive scale of rates or a minimum rate, this should not conflict with the principle of the distinct and separate enterprise, according to which the profits of the permanent establishment must be determined under paragraph 2 of Article 7. The minimum amount of the tax levied in the State where the permanent establishment is situated is, therefore, the amount which would be due if it were a distinct and separate enterprise, without reference to the profits of the whole enterprise to which it belongs. The State where the permanent establishment is situated is, therefore, justified in applying the progressive scale applicable to resident enterprises solely to the profits of the permanent establishment, leaving aside the profits of the whole enterprise when the latter are less than those of the permanent establishment. This State may likewise tax the profits of the permanent establishment at a minimum rate, provided that the same rate applies also to resident enterprises, even if taking into account the profits of the whole enterprise to which it belongs would result in a lower amount of tax, or no tax at all." [para. 39]

"As regards the split-rate system of company tax, it should first be pointed out as being a fact central to the issue here that most OECD Member countries which have adopted this system do not consider themselves bound by the provisions of paragraph 3 to extend it to permanent establishments of non-resident companies. This attitude is based, in particular, on the view that the split rate is only one element amongst others (in particular a withholding tax on distributed income) in a system of taxing company profits and dividends which must be considered as a whole and is therefore, both for legal and technical reasons, of domestic application only. The State where the permanent establishment is situated could claim the right not to tax such profits at the reduced rate, as generally, it does not tax the dividends distributed by the company to which the permanent establishment belongs. Moreover, a State which has adopted a split-rate system usually has other economic policy objectives such as the promotion of the capital market, by encouraging resident companies to distribute dividends. The extension of the reduced rate to the profits of the permanent establishment would not serve such a purpose at all, as the company distributing the dividends is not a resident of the State concerned." [para. 40]

"This view is, however, disputed. The States in favour of extending the split-rate system to permanent establishments urge that as the essential feature of this system is a special technique of taxing profits which enterprises in a corporate form derive from their activities, and is designed to afford immediate relief from the double taxation levied on the profits distributed, it should be applied to permanent establishments in bilateral conventions against double taxation. It is generally recognized that, by the effects of their provisions, such conventions necessarily result in some integration of the taxation systems of the Contracting States. On this account, it is perfectly conceivable that profits made in a State (A) by a permanent establishment of a company resident in another State (B) should be taxed in State A according to the split-rate system. As a practical rule, the tax could in such case be calculated at the reduced rate (applicable to distributed profits) on that proportion of an establishment's profits which corresponds to the ratio between the profit distributed by the company to which it belongs and the latter's total profit; the remaining profit could be taxed at the higher rate. Of course, the two Contracting States would have to consult together and exchange all information necessary for giving practical effect to this solution. Similar considerations apply to systems where distributions of profits made can be deducted from the taxable income of a company." [para. 41]

"As regards the imputation system ('*avoir fiscal*' or 'tax credit'), it seems doubtful, at least on a literal interpretation of the provisions of paragraph 3, whether it should be extended to non-resident companies in respect of dividends paid out of profits made by their permanent establishment. In fact, it has identical effects to those of the split-rate system but these effects are not immediate as they occur only at the time of the shareholder's personal taxation. From a purely economic and financial standpoint, however, it is conceivable that such profits should be treated as though they were profits of a distinct company in State A where the permanent establishment of a company which is a resident of State B is situated, and, to the extent that they are distributed, carry the '*avoir fiscal*' or 'tax credit'. But to take the matter further, to avoid all discrimination it is necessary that this advantage should already have been accorded to shareholders who are residents of State B of companies which are residents of State A. From the practical standpoint, the two States concerned should, of course, agree upon the conditions and procedures for allowing the '*avoir fis-*

cal' or 'tax credit' to shareholders who are themselves residents of either State, of the companies concerned that are residents of State B." [para. 42]

"Contracting States which are faced with the problems described above may settle them in bilateral negotiations in the light of their peculiar circumstances." [para. 43]

"D. *Withholding tax on dividends, interest and royalties received by a permanent establishment*

When permanent establishments receive dividends, interest or royalties such income, by virtue of paragraph 4 of Articles 10 and 11 and paragraph [4] of Article 12, respectively, comes under the provisions of Article 7 and consequently—subject to the observations made in paragraph 34 above as regards dividends received on holdings of permanent establishment—falls to be included in the taxable profits of such permanent establishments. (Cf. paragraph 35 of the Commentary on Article 7.)" [para. 44]

"According to the respective Commentaries on the above-mentioned provisions of Articles 10, 11 and 12 . . . these provisions dispense the State of source of the dividends, interest or royalties received by the permanent establishment from applying any limitation provided for in those Articles, which means—and this is the generally accepted interpretation—that they leave completely unaffected the right of the State of source, where the permanent establishment is situated, to apply its withholding tax at the full rate." [para. 45]

"While this approach does not create any problems with regard to the provisions of paragraph 3 of Article 24 in the case of countries where a withholding tax is levied on all such income, whether the latter be paid to residents (permanent establishments, like resident enterprises, being allowed to set such withholding tax off against the tax on profits due by virtue of Article 7) or to non-residents (subject to the limitations provided for in Articles 10, 11 and 12), the position is different when withholding tax is applied exclusively to income paid to non-residents." [para. 46]

"In this latter case, in fact, it seems difficult to reconcile the levy of withholding tax with the principle set out in paragraph 3 that for the purpose of taxing the income which is derived from their activity or which is normally connected with it—as is recognized to be the case with dividends, interest and royalties referred to in paragraph 4 of Articles 10 and 11 and in paragraph [4] of Article 12—permanent establishments must be treated as resident enterprises and hence in respect of such income be subjected to tax on profits solely." [para. 47]

"In any case, it is for Contracting States which have this difficulty to settle it in bilateral negotiations in the light of their peculiar circumstances." [para. 48]

"E.   *Credit for foreign tax*

In a related context, when a permanent establishment receives foreign income which is included in its taxable profits, it is right by virtue of the same principle to grant to the permanent establishment credit for foreign tax borne by such income when such credit is granted to resident enterprises under domestic laws." [para. 49]

"If in a Contracting State (A) in which is situated a permanent establishment of an enterprise of the other Contracting State (B) credit for tax levied in a third State (C) can be allowed only by virtue of a convention, then the more general question arises, as to the extension to permanent establishments of the benefit of conventions concluded with third States . . ." [para. 50]

"F.   *Extension to permanent establishments of the benefit of double taxation conventions concluded with third States*

When the permanent establishment in a Contracting State of a resident enterprise of another Contracting State receives dividends, interest or royalties from a third State, then the question arises as to whether and to what extent the Contracting State in which the permanent establishment is situated should credit the tax that cannot be recovered from the third State." [para. 51]

"There is agreement that double taxation arises in these situations and that some method of relief should be found. The majority of Member countries are able to grant credit in these cases on the basis of their domestic law or under paragraph 3. States that cannot give credit in such a way or that wish to clarify the situation may wish to supplement the provision in their convention with the Contracting State in which the enterprise is resident by wording that allows the State in which the permanent establishment is situated to credit the tax liability in the State in which the income originates to an amount that does not exceed the amount that resident enterprises in the Contracting State in which the permanent establishment is situated can claim on the basis of the Contracting State's convention with the third State. If the tax that cannot be recovered under the convention between the third State and the State of residence of the enterprise which has a permanent establishment in the other Contracting State is lower than that under the convention between the third State and the Contracting State in which the permanent establishment is situated, then only the lower tax collected in the third State shall be credited. This result would be achieved by adding the following words after the first sentence of paragraph 3:

'When a permanent establishment in a Contracting State of an enterprise of the other Contracting State receives dividends, interest or royalties from a third State and the right or the asset in respect of which the dividends, interest or royalties are paid is effectively connected with that permanent establishment, the first-mentioned State shall grant a tax credit in respect of the tax paid in the third State on the dividends, interest or royalties, as the case may be, by applying the rate of tax provided in the convention with respect to taxes on income and capital between the State of which the enterprise is a resident and the third State. However, the amount of the credit shall not exceed the amount that an enterprise that is a resident of the first-mentioned State can claim under that State's convention on income and capital with the third State.' " [para. 52]

"Where a permanent establishment situated in a Contracting State of an enterprise resident of another Contracting State (the State of residence) receives dividends, interest or royalties from a third State (the State of source) and, according to the procedure agreed to between the State of residence and the State of source, a certificate of domicile is requested by the State of source for the application of the withholding tax at the rate provided for in the convention between the State of source and the State of residence, this certificate must be issued by the latter State. While this procedure may be useful where the State of residence employs the credit method, it seems to serve no purposes where that State uses the exemption method as the income from the third State is not liable to tax in the State of residence of the enterprise. On the other hand, the State in which the permanent establishment is located could benefit from being involved in the certification procedure as this procedure would provide useful information for audit purposes. Another question that arises with triangular cases is that of abuses. If the Contracting State of which the enterprise is a resident exempts from tax the profits of the permanent establishment located in the other Contracting State, there is a danger that the enterprise will transfer assets such as shares, bonds or patents to permanent establishments in States that offer very favourable tax treatment, and in certain circumstances the resulting income may not be taxed in any of the three States. To prevent such practices, which may be regarded as abusive, a provision can be included in the convention between the State of which the enterprise is a resident and the third State (the State of source) stating that an enterprise can claim the benefits of the convention only if the income obtained by the permanent establishment situated in the other State is taxed normally in the State of the permanent establishment." [para. 53]

"In addition to the typical triangular case considered here, other triangular cases arise, particularly that in which the State of the enterprise is also the State from which the income ascribable to the permanent establishment in the other State originates (see also paragraph 5 of the Commentary on Article 21). States can settle these matters in bilateral negotiations." [para. 54]

Paragraph 4

5.   Since this paragraph reproduces Article 24, paragraph 4, of the OECD Model Convention, the Commentary on that paragraph is fully relevant:

"This paragraph is designed to end a particular form of discrimination resulting from the fact that in certain countries the deduction of interest, royalties and other disbursements allowed without restriction when the recipient is resident, is restricted or even prohibited when he is a non-resident. The same situation may also be found in the sphere of capital taxation, as regards debts contracted to a non-resident. It is however open to Contracting States to modify this provision in bilateral conventions to avoid its use for tax avoidance purposes." [para. 55]

"Paragraph 4 does not prohibit the country of the borrower from treating interest as a dividend under its domestic rules on thin capitalization in so far as these are compatible with paragraph 1 of Article 9 or paragraph 6 of Article 11. However, if such treatment results from rules which are not compatible with the said Articles and which only apply to non-resident creditors (to the exclusion of resident creditors), then such treatment is prohibited by paragraph 4." [para. 56]

6.   In the course of the discussion by the Group of Experts of paragraph 4, a question was raised whether such a paragraph was suitable for inclusion in a tax treaty between developed and developing countries. It was suggested that the paragraph would not be acceptable to those countries that made deductibility of disbursements

made abroad by foreign-owned corporations conditional on the recipient being taxed in such countries. After substantial discussion, the feeling of the Group was that the special circumstances mentioned above ought not to be the basis for treaty articles of broad application but that in cases where they were likely to create a problem they should be raised in bilateral negotiations.

Paragraph 5

7.   Since this paragraph reproduces Article 24, paragraph 5, of the OECD Model Convention, the Commentary on that paragraph is fully relevant:

> "This paragraph forbids a Contracting State to give less favourable treatment to an enterprise, the capital of which is owned or controlled, wholly or partly, directly or indirectly, by one or more residents of the other Contracting State. This provision, and the discrimination which it puts an end to, relates to the taxation only of enterprises and not of the persons owning or controlling their capital. Its object therefore is to ensure equal treatment for taxpayers residing in the same State, and not to subject foreign capital, in the hands of the partners or shareholders, to identical treatment to that applied to domestic capital." [para. 57]

> "Paragraph 5, though relevant in principle to thin capitalization, is worded in such general terms that it must take second place to more specific provisions in the Convention. Thus paragraph 4 (referring to paragraph 1 of Article 9 and paragraph 6 of Article 11) takes precedence over this paragraph in relation to the deduction of interest." [para. 58]

> "In the case of transfer pricing enquiries, almost all Member countries consider that additional information requirements which would be more stringent than the normal requirements, or even a reversal of the burden of proof, would not constitute discrimination within the meaning of the Article." [para. 59]

8.   In the course of the Group's discussion of paragraph 5, some members from developing countries proposed that special measures applicable to foreign-owned enterprises should not be construed as constituting prohibited discrimination as long as all foreign-owned enterprises are treated alike; they said that change represented a notable departure from the general principle of taxing foreign persons on the same basis as nationals but that the problems of tax compliance in cases in which foreign ownership was involved and the politically sensitive position of foreign-owned enterprises in developing countries warranted the change. Therefore, they proposed that Article 24, paragraph 5, of the OECD Model Convention be amended to read as follows:

> "5.   Enterprises of a Contracting State, the capital of which is wholly or partly owned or controlled, directly or indirectly, by one or more residents of the other Contracting State, shall not be subjected in the first-mentioned State to any taxation or any requirement connected therewith which is other or more burdensome than the taxation and connected requirements to which are subjected other similar enterprises *the capital of which is wholly or partly owned or controlled, directly or indirectly, by residents of third countries.*"

They further pointed out that the proposed change in paragraph 5 had been included in several tax treaties to which developed countries were parties. Some members from developed countries noted that such a proposal would limit the effect of the non-discrimination article to the prevention of discrimination between enterprises owned by non-residents, thus leaving the door open to discrimination against enterprises owned by non-residents as a class.

9.   Several members from developed countries expressed reservations concerning the proposed change and said that they considered the OECD non-discrimination Article as the backbone of the Convention. They recalled that the antecedents of the non-discrimination Article in the present OECD Model Convention dated from the nineteenth century. They felt that if such a fundamental principle were to be altered, it would have a significant effect on international tax rela-

tions generally. Further, since the proposed change was motivated in part by problems with tax compliance where foreign ownership was involved—essentially, problems with transfer pricing—it was suggested that the problem might be dealt with more properly in other parts of the Model Convention, such as in article 9 dealing with associated enterprises.

10.　Some members from developing countries indicated that, while recognizing the essential importance of and need for the article on non-discrimination, some countries might wish to modify certain paragraphs of that article in bilateral negotiations. It was suggested for example that, because of the difficulties involved in determining what constituted reasonable amounts in the case of transfer payments on account of royalties, technical assistance fees, head office expenses and so on, a country might desire to deny deductions for such payments or compute the amount of deduction in accordance with the domestic law of the country when such payments were made by an enterprise situated within its territory to a foreign controlling company, whether the latter was resident in another Contracting State or in a third country. Another example cited was that of a country which granted tax preferences with a view to the attainment of certain national objectives which might wish to make a given percentage of local ownership of the enterprise involved a condition for the granting of such tax preferences. The Group recognized that special situations such as those mentioned as examples should be resolved in bilateral negotiations.

Paragraph 6

11.　Since this paragraph reproduces Article 24, paragraph 6, of the OECD Model Convention, the Commentary on that paragraph is fully relevant:

> "This paragraph states that the scope of the Article is not restricted by the provisions of Article 2. The Article therefore applies to taxes of every kind and description levied by, or on behalf of, the State, its political subdivisions or local authorities." [para. 60]

Article 25

MUTUAL AGREEMENT PROCEDURE

A. GENERAL CONSIDERATIONS

1.   Article 25 of the United Nations Model Convention reproduces Article 25 of the OECD Model Convention with one substantive change, namely, the addition of the second and third sentences in
paragraph 4.

2.   The mutual agreement procedure is designed not only to furnish a means of settling questions relating to the interpretation and
application of the Convention, but also to provide (*a*) a forum in
which residents of the States involved can protest actions not in accordance with the Convention and (*b*) a mechanism for eliminating
double taxation in cases not provided for in the Convention. The mutual agreement procedure applies in connection with all articles of
the Convention, and, in particular, to article 7 on business profits, article 9 on associated enterprises, article 11 on interest, article 12 on
royalties and article 23 on methods for the elimination of double taxation. However, some countries may need to modify this grant of
power to their competent authorities in conformity with their domestic laws.

Paragraphs 1 *and* 2

3.   These paragraphs reproduce the full text of paragraphs 1 and 2
of Article 25 of the OECD Model Convention. The Group decided,
however, that an alternative time limit could be left to bilateral negotiations. The following passages of the Commentary on Article 25,
paragraphs 1 and 2, of the OECD Model Convention are therefore
relevant.

> "The rules laid down in paragraphs 1 and 2 provide for the
> elimination in a particular case of taxation which does not ac-
> cord with the Convention. As is known, in such cases it is nor-
> mally open to taxpayers to litigate in the tax court, either
> immediately or upon the dismissal of their objections by the

taxation authorities. When taxation not in accordance with the Convention arises from an incorrect application of the Convention in both States, taxpayers are then obliged to litigate in each State, with all the disadvantages and uncertainties that such a situation entails. So paragraph 1 makes available to taxpayers affected, without depriving them of the ordinary legal remedies available, a procedure which is called the mutual agreement procedure because it is aimed, in its second stage, at resolving the dispute on an amicable basis, i.e., by agreement between competent authorities, the first stage being conducted exclusively in the State of residence (except where the procedure for the application of paragraph 1 of Article 24 is set in motion by the taxpayer in the State of which he is a national) from the presentation of the objection up to the decision taken regarding it by the competent authority on the matter." [para. 6]

"In any case, the mutual agreement procedure is clearly a special procedure outside the domestic law. It follows that it can be set in motion solely in cases coming within paragraph 1, i.e., cases where tax has been charged, or is going to be charged, in disregard of the provisions of the Convention. So where a charge of tax has been made contrary both to the Convention and the domestic law, this case is amenable to the mutual agreement procedure to the extent only that the Convention is affected, unless a connecting link exists between the rules of the Convention and the rules of the domestic law which have been misapplied." [para. 7]

"In practice, the procedure applies to cases—by far the most numerous—where the measure in question leads to double taxation which it is the specific purpose of the Convention to avoid. Among the most common cases, mention must be made of the following:

—the questions relating to attribution to a permanent establishment of a proportion of the executive and general administrative expenses incurred by the enterprise, under paragraph 3 of Article 7;

—the taxation in the State of the payer—in case of a special relationship between the payer and the beneficial owner—of the excess part of interest and royalties, under the provisions of Article 9, paragraph 6 of Article 11 or paragraph [6] of Article 12;

—cases of application of legislation to deal with thin capitalization when the State of the debtor company has treated interest as dividends, in so far as such treatment is based on clauses of a convention corresponding for example to Article 9 or paragraph 6 of Article 11;

—cases where lack of information as to the taxpayer's actual situation has led to misapplication of the Convention, especially in regard to the determination of residence (paragraph 2 of Article 4), the existence of a permanent establishment (Article 5), or the temporary nature of the services performed by an employee (paragraph 2 of Article 15)." [para. 8]

"Article 25 also provides machinery to enable competent authorities to consult with each other with a view to resolving, in the context of transfer pricing problems, not only problems of juridical double taxation but also those of economic double taxation, and especially those resulting from the inclusion of profits of associated enterprises under paragraph 1 of Article 9; the corresponding adjustments to be made in pursuance of paragraph 2 of the same Article thus fall within the scope of the mutual agreement procedure, both as concerns assessing whether they are well-founded and for determining their amount." [para. 9]

"This in fact is implicit in the wording of paragraph 2 of Article 9 when the bilateral convention in question contains a clause of this type. When the bilateral convention does not contain rules similar to those of paragraph 2 of Article 9 (as is usually the case for conventions signed before 1977) the mere fact that Contracting States inserted in the convention the text of Article 9, as limited to the text of paragraph 1—which usually only confirms broadly similar rules existing in domestic laws—indicates that the intention was to have economic double taxation covered by the Convention. As a result, most Member countries consider that economic double taxation resulting from adjustments made to profits by reason of transfer pricing is not in accordance with—at least—the spirit of the Convention and falls within the scope of the mutual agreement procedure set up under Article 25. States which do not share this view do, however, in practice, find the means of remedying economic double taxation in most cases involving bona fide companies by making use of provisions in their domestic laws." [para. 10]

"The mutual agreement procedure is also applicable in the absence of any double taxation contrary to the Convention, once the taxation in dispute is in direct contravention of a rule in the Convention. Such is the case when one State taxes a particular class of income in respect of which the Convention gives an exclusive right to tax to the other State even though the latter is unable to exercise it owing to a gap in its domestic laws. Another category of cases concerns persons who, being nationals of one Contracting State but residents of the other State, are subjected in that other State to taxation treatment which is discriminatory under the provisions of paragraph 1 of Article 24." [para. 11]

"It should be noted that the mutual agreement procedure, unlike the disputed claims procedure under domestic law, can be set in motion by a taxpayer without waiting until the taxation considered by him to be 'not in accordance with the Convention' has been charged against or notified to him. To be able to set the procedure in motion, he must, and it is sufficient if he does, establish that the 'actions for one or both of the Contracting States' will result in such taxation, and that this taxation appears as a risk which is not merely possible but probable. Such actions mean all acts or decisions, whether of a legislative or a regulatory nature, and whether of general or individual application, having as their direct and necessary consequence the charging of tax against the complainant contrary to the provisions of the Convention." [para. 12]

"To be admissible objections presented under paragraph 1 must first meet a twofold requirement expressly formulated in that paragraph: in principle, they must be presented to the competent authority of the taxpayer's State of residence (except where the procedure for the application of paragraph 1 of Article 24 is set in motion by the taxpayer in the State of which he is a national), and they must be so presented within three years of the first notification of the action which gives rise to taxation which is not in accordance with the Convention. The Convention does not lay down any special rule as to the form of the objections. The competent authorities may prescribe special procedures which they feel to be appropriate. If no special procedure has been specified, the objections may be presented in the same way as objections regarding taxes are presented to the tax authorities of the State concerned." [para. 13]

"The requirement laid on the taxpayer to present his case to the competent authority of the State of which he is a resident (except where the procedure for the application of paragraph 1 of Article 24 is set in motion by the taxpayer in the State of which he is a national) is of general application, regardless of whether the taxation objected to has been charged in that or the other State and regardless of whether it has given rise to double taxation or not. If the taxpayer should have transferred his residence to the other Contracting State subsequently to the measure or taxation objected to, he must nevertheless still present his objection to the competent authority of the State of which he was a resident during the year in respect of which such taxation has been or is going to be charged." [para. 14]

"However, in the case already alluded to where a person who is a national of one State but a resident of the other complains of having been subjected in that other State to an action or taxation which is discriminatory under paragraph 1 of Article 24, it appears more appropriate for obvious reasons to allow him, by way of exception to the general rule set forth above, to present his objection to the competent authority of the Contracting State of which he is a national. Finally, it is to the same competent authority that an objection has to be presented by a person who, while not being a resident of a Contracting State, is a national of a Contracting State, and whose case comes under paragraph 1 of Article 24." [para. 15]

"On the other hand, Contracting States may, if they consider it preferable, give taxpayers the option of presenting their cases to the competent authority of either State. In such a case, paragraph 1 would have to be modified as follows:

'1.   Where a person considers that the actions of one or both of the Contracting States result or will result for him in taxation not in accordance with the provisions of this Convention, he may, irrespective of the remedies provided by the domestic law of those States, present his case to the competent authority of either Contracting State. The case must be presented within three years from the first notification of the action resulting in taxation not in accordance with the provisions of the Convention.' " [para. 16]

"The time limit of three years set by the second sentence of paragraph 1 for presenting objections is intended to protect administrations against late objections. This time limit must be regarded as a minimum, so that Contracting States are left free to agree in their bilateral conventions upon a longer period in the interests of taxpayers, e.g., on the analogy in particular of the time limits laid down by their respective domestic regulations in regard to tax conventions. Contracting States may omit the second sentence of paragraph 1 if they concur that their respective domestic regulations apply automatically to such objections and are more favourable in their effects to the taxpayers affected, either because they allow a longer time for presenting objections or because they do not set any time limits for such purpose." [para. 17]

"The provision fixing the starting point of the three-year time limit as the date of the 'first notification of the action resulting in taxation not in accordance with the provisions of the

Convention' should be interpreted in the way most favourable to the taxpayer. Thus, even if such taxation should be directly charged in pursuance of an administrative decision or action of general application, the time limit begins to run only from the date of the notification of the individual action giving rise to such taxation, that is to say, under the most favourable interpretation, from the act of taxation itself, as evidenced by a notice of assessment or an official demand or other instrument for the collection or levy of tax. If the tax is levied by deduction at the source, the time limit begins to run from the moment when the income is paid; however, if the taxpayer proves that only at a later date did he know that the deduction had been made, the time limit will begin from that date. Furthermore, where it is the combination of decisions or actions taken in both Contracting States resulting in taxation not in accordance with the Convention, it begins to run only from the first notification of the most recent decision or action." [para. 18]

"As regards the procedure itself, it is necessary to consider briefly the two distinct stages into which it is divided . . ." [para. 19]

"In the first stage, which opens with the presentation of the taxpayer's objections, the procedure takes place exclusively at the level of dealings between him and the competent authorities of his State of residence (except where the procedure for the application of paragraph 1 of Article 24 is set in motion by the taxpayer in the State of which he is a national). The provisions of paragraph 1 give the taxpayer concerned the right to apply to the competent authority of the State of which he is a resident, whether or not he has exhausted all the remedies available to him under the domestic law of each of the two States. On the other hand, that competent authority is under an obligation to consider whether the objection is justified and, if it appears to be justified, take action on it in one of the two forms provided for in paragraph 2." [para. 20]

"If the competent authority duly approached recognizes that the complaint is justified and considers that the taxation complained of is due wholly or in part to a measure taken in the taxpayer's State of residence, it must give the complainant satisfaction as speedily as possible by making such adjustments or allowing such reliefs as appear to be justified. In this situation, the issue can be resolved without resort to the mutual agreement procedure. On the other hand, it may be found useful to exchange views and information with the competent authority of the other Contracting State, in order, for example, to confirm a given interpretation of the Convention." [para. 21]

"If, however, it appears to that competent authority that the taxation complained of is due wholly or in part to a measure taken in the other State, it will be incumbent on it, indeed it will be its duty—as clearly appears by the terms of paragraph 2—to set in motion the mutual agreement procedure proper. It is important that the authority in question carry out this duty as quickly as possible, especially in cases where the profits of associated enterprises have been adjusted as a result of transfer pricing adjustments." [para. 22]

"A taxpayer is entitled to present his case under paragraph 1 to the competent authority of the State of which he is a resident whether or not he may also have made a claim or commenced litigation under the domestic law of that State. If litigation is pending, the competent authority of the State of residence should not wait for the final adjudication, but should say whether it considers the case to be eligible for the mutual agreement procedure. If it so decides, it has to determine whether it is itself able to arrive at a satisfactory solution or whether the case has to be submitted to the competent authority of the other Contracting State. An application by a taxpayer to set the mutual agreement procedure in motion should not be rejected without good reason." [para. 23]

"If a claim has been finally adjudicated by a court in the State of residence, a taxpayer may wish even so to present or pursue a claim under the mutual agreement procedure. In some States, the competent authority may be able to arrive at a satisfactory solution which departs from the court decision. In other States, the competent authority is bound by the court decision. It may nevertheless present the case to the competent authority of the other Contracting State and ask the latter to take measures for avoiding double taxation." [para. 24]

"In its second stage—which opens with the approach to the competent authority of the other State by the competent authority to which the taxpayer has applied—the procedure is henceforward at the level of dealings between States, as if, so to speak, the State to which the complaint was presented had given it its backing. But while this procedure is indisputably a procedure between States, it may, on the other hand, be asked:

—whether, as the title of the Article and the terms employed in the first sentence of paragraph 2 suggest, it is no more than a simple procedure of mutual agreement, or constitutes the implementation of a *'pactum de contrahendo'* laying on the parties a mere duty to negotiate but in no way laying on them a duty to reach agreement;

—or whether on the contrary, it is to be regarded (on the assumption of course that it takes place within the framework of a joint commission) as a procedure of a jurisdictional nature laying on the parties a duty to resolve the dispute." [para. 25]

"Paragraph 2 no doubt entails a duty to negotiate; but as far as reaching mutual agreement through the procedure is concerned, the competent authorities are under a duty merely to use their best endeavours and not to achieve a result. However, Contracting States could agree on a more far-reaching commitment whereby the mutual agreement procedure, and above all the discussions in the joint commission, would produce a solution to the dispute. Such a rule could be established either by an amendment to paragraph 2 or by an interpretation specified in a protocol or an exchange of letters annexed to the Convention." [para. 26]

"In seeking a mutual agreement, the competent authorities must first, of course, determine their position in the light of the rules of their respective taxation laws and of the provisions of the Convention, which are as binding on them as much as they are on the taxpayer. Should the strict application of such rules or provisions preclude any agreement, it may reasonably be held that the competent authorities, as in the case of international arbitration, can, subsidiarily, have regard to considerations of equity in order to give the taxpayer satisfaction." [para. 27]

"The purpose of the last sentence of paragraph 2 is to enable countries with time limits relating to adjustments of assessments and tax refunds in their domestic law to give effect to an agreement despite such time limits. This provision does not prevent, however, such States as are not, on constitutional or other legal grounds, able to overrule the time limits in the domestic law from inserting in the mutual agreement itself such time limits as are adapted to their internal statute of limitation. In certain extreme cases, a Contracting State may prefer not to enter into a mutual agreement, the implementation of which would require that the internal statute of limitation had to be disregarded. Apart from time limits there may exist other obstacles such as 'final court decisions' to giving effect to an agreement. Contracting States are free to agree on firm provisions for the removal of such obstacles. As regards the practical implementation of the procedure, it is generally recommended that every effort should be made by tax administrations to ensure that as far as possible the mutual agreement procedure is not in any case frustrated by operational delays or, where time limits would be in point, by the combined effects of time limits and operational delays." [para. 28]

"The Committee on Fiscal Affairs made a number of recommendations on the problems raised by corresponding adjustments of profits following transfer pricing adjustments (implementation of paragraphs 1 and 2 of Article 9) and of the difficulties of applying the mutual agreement procedure to such situations:

(*a*) Tax authorities should notify taxpayers as soon as possible of their intention to make a transfer pricing adjustment (and, where the date of any such notification may be important, to ensure that a clear formal notification is given as soon as possible), since it is particularly useful to ensure as early and as full contacts as possible on all relevant matters between tax authorities and taxpayers within the same jurisdiction and, across national frontiers, between the associated enterprises and tax authorities concerned.

(*b*) Competent authorities should communicate with each other in these matters in as flexible a manner as possible, whether in writing, by telephone, or by face-to-face or round-the-table discussion, whichever is most suitable, and should seek to develop the most effective ways of solving relevant problems. Use of the provisions of Article 26 on the exchange of information should be encouraged in order to assist the competent authority in having well-developed factual information on which a decision can be made.

(*c*) In the course of mutual agreement proceedings on transfer pricing matters, the taxpayers concerned should be given every reasonable opportunity to present the relevant facts and arguments to the competent authorities both in writing and orally." [para. 29]

"As regards the mutual agreement procedure in general, the Committee recommended that:

(*a*) The formalities involved in instituting and operating the mutual agreement procedure should be kept to a minimum and any unnecessary formalities eliminated.

(*b*) Mutual agreement cases should each be settled on their individual merits and not by reference to any balance of the results in other cases.

(*c*) Competent authorities should, where appropriate, formulate and publicize domestic rules, guidelines and procedures concerning use of the mutual agreement procedure." [para. 30]

"Finally, the case may arise where a mutual agreement is concluded in relation to a taxpayer who has brought a suit for the same purpose in the competent court of either Contracting State and such suit is still pending. In such a case, there would be no grounds for rejecting a request by a taxpayer that he be allowed to defer acceptance of the solution agreed upon as a result of the mutual agreement procedure until the court had delivered its judgement in the suit still pending. On the other hand, it is necessary to take into account the concern of the competent authority to avoid any divergence or contradiction between the decision of the court and the mutual agreement, with the difficulties or risks of abuse that they could entail. In short, therefore, it seems normal that the implementation of a mutual agreement should be made subject:

—to the acceptance of such mutual agreement by the taxpayer, and

—to the taxpayer's withdrawal of his suit at law concerning the points settled in the mutual agreement." [para. 31]

Paragraph 3

4.   This paragraph reproduces Article 25, paragraph 3, of the OECD Model Convention. The OECD Commentary on that paragraph is therefore relevant:

"The first sentence of this paragraph invites and authorizes the competent authorities to resolve, if possible, difficulties of interpretation or application by means of mutual agreement. These are essentially difficulties of a general nature which concern, or which may concern, a category of taxpayers, even if they have arisen in connection with an individual case normally coming under the procedure defined in paragraphs 1 and 2." [para. 32]

"This provision makes it possible to resolve difficulties arising from the application of the Convention. Such difficulties are not only those of a practical nature, which might arise in connection with the setting up and operation of procedures for the relief from tax deducted from dividends, interest and royalties in the Contracting State in which they arise, but also those which could impair or impede the normal operation of the clauses of the Convention as they were conceived by the negotiators, the solution of which does not depend on a prior agreement as to the interpretation of the Convention." [para. 33]

"Under this provision the competent authorities can, in particular:

—where a term has been incompletely or ambiguously defined in the Convention, complete or clarify its definition in order to obviate any difficulty;

—where the laws of a State have been changed without impairing the balance or affecting the substance of the Convention, settle any difficulties that may emerge from the new system of taxation arising out of such changes;

—determine whether, and if so under what conditions, interest may be treated as dividends under thin capitalization rules in the country of the borrower and give rise to relief for double taxation in the country of residence of the lender in the same way as for dividends (for example, relief under a parent/subsidiary regime when provision for such relief is made in the relevant bilateral convention)." [para. 34]

"Paragraph 3 confers on the 'competent authorities of the Contracting States', i.e., generally the Ministers of Finance or their authorized representatives normally responsible for the administration of the Convention, authority to resolve by mutual agreement any difficulties arising as to the interpretation of the Convention. However, it is important not to lose sight of the fact that, depending on the domestic law of Contracting States, other authorities (Ministry of Foreign Affairs, courts) have the right to interpret international treaties and agreements as well as the 'competent authority' designated in the Convention, and that this is sometimes the exclusive right of such other authorities." [para. 35]

"Mutual agreements resolving general difficulties of interpretation or application are binding on administrations as long as the competent authorities do not agree to modify or rescind the mutual agreement." [para. 36]

"The second sentence of paragraph 3 enables the competent authorities to deal also with such cases of double taxation as do not come within the scope of the provisions of the Convention. Of special interest in this connection is the case of a resident of a third State having permanent establishments in both Contracting States. It is of course desirable that the mutual agreement procedure should result in the effective elimination of the double taxation which can occur in such a situation. An exception must, however, be made for the case of Contracting States whose domestic law prevents the Convention from being complemented on points which are not explicitly or at least implicitly dealt with; in such a case, the Convention could be complemented only by a protocol subject, like the Convention itself, to ratification or approval." [para. 37]

Paragraph 4

5.   This paragraph consists of three sentences, the first of which reproduces the first sentence of Article 25, paragraph 4, of the OECD Model Convention, while the second and third sentences are not contained in that Model. In the first sentence, the words "including through a joint commission consisting of themselves or their representatives" have been inserted in 1999 between the words "with each other directly" and ". . . for the purpose of reaching", so as to bring the provision on a par with that of the corresponding provision in the OECD Model Convention. The OECD Commentary on that paragraph is relevant:

"It provides first that the competent authorities may communicate with each other directly. It would therefore not be necessary to go through diplomatic channels." [para. 39]

"The competent authorities may communicate with each other by letter, facsimile transmission, telephone, direct meetings, or any other convenient means. They may, if they wish, formally establish a joint commission for this purpose." [para. 40]

"As to this joint commission, paragraph 4 leaves it to the competent authorities of the Contracting States to determine the number of members and the rules of procedure of this body." [para. 41]

"However, while the Contracting States may avoid any formalism in this field, it is nevertheless their duty to give taxpayers whose cases are brought before the joint commission, under paragraph 2, certain essential guarantees, namely:

—the right to make representation in writing or orally, either in person or through a representative;

—the right to be assisted by a counsel." [para. 42]

6.   With regard to this paragraph the following essential elements in respect of income and expense allocations, including transfer pricing, are to be emphasized:

First, transactions between related entities should be governed by the standard of "arm's length dealing"; as a consequence, if an actual allocation is considered by the tax authorities of a treaty country to depart from that standard, the taxable profits may be redetermined;

Secondly, taxpayers are entitled to invoke the mutual agreement procedure where they consider that such action by one or both of the tax authorities regarding such redetermination is contrary to the arm's length standard;

Thirdly, the implementation of the mutual agreement procedure is delegated to the competent authorities of the treaty countries, with adequate powers to ensure full implementation and with the expectation that such implementation will enable the mutual agreement procedure to be an effective instrument for carrying out the purpose of the treaty. Such delegation includes the establishment of time limits within which matters should be presented by the interested parties to the appropriate competent authority, and hence makes unnecessary the last sentence of paragraph 1 of OECD article 25 dealing with this aspect, except for those countries whose domestic law requires the insertion of the sentence.

7.   In order to assist the competent authorities in applying the mutual agreement procedure, the Group of Experts discussed a number of possible arrangements. The Group stressed that those arrangements were not intended to be exhaustive and could be extended as appropriate in the light of experience.

8.   In this connection, it is relevant to note paragraph 50 (c) of the Report of the Ad Hoc Group of Experts on International Cooperation in Tax Matters on the Work of its Seventh Meeting held in 1995, namely:

> "With regard to dispute resolution: greater cooperation must be the goal of the Ad Hoc Group of Experts and other multinational institutions. Resolution of transfer-pricing disputes may increase international investment by assuring investors that they will not be subject to double taxation because of inconsistent and incorrect transfer prices imposed by different countries. So far, most countries have refused to cede their authority to any sort of arbitration that is outside the formal jurisdiction of the countries involved. It is proposed that the experience of such arbitrations, where they are authorized, be studied. It may be appropriate in the future for the Ad Hoc Group of Experts to initiate study of bilateral or multilateral approaches to dispute resolution (mandatory arbitration, voluntary arbitration or mediation). At present, countries may consider, in bilateral negotiations, an arbitration provision or other dispute resolution provision within the mutual agreement procedure article."

9.   It would be instructive to consider the interaction of the mutual agreement procedure with the dispute resolution mechanism which is discussed in paragraphs 44.1 to 44.7 of the OECD Model Convention, reproduced below:

> *"Interaction of the mutual agreement procedure with the dispute resolution mechanism provided by the General Agreement on Trade in Services*
>
> The application of the General Agreement on Trade in Services (GATS), which entered into force on 1 January 1995 and which all Member countries have signed, raises particular concerns in relation to the mutual agreement procedure." [para. 44.1]

> "Paragraph 3 of Article XXII of the GATS provides that a dispute as to the application of Article XVII of the Agreement, a national treatment rule, may not be dealt with under the dispute resolution mechanisms provided by Articles XXII and XXIII of the Agreement if the disputed measure 'falls within the scope of an international agreement between them relating to the avoidance of double taxation' (e.g., a tax convention). If there is disagreement over whether a measure 'falls within the scope' of such an international agreement, paragraph 3 goes on to provide that either State involved in the dispute may bring the matter to the Council on Trade in Services, which shall refer the dispute for binding arbitration. A footnote to paragraph 3, however, contains the important exception that if the dispute relates to an international agreement 'which exist(s) at the time of the entry into force' of the Agreement, the matter may not be brought to the Council on Trade in Services unless both States agree." [para. 44.2]

> "That paragraph raises two particular problems with respect to tax treaties." [para. 44.3]

> "First, the footnote thereto provides for the different treatment of tax conventions concluded before and after the entry into force of the GATS, something that may be considered inappropriate, in particular where a convention in existence at the time of the entry into force of the GATS is subsequently

renegotiated or where a protocol is concluded after that time in relation to a convention existing at that time." [para. 44.4]

"Second, the phrase 'falls within the scope' is inherently ambiguous, as indicated by the inclusion in paragraph 3 of Article XXII of the GATS of both an arbitration procedure and a clause exempting pre-existing conventions from its application in order to deal with disagreements related to its meaning. While it seems clear that a country could not argue in good faith[19] that a measure relating to a tax to which no provision of a tax convention applied fell within the scope of that convention, it is unclear whether the phrase covers all measures that relate to taxes that are covered by all or only some provisions of the tax convention." [para. 44.5]

"Contracting States may wish to avoid these difficulties by extending bilaterally the application of the footnote to paragraph 3 of Article XXII of the GATS to conventions concluded after the entry into force of the GATS. Such a bilateral extension, which would supplement—but not violate in any way—the Contracting States' obligations under the GATS, could be incorporated in the Convention by the addition of the following provision:

'For purposes of paragraph 3 of Article XXII (Consultation) of the General Agreement on Trade in Services, the Contracting States agree that notwithstanding that paragraph, any dispute between them as to whether a measure falls within the scope of this Convention may be brought before the Council on Trade in Services, as provided by that paragraph, only with the consent of both Contracting States. Any doubts as to the interpretation of this paragraph shall be resolved under paragraph 3 of Article 25 (Mutual Agreement Procedure) or, failing agreement un-

---

[19]The obligation of applying and interpreting treaties in good faith is expressly recognized in articles 26 and 31 of the Vienna Convention on the Law of Treaties; thus, the exception in paragraph 3 of article XXII of the GATS applies only to good-faith disputes.

der that procedure, pursuant to any other procedure agreed to by both Contracting States.' " [para. 44.6]

"Problems similar to those discussed above may arise in relation with other bilateral or multilateral agreements related to trade or investment. Contracting States are free, in the course of their bilateral negotiations, to amend the provision suggested above so as to ensure that issues relating to the taxes covered by their tax convention are dealt with through the mutual agreement procedure rather than through the dispute settlement mechanism of such agreements." [para. 44.7]

Other issues

10.   The procedural arrangements for mutual agreements in general should be suitable to the number and types of issues expected to be dealt with by the competent authorities and to the administrative capability and resources of those authorities. The arrangements should not be rigidly structured but instead should embody the degree of flexibility required to facilitate consultation and agreement rather than hinder them by elaborate procedural requirements and mechanisms. But even relatively simple procedural arrangements must incorporate certain minimum rules that inform taxpayers of their essential rights and obligations under the mutual agreement procedure. Such minimum rules would appear to involve such questions as:

—At what stage in his tax matter a taxpayer can invoke action by the competent authority under the mutual agreement procedure;

—Whether any particular form must be followed by a taxpayer in invoking action by the competent authority;

—Whether any time limits are applicable to a taxpayer's invocation of action by the competent authority;

—If a taxpayer invokes action by the competent authority, whether he is bound by the decision of the competent authorities and whether he must waive recourse to other administrative or judicial processes;

—In what manner, if at all, a taxpayer can participate in the competent authority proceedings and what requirements regarding the furnishing of information by a taxpayer are involved.

(a) Information on adjustments

11.   The competent authorities should decide on the extent of the information to be provided on adjustments involving income allocation and the time when it is to be given by one competent authority to the other. Thus, the information could cover adjustments proposed or concluded by the tax administration of one country, the related entities involved and the general nature of the adjustments.

12.   Generally speaking, most competent authorities are likely to conclude that the automatic transmittal of such information is not needed or desirable. The competent authority of the country making an adjustment may find it difficult or time-consuming to gather the information and prepare it in a suitable form for transmission. In addition, the other competent authority may find it burdensome merely to process a volume of data routinely transmitted by the first competent authority. Moreover, a taxpaying corporation can usually be counted upon to inform its related entity in the other country of the proceedings and the latter is thus in a position to inform, in turn, its competent authority. For this reason, the functioning of a consultation system would be aided if a tax administration considering an adjustment possibly involving an international aspect were to give the taxpayer as much warning as possible.

13.   Some competent authorities, while not wishing to be informed routinely of all adjustments in the other country, may desire to receive, either from their own taxpayers or from the other competent authority, "early warning" of serious cases or of the existence of a significant degree or pattern of activity respecting particular types of cases; similarly, they may want to transmit such information. In this event, a process should be worked out for obtaining the information. Some competent authorities may want to extend this early warning system to less serious cases, thus covering a larger number of cases.

(b) Invocation of competent authority consultation at the point of proposed or concluded adjustments

14.   The competent authorities must decide at what stage the competent authority consultation process may be invoked by a taxpayer and which competent authority a taxpayer should go to in order to initiate that process. For example, suppose an adjustment is proposed by State A that would increase the income of a parent company in State A and the adjustment would have a correlative effect on a related entity in State B. May the company go to its competent authority in State A, asserting that the adjustment is contrary to the treaty, and ask that the bilateral competent authority process commence? (It is assumed, as stated earlier, that if the bilateral competent authority process is properly invoked, the two competent authorities must enter the process of consultation.) As another example, may the related entity in State B invoke its competent authority?

15.   Probably most competent authorities, at least in the early stages of their experience, would prefer that the process not be invoked at the point of a proposed adjustment and probably not even at the point of a concluded adjustment. A proposed adjustment may never result in final action and even a concluded adjustment may or may not trigger a claim for a correlative adjustment; even if it does, the latter adjustment may occur without problems. As a consequence, many competent authorities may decide that the process should not be invoked until the correlative adjustment (or other tax consequence in the second country) is involved at some point.

16.   However, some competent authorities may prefer that the bilateral process be invoked earlier, perhaps at the proposed adjustment stage. Such involvement may make the process of consultation easier, in that the first country will not have an initial fixed position. In such a case, the other competent authority should be prepared to discuss the case at this early stage with the first competent authority. Other competent authorities may be willing to let the taxpayer decide, and thus stand ready to have the process invoked at any point starting with the proposed adjustment.

17.   In any event, at a minimum, taxpayers must be informed when they can invoke the mutual agreement procedure and which competent authority is to be addressed (presumably it would be the competent authority of the country where the invoking taxpayer resides). Taxpayers should also be informed in what form the request should be submitted, although it is likely that a simple form would normally be suitable.

(c)   Correlative adjustments

(i)   *Governing rule*

18.   It is the general view that a tax treaty should provide that if one country makes an adjustment in the tax liabilities of an entity under the rules governing the allocation of income and expense, thereby increasing the tax liabilities of that entity, and if the effect of this adjustment, when reflected in the tax status of a related entity in the other country, would require a change in the tax liabilities of the related entity, then a correlative adjustment should be made by the second country at the related entity's request if the initial adjustment is in accord with the treaty standard governing allocation of income and expense. The purpose of such a treaty provision is to avoid economic double taxation. It is clear that the key aspect of a treaty provision requiring a correlative adjustment is that the initial adjustment itself must conform to the appropriate arm's length standard. Such conformity thus becomes for this purpose an important facet of competent authority consultation.

19.   While many countries may be willing to agree that a correlative adjustment should be made, some countries may believe it appropriate to reserve a degree of discretion to the competent authorities, which could then decide that a correlative adjustment need not be made where they conclude that the actual allocations of the related entities which provoked the initial adjustment involved fraud, evasion, intent to avoid taxes or gross abuse in the allocation method utilized. Such countries may take the view that, if a correlative adjustment were required in such situations and the taxpayer were

thus given, in effect, an almost automatic guarantee against the consequence of double taxation, the taxpayer would generally have little to lose in initially using clearly improper allocations. Hence, if the competent authorities possess such discretion and there were a risk to the taxpayer of economic double taxation, he would be deterred from taking such action and would be more careful in his allocations. Other countries may feel, however, that the key objective of the treaty should be to avoid double taxation and, hence, matters such as fraud should be left to other provisions of law, although even here they might concede some modicum of discretion to be used in outrageous cases.

20.   Putting such situations to one side, some countries may not desire a provision requiring correlative adjustments but would leave the entire matter to the discretionary agreement of the competent authorities in the view that the requirement of a correlative adjustment is too strong an invitation to a country to make a large number of initial adjustments. Other countries, however, may believe that the constraint that competent authorities must agree that the initial adjustment conforms to an arm's length standard is itself a sufficient safeguard.

21.   It is recognized that, to be effective, a treaty with a correlative adjustment provision must also provide that any domestic law procedural or other barriers to the making of the correlative adjustment are to be disregarded. Thus, such provisions as statutes of limitations and finality of assessments would have to be overridden to permit the correlative adjustment to be made. If a particular country cannot, through a treaty, override such aspects of its domestic law, this would have to be indicated as an exception to the correlative adjustment provision, although it would be hoped that domestic law could be amended to permit the treaty to operate.

22.   The treaty need not prescribe the method of the correlative adjustment since this depends on the nature of the initial adjustment and its effect on the tax status of the related entity. The method of the correlative adjustment is thus an aspect of the substantive issue underlying the initial adjustment.

(ii)   Competent authority procedure

23.   Given this correlative adjustment requirement, it is clear that the competent authority process must be available at this point. Thus, if the tax authorities of the second country do not themselves work out the correlative adjustment, the taxpayers should be entitled to invoke the competent authority procedure. Hence as one of the minimum aspects of the competent authority procedure, the competent authorities must establish rules as to which competent authority the taxpayers may go to, i.e., the competent authority of the country in which the related entity seeking the correlative adjustment is situated or the competent authority of the country of the initial adjustment, or both. If a time limit on the invocation is to be imposed, then the limit must be stated and the stage at which the time begins to run must be defined. In some countries, when a taxpayer invokes the competent authority of its country, that competent authority may be in a position to dispose of the matter without having to consult the competent authority of the other country. For example, the first competent authority may be in a position to handle a matter having potential international consequences that arises from an adjustment proposed by a taxing unit in the country other than the central body. This is, of course, an aspect of domestic law as affected by the treaty.

24.   As another minimum procedural aspect, the competent authorities must indicate the extent to which a taxpayer may be allowed to participate in the competent authority procedure and the manner of his participation. Some countries may wish to favour a reasonable degree of taxpayer participation. Some countries may wish to allow a taxpayer to present information and even to appear before them; others may restrict the taxpayer to presentation of data. Presumably, the competent authorities would make it a condition that a taxpayer invoking the procedure be required to submit to them relevant information needed to decide the matter. In addition, some competent authorities may, where appropriate, require that data furnished by a taxpayer be prepared as far as possible in accordance with internationally accepted accounting standards so the data provided will have some uniformity and objectivity. It is to be noted that rapid progress

is being made in developing international accounting standards and the work of competent authorities should be aided by this development. As a further aspect concerning the taxpayer's participation, there should be a requirement that the taxpayer who invokes the competent authority procedure should be informed of the response of the competent authority.

25.   The competent authorities will have to decide how their consultation should proceed once the procedure comes into operation. Presumably, the nature of the consultation will depend on the number and character of the cases involved. The competent authorities should keep the consultation procedure flexible and leave every method of communication open, so that the method appropriate to the matter at hand can be used.

26.   Various alternatives are available, such as informal consultation by communication or in person; meetings between technical personnel or auditors of each country, whose conclusions are to be accepted or ratified by the competent authorities; appointment of a joint commission for a complicated case or a series of cases; formal meetings of the competent authorities in person etc. It does not seem desirable to place a time limit on when the competent authorities must conclude a matter, since the complexities of particular cases may differ. Nevertheless, competent authorities should develop working habits that are conducive to prompt disposition of cases and should endeavour not to allow undue delay.

27.   An important minimum procedural aspect of the competent authority procedure is the effect of a taxpayer's invocation of that procedure. Must a taxpayer who invokes that process be bound by the decision of the competent authorities in the sense that he gives up rights to alternative procedures, such as recourse to domestic administrative or judicial procedures? If the competent authorities want their procedure to be exclusive and binding, it would be necessary that the treaty provisions be so drawn as to permit this result. Presumably, this may be accomplished under the general delegation in article 25, paragraph 4, by requiring the taxpayer to waive recourse to those alternative procedures. (However, even with this guideline

paragraph, some countries may consider that their domestic law requires a more explicit statement to permit the competent authority procedure to be binding, especially in view of paragraph 1 of guideline 25[20] referring to remedies under national laws and of the present practice under treaties not to make the procedure a binding one.) Some competent authorities may desire that their actions be binding, since they will not want to go through the effort of reaching agreements only to have the taxpayer reject the result if he feels he can do better in the courts or elsewhere. Other competent authorities may desire to follow the present practice and thus may not want to bind taxpayers or may not be in a position to do so under domestic law. This would appear to be a matter on which developing experience would be a useful guide.

28.   A basic issue regarding the competent authority procedure is the extent to which the competent authorities should consider themselves under obligation to reach an agreement on a matter that comes before them. At a minimum, the treaty requires consultation and the obligation to endeavour to find a solution to economic double taxation. But must the consultation end in agreement? Presumably, disagreement would, in general, leave the related entities in a situation where double taxation may result contrary to the treaty, for example, when a country has opposed a correlative adjustment on the grounds that the initial adjustment was not in conformity with the arm's length standard. On the other hand, an agreement would mean a correlative adjustment made, or a change in the initial adjustment followed then by a correlative adjustment, or perhaps the withdrawal of the initial adjustment. In essence, the general question is whether the competent authority consultation is to be governed by the requirement that there be an "agreement to agree".

29.   In practice, this question is not as serious as it may seem. The experience of most competent authorities, at least as concerns dis-

---

[20]For any reference to "guideline", please refer to the *Manual for the Negotiation of Bilateral Tax Treaties between Developed and Developing Countries* (United Nations publication, Sales No. E.79.XVI.3).

putes between developed countries, is that in the end an agreement or solution is almost always reached. Of course, the solution may often be a compromise, but compromise is an essential aspect of the process of consultation and negotiation. Hence, in reality, it would not be much of a further step for competent authorities to decide that their procedure should be governed by the standard of "agreement to agree". However, some countries would consider the formal adoption of such standard as a step possessing significant juridical consequences and hence would not be disposed to adopt such a requirement.

30.   It is recognized that, for some countries, the process of agreement might well be facilitated if competent authorities, when faced with an extremely difficult case or an impasse, could call, either informally or formally, upon outside experts to give an advisory opinion or otherwise assist in the resolution of the matter. Such experts could be persons currently or previously associated with other tax administrations and possessing the requisite experience in this field. In essence, it would largely be the personal operation of these experts that would be significant. This resort to outside assistance could be useful even where the competent authorities are not operating under the standard of an "agreement to agree", since the outside assistance, by providing a fresh point of view, may help to resolve an impasse.

(*d*)   *Publication of competent authority procedures and determinations*

31.   The competent authorities should make public the procedures they have adopted with regard to their consultation procedure. The description of the procedures should be as complete as is feasible and at the least should contain the minimum procedural aspects discussed above.

32.   Where the consultation procedure has produced a substantive determination in an important area that can reasonably be viewed as providing a guide to the viewpoints of the competent authorities, the

competent authorities should develop a procedure for publication in their countries of that determination or decision.

(e) Procedures to implement adjustments

33. The competent authorities should consider what procedures may be required to implement the various adjustments involved. For example:

(i) The first country may consider deferring a tax payment under the adjustment or even waiving the payment if, for example, payment or reimbursement of an expense charge by the related entity is prohibited at the time because of currency or other restrictions imposed by the second country.

(ii) The first country may consider steps to facilitate carrying out the adjustment and payment of a reallocated amount. Thus, if income is imputed and taxed to a parent corporation because of service to a related foreign subsidiary, the related subsidiary may be allowed, as far as the parent country is concerned, to establish on its book an account payable in favour of the parent, and the parent will not be subject to a second tax in its country on the establishment or payment of the amount receivable. Such payment should not be considered a dividend by the country of the subsidiary.

(iii) The second country may consider steps to facilitate carrying out the adjustment and payment of a reallocated amount. This may, for example, involve recognition of the payment made as a deductible item, even though prior to the adjustment there was no legal obligation to pay such amount. This is really an aspect of the correlative adjustment.

(f) Unilateral procedures

34.   The above discussion has related almost entirely to bilateral procedures to be agreed upon by the competent authorities to implement the mutual agreement procedure. In addition, a competent authority may consider it useful to develop certain unilateral rules or procedures involving its relationship to its own taxpayers, so that these relationships may be better understood. These unilateral rules can cover such matters as the form to be followed in bringing matters to the attention of the competent authority; the permission to taxpayers to bring matters to the competent authority at an early stage even where the bilateral procedure does not require consultation at that stage; the question whether the competent authority will raise new domestic issues (so-called affirmative issues) between the tax authorities and the taxpayer if he goes to the competent authority; and requests for information that will assist the competent authority in handling cases.

35.   Unilateral rules regarding the operation of a competent authority would not require agreement to them by the other competent authority, since the rules are limited to the domestic relationship with its own taxpayers. However, it would seem appropriate to communicate such unilateral rules to the other treaty competent authorities, and to avoid wherever possible material differences, if any, in such rules in relation to the various treaties.

36.   Some members of the Group of Experts supported the idea of adding to article 25 a paragraph providing for arbitration in case the competent authorities cannot resolve in mutual agreement any difficulty or doubt arising as to the interpretation or application of the Convention. An example of such an additional paragraph could read:

> "If any difficulty or doubt arising as to the interpretation or application of this Convention cannot be resolved by the competent authorities in a mutual agreement procedure pursuant to the previous paragraphs of this article, the case may, if both competent authorities and taxpayer(s) agree, be submitted for arbitration, provided the taxpayer agrees in writing to be

bound by the decision of the arbitration board. The decision of the arbitration board in a particular case shall be binding on both States with respect to that case. The competent authorities shall by mutual agreement settle the procedures for such an arbitration board."

Article 26

EXCHANGE OF INFORMATION

A. GENERAL CONSIDERATIONS

1.   Article 26 of the United Nations Model Convention reproduces Article 26 of the OECD Model Convention with three substantive changes in paragraph 1, namely, the insertion of the phrase "in particular for the prevention of fraud or evasion of such taxes" in the first sentence, the insertion of the phrase "However, if the information is originally regarded as secret in the transmitting State" in the fourth sentence and the addition of a new sentence (sixth and last sentence). The latter sentence is the key to the approach advocated by the Group; it would stress the importance of the competent authorities in implementing fully the provisions on the exchange of information and will give them the necessary authority.

2.   The words "in particular for the prevention of fraud or evasion of such taxes" were inserted at the request of members of the Group, mainly from developing countries, who wanted to emphasize that the exchange of information under article 26 covers the purpose of preventing fraud or evasion. The exchange of information for the prevention of fraud or evasion is subject to the general condition embodied in the first sentence of paragraph 1, that the taxation involved is not contrary to the Convention.

3.   Since article 26 of the United Nations Model Convention reproduces the substance of all the provisions of Article 26 of the OECD Model Convention, the preliminary remarks contained in the

351

Commentary on the latter Article are relevant. These remarks read as follows:

> "There are good grounds for including in a convention for the avoidance of double taxation provisions concerning cooperation between the tax administrations of the two Contracting States. In the first place it appears to be desirable to give administrative assistance for the purpose of ascertaining facts in relation to which the rules of the Convention are to be applied. Moreover, in view of the increasing internationalization of economic relations, the Contracting States have a growing interest in the reciprocal supply of information on the basis of which domestic taxation laws have to be administered, even if there is no question of the application of any particular Article of the Convention." [para. 1]

> "Therefore the present Article embodies the rules under which information may be exchanged to the widest possible extent, with a view to laying the proper basis for the implementation of the domestic laws of the Contracting States concerning taxes covered by the Convention and for the application of specific provisions of the Convention. The text of the Article makes it clear that the exchange of information is not restricted by Article 1, so that the information may include particulars about non-residents." [para. 2]

> "The matter of administrative assistance for the purpose of tax collection is not dealt with in the Article. This matter is dealt with in the Convention on Mutual Administrative Assistance in Tax Matters, a multilateral convention that entered into force on 1 April 1995. This Convention was drawn up within the Council of Europe on the basis of a first draft prepared by the Committee on Fiscal Affairs and is open to the signature of the Member States of the Council of Europe and Member countries of the OECD. This matter can also form the subject of a separate bilateral agreement that can be negotiated between the Contracting States on the basis of the Model Convention for Mutual Administrative Assistance in the Recovery of Tax Claims adopted by the Committee on Fiscal Affairs on

29 June 1979; alternatively, the provisions on assistance in the field of tax collection may be introduced in the double taxation convention, whenever Contracting States find it preferable." [para. 3]

4.   The Group emphasized that in negotiating treaties for the avoidance of double taxation and tax evasion the competent authorities might wish to provide for the exchange of such information as was necessary for carrying out the provisions of the treaty or of the domestic laws of the Contracting States concerning taxes covered by the treaty. In that regard, the Group suggested guidelines[21] for arrangements regarding the implementation of appropriate exchanges of information. Those guidelines are in the form of an inventory of possible arrangements from which the competent authorities under a tax treaty may select the particular arrangements which they decide should be used. The inventory is not intended to be exhaustive nor is it to be regarded as listing matters all of which are to be drawn on in every case. Instead, the inventory is a listing of suggestions to be examined by competent authorities in deciding on the matters they wish to cover.

5.   The Group also emphasized that the term "exchange of information" included an exchange of documents and that, subject to the provisions of paragraph 2 of the article if specifically requested by the competent authority of a Contracting State, the competent authority of the other Contracting State should provide information under that article in the form of depositions of witnesses and authenticated copies of unedited original documents (including books, papers, statements, records, accounts or writings), to the extent that it could obtain such depositions and documents under the laws and administrative practices applying in respect to its own taxes.

---

[21]Please refer to the *Manual for the Negotiation of Bilateral Tax Treaties between Developed and Developing Countries* (United Nations publication, Sales No. E.79.XVI.3).

Routine transmittal of information[22]

6.   A method of exchange of information is that of the routine or automatic flow of information from one treaty country to another. The following are various aspects that the competent authorities should focus on in developing a structure for such routine exchange. In considering routine exchanges of information it should be recognized that some countries not desiring to receive such information in a routine fashion (or unable to receive it routinely because the transmitting countries do not routinely collect such information) may desire to obtain information of this type under a specific request. Hence, in these situations, items mentioned in the present section should be considered as available for coverage under the next section, "Transmittal on specific request".

Items covered

7.   *Regular sources of income.* The items covered under a routine transmittal or exchange of information may extend to regular sources of income flowing between countries, such as dividends, interest, compensation (including wages, salaries, fees and commissions), royalties, rents and other possible items whose regular flow between the two countries is significant. It should be recognized that at present a few countries are not in a position to supply routine information of this type because their tax collection procedures do not provide the needed data.

   Transactions involving taxpayer activity. A routine exchange of information may cover certain significant transactions involving taxpayer activity.

   (*a*)   Transactions relevant to the treaty itself:

      —Claims for refund of transmitting country tax made by residents of receiving country;

---

[22]In the following text, "transmitting country" refers to the country transmitting information and "receiving country" refers to the country receiving information.

—Claims for exemption or particular relief from transmitting country tax made by residents of receiving country;

(*b*) Transactions relevant to special aspects of the legislation of the transmitting country:

—Items of income derived by residents of the receiving country that receive exemption or partial relief under special provisions of the national law of the transmitting country;

(*c*) Transactions relating to activities in the transmitting country of residents of the receiving country:

—Opening and closing by receiving country residents of a branch, office etc. in the transmitting country;

—Creation or termination by receiving country residents of a corporation in the transmitting country;

—Creation or termination by receiving country residents of a trust in the transmitting country;

—Opening and closing by receiving country residents of bank accounts in the transmitting country;

—Property in the transmitting country acquired by residents of the receiving country by inheritance, bequest or gift;

—Ancillary probate proceedings in the transmitting country concerning receiving country residents;

(*d*) General information:

—Tax laws, administrative procedures etc. of the transmitting country;

—Changes in regular sources of income flowing between countries, especially as they affect the treaty, including administrative interpretations of and court decisions on treaty provisions and administrative practices or developments affecting application of the treaty;

—Activities that affect or distort application of the treaty, including new patterns or techniques of evasion or avoidance used by residents of the transmitting or receiving country;

—Activities that have repercussions regarding the tax system of the receiving country, including new patterns or techniques of evasion or avoidance used by residents of either country that significantly affect the receiving country's tax system.

General operational aspects to be considered

8.   The competent authorities should consider various factors that may have a bearing on the operational character of the routine exchange, including its effectiveness. For example:

(*a*)   Countries that are more interested in receiving information on a specific request basis than on a routine basis, in their consideration of the specific request area, should keep in mind items mentioned in this inventory under the heading of routine information.

(*b*)   A minimum floor amount may be fixed to limit minor data.

(*c*)   The routine source of income items may be rotated from year to year, for example, dividends only in one year, interest in another etc.

(*d*)   The information to be exchanged routinely need not be strictly reciprocal in all items. Country A may be interested in receiving information on some items but not others; the preferences of country B may extend to different items; it is not necessary for either country to receive items in which it is not interested, nor should either country refuse to transmit information on certain items simply because it is not interested in receiving information on those items.

(*e*)   While the information to be exchanged on income items may not always be significant in itself as regards the income flows escaping tax, the routine exchange may provide indications respecting the degree to which the capital or other assets producing the income flows are escaping tax.

(*f*)   Whether the information on items of income should cover the payee only or also the payer is a further point to be taken into account.

(g) Another factor to be considered is whether the information should cover only residents of the receiving country or also those domiciled therein or citizens thereof, or be limited to any of these categories.

(h) The degree of detail involved in the reporting, e.g., name of taxpayer or recipient, profession, address etc., may need to be taken into account.

(i) The form and the language in which the information should be provided is a further point to be considered.

Factors to be considered by the transmitting country

9.   The transmitting country may wish to give consideration to factors affecting its ability to fulfil the requirements of a routine exchange of information. Such a consideration would presumably lead to a more careful selection of the information to be routinely exchanged rather than to a decision not to exchange information that could be of practical use.

10.   Among the factors to be considered are the administrative ability of the transmitting country to obtain the information involved. This in turn is governed by the general effectiveness of its administrative procedures, its use of withholding taxes, its use of information returns from payers or others and the overall costs of obtaining the information involved.

Factors to be considered by receiving country

11.   The receiving country may wish to give consideration to factors affecting its ability to use the information that could be received under a routine exchange of information, such as the administrative ability of the receiving country to use the information on a reasonably current basis and effectively to associate such information with its own taxpayers, either routinely or on a sufficient scale to justify the routine receipt of the information.

Transmittal on specific request

12.   A method of exchange of information that is in current use is that of a request for specific information made by one treaty country to another. The specific information may relate to a particular taxpayer and certain facets of his situation or to particular types of transactions or activities or to information of a more general character. The following are various aspects of the question that the competent authorities should focus on in developing a structure for such exchange of information pursuant to specific requests.

Items covered

13.   *Particular taxpayers.* The information that may be desired from a transmitting country with respect to a receiving country taxpayer is essentially open-ended and depends on the factors involved in the situation of the taxpayer under the tax system of the receiving country and the relationship of the taxpayer and his activities to the transmitting country. A specific enumeration in advance of the type of information that may be within the scope of an exchange pursuant to specific request does not seem to be a fruitful or necessary task. The agreement to provide information pursuant to specific request may thus be open-ended as to the range, scope and type of information, subject to the overall constraints to be discussed herein.

14.   The request for specific information may arise in a variety of ways. For example:

   (*a*) Information needed to complete the determination of a taxpayer's liability in the receiving country when that liability depends on the taxpayer's worldwide income or assets; the nature of the stock ownership in the transmitting country of the receiving country corporation; the amount or type of expense incurred in the transmitting country; and the fiscal domicile of an individual or corporation;

   (*b*) Information needed to determine the accuracy of a taxpayer's tax return to the tax administration of the receiving country or the accuracy of the claims or proof asserted by the taxpayer in defence of the tax return when the return is regarded as suspect or is under actual investigation;

(*c*) Information needed to determine the true liability of a taxpayer in the receiving country when it is suspected that his reported liability is wrong.

Particular types of transactions or activities. The exchange on specific request need not be confined to requests regarding particular taxpayers but may extend to requests for information on particular types of transactions or activities. For example:

(*a*) Information on price, cost, commission or other such patterns in the transmitting country necessary to enable the tax administration of the receiving country either to determine tax liability in a particular situation or to develop standards for investigation of its taxpayers in situations involving possible under- or over-invoicing of exported or imported goods, the payment of commissions on international transactions and the like;

(*b*) Information on the typical methods by which particular transactions or activities are customarily conducted in the transmitting country;

(*c*) Information on whether a particular type of activity is being carried on in the transmitting country that may have effects on taxpayers or tax liabilities in the receiving country.

15. *Economic relationships between the countries.* The specific request may extend to requests for information regarding certain economic relationships between the countries which may be useful to a country as a check on the effectiveness of its tax administration activities, for example:

(*a*) The volume of exports from the transmitting country to the receiving country;

(*b*) The volume of imports into the transmitting country from the receiving country;

(*c*) Names of banks dealing in the transmitting country with branches, subsidiaries etc. of residents of the receiving country.

It should be noted that since items in this category, such as the volume of exports between the countries, are presumably not regarded as secret to the tax authorities in the transmitting country, they may be disclosed generally in the receiving country, as provided in article 26.

Rules applicable to the specific request

16.   The competent authorities should develop rules applicable to the transmission of specific requests by the receiving country and to the response by the transmitting country. These rules should be designed to facilitate a systematic operational procedure regarding such exchange that is both efficient and orderly. While the rules may be general in character in the sense that they set standards or guidelines governing the specific request procedures, the rules should also permit discussion between the competent authorities of special situations that either country believes require special handling.

The rules should pertain to:

(*a*) The specificity of detail required in the request by the receiving country, the form of such request and the language of the request and reply;

(*b*) The extent to which the receiving country must pursue or exhaust its own administrative processes and possibilities before making a specific request; presumably the receiving country should make a bona fide effort to obtain the information for itself before resorting to the specific request procedure;

(*c*) The conditions affecting the nature and extent of the response by the transmitting country. This aspect should cover the ability of the transmitting country to provide documentary material when the receiving country needs material in that form for use in judicial or other proceedings, including the appropriate authentication of the documents.

Transmittal of information on discretionary initiative of transmitting country (spontaneous exchange)

17.   The competent authorities should determine whether, in addition to the routine and specific request methods of exchange of information under which a transmitting country is automatically transmitting information or systematically responding to specific requests by the receiving country, they desire a transmittal of information on the discretionary initiative of the transmitting country itself. Such a transmittal could occur when, in the course of its own activities, the tax administration of the transmitting country obtains information that it considers would be of importance to the receiving country. The information may relate to facets of a particular taxpayer's situation and the relationship of that situation to his liability in the receiving country or to the liability of other taxpayers in the receiving country. Or the information may relate to a pattern of transactions or conduct by various taxpayers or groups of taxpayers occurring in either country that is likely to affect the tax liabilities or tax administration of the receiving country in relation either to its national laws or to the treaty provisions.

18.   The competent authorities will have to determine, under the standards governing the exchange of information developed pursuant to the treaty, whether it is the duty of a transmitting country affirmatively to develop a procedure and guidelines governing when such information is to be transmitted, whether such transmittal is to be considered by the transmitting country but is fully discretionary, or whether such transmittal need not even be considered by the transmitting country. Even if it is agreed that it is the duty of the transmitting country to develop a system for such transmittal, presumably the decision on when the conditions under that system have been met will rest on the discretionary judgement of the latter country.

Use of information received

19.　The competent authorities will have to decide on the permissible use of the information received. The decisions on this matter basically depend on the legal requirements set forth in article 26 itself. Under the guideline,[23] the extent of the use of information depends primarily on the requirements of national law regarding the disclosure of tax information or on other "security requirements" regarding tax information. This being so, it is possible that the extent of the disclosure or the restrictions on disclosure may vary between the two countries. However, such possible variance need not be regarded as inappropriate or as negating exchanges of information that would otherwise occur if the countries involved are satisfied with such a consequence under article 26 as adopted in their convention.

Recipients of information received through exchange

20.　The competent authorities will have to specify, either in detail or by reference to existing comparable rules in the receiving country, who the qualifying recipients of information in that country are. Under article 26 the information can be disclosed, for example:

(*a*)　To administrators of the taxes covered in the convention;

(*b*)　To enforcement officials and prosecutors for such taxes;

(*c*)　To administrative tribunals for such taxes;

(*d*)　To judicial tribunals for such taxes;

(*e*)　In public court proceedings or in judicial decisions where it may become available to the public if considered appropriate;

(*f*)　To the competent authority of another country (see the section below entitled "Consultation among several competent authorities").

---

[23]Please refer to the *Manual for the Negotiation of Bilateral Tax Treaties between Developed and Developing Countries* (United Nations publication, Sales No. E.79.XVI.3).

The form in which information is provided

21.   The permissible extent of the disclosure may affect the form in which the information is to be provided if it is to be useful to the receiving country. Thus, if the information may be used in judicial tribunals and if, to be so used, it must be of a particular character or form, then the competent authorities will have to consider how to provide for a transmittal that meets this need. (See also the comment on documents in the section above dealing with rules applicable to the specific request.)

Consultation among several competent authorities

22.   Countries may wish to give consideration to procedures developed by the competent authorities for consultations covering more than the two competent authorities under a particular treaty. Thus, if countries A, B and C are joined in a network of treaties, the competent authorities of A, B and C might desire to hold a joint consultation. This could be desired whether all three countries are directly intertwined, for example, where there are A-B, A-C and B-C treaties, or where one country is a link in a chain but not fully joined, for example, where there are A-B and B-C treaties but not an A-C treaty. Countries desiring to have their competent authorities engage in such consultations should provide the legal basis for the consultations by adding the necessary authority in their treaties. Some countries may feel that article 26 permits joint consultation where all three countries are directly linked by bilateral treaties. However, the guideline does not cover joint consultation where a link in the chain is not fully joined, as in the second situation described above. In such a case, it would be necessary to add a treaty provision allowing the competent authority of country B to provide information received from country A to the competent authority of country C. Such a treaty provision could include a safeguard that the competent authority of country A must consent to the action of the competent authority of country B. Presumably, it would so consent only where it was satisfied as to the provisions regarding protection of secrecy in the B-C treaty.

Overall factors

23.   There are a variety of overall factors affecting the exchanges of information that the competent authorities will have to consider and decide upon, either as to their specific operational handling in the implementation of the exchange of information or as to their effect on the entire exchange process itself. Among such overall factors are:

Factors affecting implementation of exchange of information

(*a*)   The competent authorities should decide on the channels of communication for the different types of exchanges of information. One method of communication that may be provided for is to permit an official of one country to go in person to the other country to receive the information from the competent authority and discuss it so as to expedite the process of exchange of information.

(*b*)   Some countries may have decided that it is useful and appropriate for a country to have representatives of its own tax administration stationed in the other treaty country. Such an arrangement would presumably rest on authority, treaty or agreements other than that in the article on exchange of information of the envisaged double taxation treaty (though, if national laws of both countries permit, this article would be treated as covering this topic) and the arrangement would determine the conditions governing the presence of such representatives and their duties. In this regard, it should be noted that it would not seem necessary that the process be reciprocal, so that it would be appropriate for country A to have its representatives in country B but not vice versa if country A considered the process to be useful and country B did not. If arrangements do exist for such representatives, then the competent authorities may want to coordinate with those representatives where such coordination would make the exchange of information process more effective and where such coordination is otherwise appropriate.

(*c*) Some countries may decide it is appropriate to have a tax official of one country participate directly with tax officials of the other country in a joint or "team" investigation of a particular taxpayer or activity. The existence of the arrangement for most countries would presumably rest on authority, treaty or agreements other than that in the envisaged treaty article on exchange of information, although, if national laws of both countries permit, this article could be treated by the countries as authorizing the competent authorities to sanction this arrangement. In either event, if the arrangement is made, it would be appropriate to extend to such an investigation the safeguards and procedures developed under the envisaged treaty article on exchange of information.

(*d*) The process of exchange of information should be developed so that it has the needed relevance to the effective implementation of the substantive treaty provisions. Thus, treaty provisions regarding intercompany pricing and the allocation of income and expenses produce their own informational requirements for effective implementation. The exchange of information process should be responsive to those requirements.

(*e*) The substantive provisions of the treaty should take account of and be responsive to the exchange of information process. Thus, if there is an adequate informational base for the exchange of information process to support allowing one country to deduct expenses incurred in another country, then the treaty should be developed on the basis of the substantive appropriateness of such deduction.

(*f*) The competent authorities will have to determine to what extent there should be cost sharing or cost reimbursement with respect to the process of exchange of information.

Factors affecting structure of exchange of information process

24. (*a*) It should be recognized that the arrangements regarding exchange of information worked out by country A with country

B need not parallel those worked out between country A and country C or between country B and country C. The arrangements should in the first instance be responsive to the needs of the two countries directly involved and need not be fully parallel in every case just for the sake of formal uniformity. However, it should be observed that prevention of international tax evasion and avoidance will often require international cooperation of tax authorities in a number of countries. As a consequence, some countries may consider it appropriate to devise procedures and treaty provisions that are sufficiently flexible to enable them to extend their cooperation to multicountry consultation and exchange arrangements.

(*b*) The competent authorities will have to weigh the effect of a domestic legal restriction on obtaining information in a country that requests information from another country not under a similar domestic legal restriction. Thus, suppose country A requests information from country B and the tax authorities in country B are able to go to their financial institutions to obtain such information, whereas the tax authorities in country A are generally not able to go to their own financial institutions to obtain information for tax purposes. How should the matter be regarded in country B? It should be noted that article 26 here permits country B to obtain the information from its financial institutions and transmit it to country A. Thus, country B is not barred by its domestic laws regarding tax secrecy if it decides to obtain and transmit the information. It thus becomes a matter of discretion in country B as to whether it should respond, and may perhaps become a matter for negotiation between the competent authorities. It should be noted that many countries in practice do respond in this situation and that such a course is indeed useful in achieving effective exchange of information to prevent tax avoidance. However, it should also be noted that country A, being anxious to obtain information in such cases from other countries, should also recognize its responsibility to try to change its domestic laws to strengthen the domestic authority of its own tax administration and to enable it to respond to requests from other countries.

(c)   In addition to situations involving the legal imbalance discussed above, the competent authorities will have to weigh the effects of a possible imbalance growing out of a divergence in other aspects of tax administration. Thus, if country A cannot respond as fully to a request as country B can because of practical problems of tax administration in country A, then might the level of the process of exchange of information be geared to the position of country A? Or, on the other hand, in general or in particular aspects, should country B be willing to respond to requests of country A even when country A would not be able to respond to requests of country B? This matter is similar to that discussed in the preceding paragraph and a similar response should be noted.

(d)   It should be noted that article 26 authorizes a transmitting country to use its administrative procedures solely to provide information to the requesting country, even when the person about whom information is sought is not involved in a tax proceeding in the transmitting country. Moreover, the transmitting country should, for the purpose of exchange of information, use its own administrative authority in the same way as if its own taxation were involved.

(e)   The competent authorities will have to weigh the effect on the process of exchange of information of one country's belief that the tax system or tax administration of the other country, either in general or in particular situations, is discriminatory or confiscatory. It may be that further exploration of such a belief could lead to substantive provisions in the treaty or in national law that would eliminate the problems perceived by the first country and thereby facilitate a process of exchange of information. One possible example of this is the treatment of non-permanent residents.

(f)   The competent authorities will have to weigh the effects that the process of exchange of information may have on the competitive position of taxpayers of the countries involved. Thus, if country A has a treaty with country B providing for exchange of information, country A will have to weigh the effect on the structure or process of that exchange of the fact that country C does not have a treaty with country B, so that firms of country C doing business in country B may be subject to a different tax posture in country B than firms of country A. Similarly, even if a treaty with an exchange of information article exists between countries C and B, if the tax administration of country A has more authority to obtain information (to be exchanged with country B) than does the tax administration of country C, or is otherwise more effective in its administration and therefore has more information, then a similar difference in tax posture may result. As a corollary, it seems clear that the adequate implementation of exchange of information provisions requires a universal effort of tax administrations to obtain and develop under national laws a capacity for securing information and a competence in utilizing information that is appropriate to a high level of efficient and equitable tax administration.

Periodic consultation and review

25. Since differences in interpretation and application, specific difficulties and unforeseen problems and situations are bound to arise, provision must be made for efficient and expeditious consultation between the competent authorities. Such consultation should extend both to particular situations and problems and to periodic review of the operations under the exchange of information provision. The periodic review should ensure that the process of exchange of information is working with the requisite promptness and efficiency, that it is meeting the basic requirements of treaty implementation and that it is promoting adequate compliance with treaty provisions and the national laws of the two countries.

B.   COMMENTARY ON THE PARAGRAPHS OF ARTICLE 26

Paragraph 1

26.   As noted above, this paragraph, while incorporating all the provisions of Article 26, paragraph 1, of the OECD Model Convention also contains three additions. The Commentary on that paragraph is therefore relevant:

> "The main rule concerning the exchange of information is contained in the first sentence of the paragraph. The competent authorities of the Contracting States shall exchange such information as is necessary to secure the correct application of the provisions of the Convention or of the domestic laws of the Contracting States concerning taxes covered by the Convention even if, in the latter case, a particular Article of the Convention need not be applied. Some countries replace 'necessary' with 'relevant' in their bilateral conventions, regarding this as a better way to express the sense of the provisions; in the view of the Committee on Fiscal Affairs, either word may be used in that context. In order to keep the exchange of information within the framework of the Convention, a limitation to the exchange of information is set so that information should be given only in so far as the national tax in question is covered by the Convention and the taxation under the domestic taxation laws concerned is not contrary to the Convention. An illustration may be cited in this connection: a request for the imposition of a sales tax need not be complied with by the requested State as it is not covered by the Convention." [para. 5]

> "The following examples may clarify the principle dealt with in paragraph 5 above. In all such cases information can be exchanged under paragraph 1." [para. 6]

> "Application of the Convention

> (*a*)   When applying Article 12, State A where the beneficiary is resident asks State B where the payer is resident

for information concerning the amount of royalty transmitted.

(*b*)   Conversely, in order to grant the relief provided for in Article 12, State B asks State A whether the recipient of the amounts paid is in fact a resident of the last-mentioned State and the beneficial owner of the royalties.

(*c*)   Similarly, information may be needed with a view to the proper allocation of taxable profits between associated companies in different States or the adjustment of the profits shown in the accounts of a permanent establishment in one State and in the accounts of the head office in the other State (Articles 7, 9, 23 A and 23 B)." [para. 7]

"Implementation of the domestic laws

(*a*)   A company in State A supplies goods to an independent company in State B. State A wishes to know from State B what price the company in State B paid for the goods with a view to a correct application of the provisions of its domestic laws.

(*b*)   A company in State A sells goods through a company in State C (possibly a low-tax country) to a company in State B. The companies may or may not be associated. There is no convention between State A and State C, nor between State B and State C. Under the convention between A and B, State A, with a view to ensuring the correct application of the provisions of its domestic laws to the profits made by the company situated in its territory, asks State B what price the company in State B paid for the goods.

(*c*)   State A, for the purpose of taxing a company situated in its territory, asks State B, under the convention between A and B, for information about the prices charged by a company in State B, or a group of companies in State B with which the company in State A has no business contacts in order to enable it to check the prices charged by the company in State A by direct comparison (e.g., prices charged by a company or a group of companies in a dominant position). It should be borne in mind that the exchange of information in this case might be a difficult and delicate matter owing in particular to the provisions of subparagraph (*c*) of paragraph 2 relating to business and other secrets." [para. 8]

"The rule laid down in paragraph 1 allows information to be exchanged in three different ways:

(*a*)   on request, with a special case in mind, it being understood that the regular sources of information available under the internal taxation procedure should be relied upon in the first place before request for information is made to the other State;

(*b*)   automatically, for example when information about one or various categories of income having their source in one Contracting State and received in the other Contracting State is transmitted systematically to the other State . . ."

(*c*)   spontaneously, for example in the case of a State having acquired, through certain investigations, information which it supposes to be of interest to the other State." [para. 9]

"The manner in which the exchange of information agreed to in the Convention will finally be effected can be decided upon by the competent authorities of the Contracting States." [para. 10]

"Reciprocal assistance between tax administrations is feasible only if each administration is assured that the other administration will treat with proper confidence the information which it will receive in the course of their cooperation. At the same time maintenance of such secrecy in the receiving Contracting State is a matter of domestic laws. It is therefore provided in paragraph 1 that information communicated under the provisions of the Convention shall be treated as secret in the receiving State in the same manner as information obtained under the domestic laws of that State. Sanctions for the violation of such secrecy in that State will be governed by the administrative and penal laws of that State." [para. 11]

"The information obtained may be disclosed only to persons and authorities involved in the assessment or collection of, the enforcement or prosecution in respect of, or the determination of appeals in relation to the taxes covered by the Convention. This means that the information may also be communicated to the taxpayer, his proxy or to the witnesses. The information received by a Contracting State may be used by such persons or authorities only for the purposes mentioned in paragraph 1. If the information appears to be of value to the receiving State for other purposes than those referred to, that State may not use the information for such other purposes but it must resort to means specially designed for those purposes (e.g., in case of a non-fiscal crime, to a treaty concerning judicial assistance)." [para. 12]

"Under this Article, information may not be disclosed to authorities that supervise the general administration of the Government of a Contracting State, but are not involved specifically in tax matters. In their bilateral negotiations, however, Member countries may agree to provide for disclosure to such supervisory bodies." [para. 12.1]

"As stated above, the information obtained can be communicated to the persons and authorities mentioned but it does not follow from this that it can be disclosed by them in court sessions held in public or in decisions which reveal the name of the taxpayer. The last sentence of the paragraph, however, opens up this possibility. Once information is used in public court proceedings or in court decisions and thus rendered public, it is clear that from that moment such information can be quoted from the court files or decisions for other purposes even as possible evidence. But this does not mean that the persons and authorities mentioned in paragraph 1 are allowed to provide on request additional information received. If either or both of the Contracting States object to the information being made public by courts in this way, or, once the information has been made public in this way, to the information being used for other purposes, because this is not the normal procedure under their domestic laws, they should state this expressly in their convention." [para. 13]

27.   With regard to the additions to Article 26, paragraph 1, of the OECD Model Convention, the Group of Experts observed that the reference to fraud or evasion in paragraph 1 was intended to focus attention on the importance of exchanges of information that would assist the treaty partners in combating such practices. Since a number of countries were concerned with the need for information to assist in the administration of specific statutory provisions against tax avoidance and others were concerned with the need for information to assist in detecting other aspects of tax avoidance, the Group considered it advisable to include the reference in the last sentence of paragraph 1 to exchanges of information regarding tax avoidance where the treaty partners deemed it appropriate. The reference in the same sentence to the consultations aimed at developing appropriate conditions, methods and techniques was designed to enable the treaty partners to work out the modalities for exchanges of information between them.

28.   In the course of the discussion, members from developing countries observed that the proliferation of transnational corporations and the ever-growing sophistication and complexity of the forms taken by international business transactions were resulting in increasing tax avoidance and evasion. The view was expressed that such a situation might have reached a point where it could negate completely the effects of treaties for the avoidance of double taxation and raised the question whether steps should be taken outside and in addition to the existing framework of such treaties. One member from a developing country, supported by other members from developing countries, suggested that the quickest and most effective way of ensuring the exchange of information required to combat tax evasion efficiently would be through the conclusion of a multilateral

agreement dealing specifically with the exchange of information and mutual assistance in tax administration.

29.   While discussing the problems of tax havens, the Group felt that as a protection against improper manipulation of treaty benefits, consideration should be given in bilateral negotiations to the inclusion of a separate article along the following lines:

> "Each of the Contracting States should endeavour to collect on behalf of the other Contracting State such taxes imposed by that other Contracting State to the extent necessary to ensure that any exemption or reduced rate of tax granted under the treaty by that other Contracting State should not be enjoyed by persons not entitled to such benefits."

Paragraph 2

30.   Since this paragraph reproduces Article 26, paragraph 2, of the OECD Model Convention, the Commentary on that paragraph is fully relevant:

> "This paragraph contains certain limitations to the main rule in favour of the requested State. In the first place, the paragraph contains the clarification that a Contracting State is not bound to go beyond its own internal laws and administrative practice in putting information at the disposal of the other Contracting State. However, types of administrative measures authorized for the purpose of the requested State's tax must be utilized, even though invoked solely to provide information to the other Contracting State. Likewise, internal provisions concerning tax secrecy should not be interpreted as constituting an obstacle to the exchange of information under the present article. As mentioned above, the authorities of the requesting State are obliged to observe secrecy with regard to information received under this Article. A Contracting State that under its domestic law is required to notify the taxpayer that an exchange of information is proposed should inform its treaty partners in writing that it has this requirement and what the

consequences are for its obligations in relation to mutual assistance." [para. 14]

"Furthermore, the requested State does not need to go so far as to carry out administrative measures that are not permitted under the laws or practice of the requesting State or to supply items of information that are not obtainable under the laws or in the normal course of administration of the requesting State. It follows that a Contracting State cannot take advantage of the information system of the other Contracting State if it is wider than its own system." [para. 15]

"Information is deemed to be obtainable in the normal course of administration if it is in the possession of the tax authorities or can be obtained by them in the normal procedure of tax determination, which may include special investigations or special examination of the business accounts kept by the taxpayer or other persons, provided that the tax authorities would make similar investigations or examination for their own purposes. This means that the requested State has to collect the information the other State needs in the same way as if its own taxation was involved, under the proviso mentioned in paragraph 15 above." [para. 16]

"The requested State is at liberty to refuse to give information in the cases referred to in the paragraphs above. However if it does give the requested information, it remains within the framework of the agreement on the exchange of information which is laid down in the Convention; consequently it cannot be objected that this State has failed to observe the obligation to secrecy." [para. 17]

"If the structure of the information systems of two Contracting States is very different, the conditions under subparagraphs (a) and (b) of paragraph 2 will lead to the result that the Contracting States exchange very little information or perhaps none at all. In such a case, the Contracting States may find it appropriate to broaden the scope of the exchange of information." [para. 18]

"In addition to the limitations referred to above, subparagraph (c) of paragraph 2 contains a reservation concerning the disclosure of certain secret information. Secrets mentioned in this subparagraph should not be taken in too wide a sense. Before invoking this provision, a Contracting State should carefully weigh if the interests of the taxpayer really justify its application. Otherwise it is clear that too wide an interpretation would in many cases render ineffective the exchange of information provided for in the Convention. The observations made in paragraph 17 above apply here as well. The requested State in protecting the interests of its taxpayers is given a certain discretion to refuse the requested information, but if it does supply the information deliberately the taxpayer cannot allege an infraction of the rules of secrecy. It is open to the Contracting States to add further dispensations from the obligation to supply information to the items listed in subparagraph (c), for example, information protected by provisions on banker's discretion. It has been felt necessary also to prescribe a limitation with regard to information which concerns the vital interests of the State itself. To this end, it is stipulated that Contracting States do not have to supply information the disclosure of which would be contrary to public policy (*ordre public*)." [para. 19]

31.   During the eighth meeting, held in December 1997, several members of the Group of Experts noted that some treaties contained provisions for collection assistance in article 26, even though neither the United Nations nor the OECD Model Convention contained such a provision. The Group decided, in its consideration of article 26, to examine whether the United Nations Model Convention or the Commentaries should include provisions for collection assistance. The Group agreed with the suggestion of a member from a developed country to include the following material dealing with "Assistance in recovery" in the Commentaries which may be considered by Contracting States during bilateral negotiations.

"ASSISTANCE IN RECOVERY

1.   The States agree to lend each other assistance and support with a view to the collection, in accordance with their respective laws or administrative practice, of the taxes to which this Convention shall apply and of any increases, surcharges, overdue payments, interests and costs pertaining to the said taxes.

2.   At the request of the applicant State the requested State shall recover tax claims of the first-mentioned State in accordance with the law and administrative practice for the recovery of its own tax claims. However, such claims do not enjoy any priority in the requested State and cannot be recovered by imprisonment for debt of the debtor. The requested State is not obliged to take any executory measures which are not provided for in the laws of the applicant State.

3.   The provisions of paragraph 2 shall apply only to tax claims which form the subject of an instrument permitting their enforcement in the applicant State and unless otherwise agreed between the competent authorities, which are not contested.

However, where the claim relates to a liability to tax of a person as a non-resident of the applicant State, paragraph 2 shall only apply, unless otherwise agreed between the competent authorities, where the claim may no longer be contested.

4.   The obligation to provide assistance in the recovery of tax claims concerning a deceased person or his estate is limited to the value of the estate or the property acquired by each beneficiary of the estate, according to whether the claim is to be recovered from the estate or from the beneficiaries thereof.

5.   The requested State shall not be obliged to accede to the request:

(*a*)   If the applicant State has not pursued all means available in its own territory, except where recourse to such means would give rise to disproportionate difficulty;

(*b*)   If and in so far as it considers the tax claim to be contrary to the provisions of this Convention or of any other convention to which both of the States are parties.

6.   The request for administrative assistance in the recovery of tax claim shall be accompanied by:

(*a*)   a declaration that the tax claim concerns a tax covered by the Convention and that the conditions of paragraph 3 are met;

(*b*)   an official copy of the instrument permitting enforcement in the applicant State;

(*c*)   any other document required for recovery;

(*d*)   where appropriate, a certified copy confirming any related decision emanating from an administrative body or a public court.

7.   The applicant State shall indicate the amounts of the tax claim to be recovered in both the currency of the applicant State and the currency of the requested State. The rate of exchange to be used for the purpose of the preceding sentence is the last selling price settled on most representative exchange market or markets of the applicant State. Each amount recovered by the requested State shall be transferred to the applicant State in the currency of the requested State. The transfer shall be carried out within a period of a month from the date of the recovery.

8.   At the request of the applicant State, the requested State shall, with a view to the recovery of an amount of tax, take measures of conservancy even if the claim is contested or is not yet the subject of an instrument permitting enforcement, in so far as such is permitted by the laws and administrative practice of the requested State.

9.   The instrument permitting enforcement in the applicant State shall, where appropriate and in accordance with the provisions in force in the requested State, be accepted, recognized, supplemented or replaced as soon as possible after the date of the receipt of the request for assistance by an instrument permitting enforcement in the requested State.

10.   Questions concerning any period beyond which a tax claim cannot be enforced shall be governed by the law of the applicant State. The request for assistance in the recovery shall give particulars concerning that period."

Article 27

MEMBERS OF DIPLOMATIC MISSIONS AND CONSULAR POSTS

Article 27 of the United Nations Model Convention reproduces Article 27 of the OECD Model Convention. The Commentary of that Article is therefore relevant:

"The aim of the provision is to secure that members of diplomatic missions and consular posts shall, under the provisions of a double taxation convention, receive no less favourable treatment than that to which they are entitled under international law or under special international agreements." [para. 1]

"The simultaneous application of the provisions of a double taxation convention and of diplomatic and consular privileges conferred by virtue of the general rules of international law, or under a special international agreement, may, under certain circumstances, have the result of discharging, in both Contracting States, tax that would otherwise have been due. As an illustration, it may be mentioned that, e.g., a diplomatic agent who is accredited by State A to State B and derives royalties or dividends from sources in State A will not, owing to international law, be subject to tax in State B in respect of this income and may also, depending upon the provisions of the bilateral convention between the two States, be entitled as a resident of State B to an exemption from, or a reduction of, the tax imposed on the income in State A. In order to avoid tax reliefs that are not intended, the Contracting States are free to adopt bilaterally an additional provision which may be drafted on the following lines:

"'In so far as, due to fiscal privileges granted to members of diplomatic missions and consular posts under the general rules of international law or under the provisions of special international agreements, income or capital are not subject to tax in the receiving State, the right to tax shall be reserved to the sending State.'" [para. 2]

"In many OECD Member countries, the domestic laws contain provisions to the effect that members of diplomatic missions and consular posts while abroad shall for tax purposes be deemed to be residents of the sending State. In the bilateral relations between Member countries in which provisions of this kind are operative internally, a further step may be taken by including in the Convention specific rules that establish, for purposes of the Convention, the sending State as the State of residence of the members of the diplomatic missions and consular posts of the Contracting States. The special provision suggested here could be drafted as follows:

'Notwithstanding the provisions of Article 4 an individual who is a member of a diplomatic mission or a consular post of a Contracting State which is situated in the other Contracting State or in a third State shall be deemed for the purposes of the Convention to be a resident of the sending State if:

(*a*) in accordance with international law he is not liable to tax in the receiving State in respect of income from sources outside that State or on capital situated outside that State, and

(*b*) he is liable in the sending State to the same obligations in relation to tax on his total income or on capital as are residents of that State.'" [para. 3]

"By virtue of paragraph 1 of Article 4,[24] the members of diplomatic missions and consular posts of a third State accredited to a Contracting State are not deemed to be residents of the

---

[24]This paragraph will not apply to those bilateral agreements which omit the second sentence of paragraph 1 of article 4.

receiving State if they are only subject to a limited taxation in that State . . . This consideration also holds true of the international organizations established in a Contracting State and their officials as they usually benefit from certain fiscal privileges either under the convention or treaty establishing the organization or under a treaty between the organization and the State in which it is established. Contracting States wishing to settle expressly this question, or to prevent undesirable tax reliefs, may add the following provision to this Article:

'The Convention shall not apply to international organizations, to organs or officials thereof and to persons who are members of a diplomatic mission or a consular post of a third State, being present in a Contracting State and not treated in either Contracting State as residents in respect of taxes on income or on capital.'

This means that international organizations, organs or officials who are liable in a Contracting State in respect only of income from sources therein should not have the benefit of the Convention." [para. 4]

"Although honorary consular officers cannot derive from the provisions of the Article any privileges to which they are not entitled under the general rules of international law (there commonly exists only tax exemption for payments received as consideration for expenses honorary consuls have on behalf of the sending State), the Contracting States are free to exclude, by bilateral agreement, expressly honorary consular officers from the application of the Article." [para. 5]

Commentary on chapter VII

FINAL PROVISIONS

Articles 28 *and* 29

ENTRY INTO FORCE AND TERMINATION

Articles 28 and 29 of the United Nations Model Convention reproduce Articles 29 and 30 of the OECD Model Convention. The Commentary on the latter Articles is therefore relevant:

"The present provisions on the procedure for entry into force, ratification and termination are drafted for bilateral conventions and correspond to the rules usually contained in international treaties." [para. 1]

"Some Contracting States may need an additional provision in the first paragraph of Article 29 indicating the authorities which have to give their consent to the ratification. Other Contracting States may agree that the Article should indicate that the entry into force takes place after an exchange of notes confirming that each State has completed the procedures required for such entry into force." [para. 2]

"It is open to Contracting States to agree that the Convention shall enter into force when a specified period has elapsed after the exchange of the instruments of ratification or after the confirmation that each State has completed the procedures required for such entry into force." [para. 3]

"No provisions have been drafted as to the date on which the Convention shall have effect or cease to have effect, since such provisions would largely depend on the domestic laws of the Contracting States concerned. Some of the States assess tax on the income received during the current year, others on the income received during the previous year, others again have a fiscal year which differs from the calendar year. Furthermore, some conventions provide, as regards taxes levied by deduction at the source, a date for the application or termination which differs from the date applying to taxes levied by assessment." [para. 4]

"As it is of advantage that the Convention should remain in force at least for a certain period, the Article on termination can only be given after a certain year—to be fixed by bilateral agreement. It is open to the Contracting States to decide upon the earliest year during which such notice can be given or even to agree not to fix any such year, if they so desire." [para. 5]

Litho in United Nations, New York
00-67665—November 2001—1,520
ISBN 92-1-159097-3

United Nations publication
Sales No.E.01.XVI.2
ST/ESA/PAD/SER.E/21